ecoPRO Handbook

ecoPRO Required Reading

Authors
Thomas W. Cook • Ann Marie VanDerZanden • Heather L. Venhaus •
Herbert Dreiseitl

Washington State Nursery & Landscape Association

ISBN 9781119819882

Copyright © 2022 John Wiley & Sons, Inc. All rights reserved. No part of this publication may be reproduced, stored in a retrieval system or transmitted in any form or by any means, electronic, mechanical, photocopying, recording, scanning or otherwise, except as permitted under Sections 107 or 108 of the 1976 United States Copyright Act, without either the prior written permission of the Publisher, or authorization through payment of the appropriate per-copy fee to the Copyright Clearance Center, Inc. 222 Rosewood Drive, Danvers, MA 01923, Web site: www.copyright.com. Requests to the Publisher for permission should be addressed to the Permissions Department, John Wiley & Sons, Inc., 111 River Street, Hoboken, NJ 07030-5774, (201)748-6011, fax (201)748-6008, Web site: http://www.wiley.com/go/permissions.

10 9 8 7 6 5 4 3 2 1

List of Titles

Designing the Sustainable Site: Integrated Design Strategies for Small Scale Sites and Residential Landscapes
    by Heather L. Venhaus and Herbert Dreiseitl
    Copyright © 2012, ISBN: 978-0-470-90009-3

Sustainable Landscape Management: Design, Construction, and Maintenance
    by Thomas W. Cook and Ann Marie VanDerZanden
    Copyright © 2011, ISBN: 978-0-470-48093-9

TABLE OF CONTENTS

How to use the ecoPRO Handbook — 7
ecoPRO: Guiding Principles & Best Practices — 8

SECTION I – SUSTAINABLE LANDSCAPE MANAGEMENT

Introduction to Sustainability — 33
Source: Chapter 1 of Sustainable Landscape Management: Design, Construction, and Maintenance

Sustainable Landscape Construction: Process, Irrigation Systems, & Hardscape Materials — 47
Source: Chapter 3 of Sustainable Landscape Management: Design, Construction, and Maintenance

Retrofitting Existing Landscapes for Sustainability — 69
Source: Chapter 4 of Sustainable Landscape Management: Design, Construction, and Maintenance

Ecosystem Development & Management in the Context of Sustainable Landscapes — 89
Source: Chapter 5 of Sustainable Landscape Management: Design, Construction, and Maintenance

Building a Sustainable Future — 109
Source: Chapter 1 of Designing the Sustainable Site: Integrated Design Strategies for Small Scale Sites & Residential Landscapes

Purpose & Principles of the Sustainable Sites Initiative, The Sustainable Sites Initiative Resource: The Case for Sustainable Landscapes — 125
Source: American Society of Landscape Architects, Lady Bird Johnson Wildflower Center at The University of Texas at Austin, and United States Botanic Garden

SECTION II – SOIL HEALTH & MANAGEMENT

Sustainable Soils for Landscapes — 135
Source: Chapter 7 of Sustainable Landscape Management: Design, Construction, and Maintenance

Building Soils: Summary of "Building Soil Best Management Practices for Western Washington" — 149
Source: Building Soils, www.BuildingSoils.org

Building Soils: When to Amend - Construction Sequencing for Soil Protection & Restoration — 151
Source: Building Soils, www.BuildingSoils.org

Building Soils: Erosion Control With Compost — 153
Source: Building Soils, www.BuildingSoils.org

WSU Resource: Estimating Soil Texture — 154
Source: Washington State University

SECTION III – PLANT HEALTH CARE

Managing Trees, Shrubs & Beds Sustainably — 157
Source: Chapter 8 of Sustainable Landscape Management: Design, Construction, and Maintenance

Sustainable Lawn Care, Installation & Maintenance — 185
Source: Seattle Public Utilities

ProIPM: Integrated Pest Management Solutions for the Landscape Professionals — 193
Source: Seattle Public Utilities

Basic Of Natural Pest Control - Integrated Pest Management Flowchart — 195
Source: Local Hazardous Waste Management Program

Gardening without Pesticides — 196
Source: Grow Smart; Grow Safe Program

TABLE OF CONTENTS

SECTION IV – WATER MANAGEMENT

Building Soils: Managing Stormwater Onsite — 200
Source: Building Soils, www.BuildingSoils.org

Best Irrigation Practices — 204
Source: Cascade Water Alliance

    Efficient Landscape Irrigation Design Checklist — 206

    Efficient Landscape Irrigation Installation Checklist — 208

    Efficient Irrigation System Management Inspection Checklist — 209

    Landscape Irrigation Schedule Evaluation Checklist — 210

    Irrigation Evaluation Form — 211

    Definitions of Efficient Irrigation Terms — 212

    Resources for Efficient Irrigation Design & Management — 215

    Elements of an Efficient Irrigation Plan — 216

Winterizing & Starting Up the Irrigation System — 217
Source: Tacoma Water

WAC 246-274-011 Greywater Irrigation Systems - General Requirements — 218
Source: https://apps.leg.wa.gov/wac/default.aspx?cite=246-274-011

SECTION V – HUMAN HEALTH & ENVIRONMENTAL ISSUES

Environmental Issues, chapter 6 — 221
Source: Chapter 1 of Sustainable Landscape Management: Design, Construction, and Maintenance

Clean Cities' Guide to Alternative Fuel Commercial Lawn Equipment — 239
Source: U.S. Department of Energy

WA State Noxious Weed Classifications & RCW — 254
Source: https://www.nwcb.wa.gov/washingtons-noxious-weed-laws

SECTION VI – ecoPRO Resources

ecoPRO Glossary of Terms — 256

ecoPRO Required Reading List, Supplemental Materials & Additional Resources for Study — 262

About the ecoPRO Handbook

The ecoPRO Required Reading Handbook is a compilation of a materials, including published work and resources developed by variety of industry experts and organizations, including:

- *Designing the Sustainable Site: Integrated Design Strategies for Small Scale Sites & Residential Landscapes.* By Heather L. Venhaus and Herbert Dreiseitl | Copyright © 2012, ISBN: 978-0-470-90009-3
- *Sustainable Landscape Management: Design, Construction & Maintenance*
  By Ann Marie VanDerZanden and Thomas W. Cook | Copyright ©2011, ISBN: 978-0-470-48093-9
- Additional resources & materials provided by:
  - Cascade Water Alliance
  - Department of Energy
  - Local Hazardous Waste Management Program
  - Seattle Public Utilities
  - Tacoma Water
  - Washington State University
  - ecoPRO Certified Sustainable Landscape Professional Certification Program

The content of the ecoPRO Required Reading Handbook is organized into sections relating to ecoPRO Best Management Practices and ecoPRO training sessions. Because material is being pulled from a variety of sources, page and chapter sequencing may conflict with the ecoPRO Required Reading Handbook Table of Contents. To help guide your study, below are tips to help navigate your ecoPRO Required Reading Handbook.

HOW TO NAVIGATE YOUR ecoPRO HANDBOOK

- **SECTION TITLE PAGES:** Section Title Pages can be found at the beginning of every section. These pages work to reorient your study by listing the various materials you will find within that ecoPRO section.
- **PAGE NUMBERS:** Use the page number in the bottom corners of the page, as this relates to the ecoPRO table of contents.
- **STUDY QUESTIONS:** Study questions can be found at the end of select chapters. Please be aware that these questions are not specific to ecoPRO exam questions. Instead, they are questions that coincide with the original published materials.
- **SUPPLEMENTAL & ADDITIONAL MATERIALS LIST:** An extensive list of supplemental and additional resources can be found at the back of your ecoPRO Required Reading Handbook. Items listed under supplemental are highly recommended to support your study. Additional resources are provided to learn more or to use as references, as desired.

Guiding Principles & Sustainable Best Practices (Revised 2/2020)

STATEMENT OF PURPOSE

ecoPRO Sustainable Landscape Professional Certification is an advanced certification for professionals working in the landscape industry in Washington. It is administered by the Washington State Nursery & Landscape Association (WSNLA) to ensure a unified standard for sustainable practices within the horticultural industry that also enhances marketing, networking, and educational opportunities.

- Certified landscape professionals will have demonstrated knowledge of, and voluntarily practice, the sustainable best landscape practices presented in this document.
- Certified landscape professionals will be able to offer knowledgeable, enthusiastic, profitable, and environmentally sound landscape design, installation, and maintenance services. Participants' work will strive to have a positive impact on the environment and on their local Washington State community.
- The Program provides science-based information that promotes, guides, and informs ecological, sustainable landscape management.

ecoPRO sustainable best practices align as much as possible with existing business and site certifications. There are several sustainable certifications applicable to landscape businesses and sites in Washington State. Some of these include: EnviroStars—a certification for businesses that reduce their use and input of toxics in the environment; Sustainable Sites Initiative (SITES)—a national certification for landscapes designed, installed, and including a maintenance plan for sustainable practices; Salmon Safe—a land management certification for sites that protect water quality and preserve and restore habitat; the regional BuiltGreen, national LEED, and Living Building Challenge--green building certifications that include site development best practices; Greenroads—for road construction; Envision—for infrastructure projects; and Oregon Tilth's Organic Land Care accreditation program, which applies USDA National Organic Program agricultural standards and policies to landscapes.

BACKGROUND & ACKNOWLEDGEMENTS

Program standards and requirements were developed by a nine-person volunteer Advisory Committee in 2011-2012 with additional input by outside reviewers. The standards and requirements were updated in 2019. The Initial Advisory Committee, convened by WSNLA, Washington Association of Landscape Professionals, and Cascadia Consulting Group in 2011, was comprised of landscape professional leaders in the private and public sectors: designers, builders, maintenance professionals, horticulture educators, and growers. The Initial Advisory Committee members, as well as subsequent committee members, are associated with other relevant initiatives and professional organizations, including the regional EnviroStars certification program and national Sustainable Sites Initiative (SITES), Association of Professional Landscape Designers (APLD), Washington Chapter of the Society of Landscape Architects (WASLA), International Society of Arboriculture (ISA), Coalition of Organic Landscape Professionals (COOL), Washington Native Plant Society, Sports Turf Management Association (STMA), and Building Owner and Management Association (BOMA).

The Initial Advisory Committee had the overarching goals of developing a program that:
- Serves landscape professionals in Washington state;
- Addresses Washington state habitat, water quality, conservation, and toxics reduction issues;
- Holistically addresses the landscape; and
- Builds on existing programs.

The Initial Advisory Committee first reviewed existing organic and sustainable landscape certification programs in California, Oregon, British Columbia, Connecticut, and nationwide, with the goal of adopting and adapting policies, standards, and material. The committee chose to develop a menu of Sustainable Best Practices that encourage professionals to consider the whole landscape, from design to installation to maintenance over time. They designed the program as a second tier certification that builds on and does not duplicate existing basic horticultural education and certification opportunities. The program is geared to professionals who already have basic landscape horticultural knowledge, experience, and certification, and who serve a wide range of clients – from public to residential to commercial.

We want to acknowledge the following individuals and entities instrumental in the initial development of this program for Washington State:

Initial Advisory Committee
Will Bailey, CLT, CLP, ISA, Signature Landscape Services
Jessica Bloom, CPH, NW Bloom Eco-Logical Landscapes
Van Bobbitt, ISA, South Seattle Community College
Barb DeCaro, Seattle Parks and Recreation
Don Marshall, CPH, Lake WA Institute of Technology
David McDonald, Seattle Public Utilities
Lisa Port, APLD, Banyon Tree Design Studio
Ladd Smith, In Harmony Sustainable Landscape Services
Jeff van Lierop, Country Green
Patty Anderson, Washington Association of Landscape Professionals (facilitator)
Jeanne McNeil, CPH, Esq, Washington State Nursery & Landscape Association (facilitator)
Gwen Vernon, Cascadia Consulting Group (facilitator)

Review and Support
Janine Anderson, CPH, Anderson LeLievre Landscape Design
Meg Angevine, City of Redmond Park Operations
Mike Brent, Cascade Water Alliance
Shannon Britton, Seattle University
Brent Chapman, South Puget Sound Community College
Sharon Collman, Washington State University – Snohomish County Extension
Sarah Gage, Washington State Recreation and Conservation Office
Mark Guthrie, QWEL, CLIA, Tacoma Water, Tacoma Public Utilities
Howard Harrison, CPH, Chinook Compost Tea
Courtney Landoll, PLA, ASLA, LEED Green Associate, The Watershed Company
Susan M. Nicol, ISA, Horticulturist
Lisa Niehaus, Local Hazardous Waste Management Program in King County
Patrick Schwarzkopf, Pacific Landscape Management
Jenna Smith, Seattle Public Utilities
Peg Tillery, CPH, Washington State University, Kitsap County Extension
Ray Willard, PLA, Washington State Department of Transportation
Burton Yuen, LEED AP B+C, Harrison Design | Landscape Architecture

Initial Funding
Seattle Public Utilities
Washington Department of Ecology
Washington State Department of Agriculture
WSNLA Scholarship & Research Charitable Fund

GUIDING PRINCIPLES

United States Environmental protection Agency (from US EPA): www.epa.gov/sustainability):
Sustainability is based on a simple principle: Everything that we need for our survival and well-being depends, either directly or indirectly on our natural environment. Sustainability creates and maintains the conditions under which

humans and nature can exist in productive harmony, that permit fulfilling the social, economic and other requirements of present and future generations.

Brundtland Commission of the United Nations 1987: *Sustainability is defined as design, construction, operations, and maintenance practices that meet the needs of the present generation without compromising the ability of future generations to meet their own needs.*

The Three Spheres of Sustainability

Social-Environmental
Environmental Justice
Natural Resources Stewardship
Locally & Globally

Environmental
Natural Resource Use
Environmental Managemet
Pollution Prevention
(air, water, land, waste)

Environmental-Economic
Energy Efficiency
Subsidies / Incentives for
use of Natural Resources

Social
Standard of Living
Education
Community
Equal Opportunity

Sustainability

Economic
Profit
Cost Savings
Economic Growth
Research &
Development

Economic-Social
Business Ethics
Fair Trade
Worker's Rights

Adopted from the 2002 University of Michigan Sustainability Assessment

Sustainable Landscaping is the work of designing, constructing, and maintaining landscapes to conserve and regenerate water, air, soil, plant, and wildlife resources, and protect and enhance human health and well-being. Sustainable practices focus on the environment of an ecoregion[1] while striving to be socially equitable and economically feasible.

Sustainable Landscape Practice is the use of ecologically sound principles to work in concert with natural ecoregional systems. It encourages working within closed systems with regard to organic matter and nutrient cycling. It aims to be pesticide-free. The goal of sustainable landscape practice is to design, construct, and maintain landscapes that will continue to be aesthetically pleasing, ecologically resilient, and enduring in the ecoregion in which they are located.

ecoPRO Certified Sustainable Landscape Professionals have passed an exam that tests their knowledge of sustainable landscaping principles and best practices. They abide by the ecoPRO Code of Conduct to design, construct, and manage landscapes using the most current, ecologically sound principles and practices. Where possible, ecoPRO certified professionals collaborate across the disciplines of design, construction, and maintenance.

---

[1] An "ecoregion" is an area that reflects broad ecological patterns occurring on the landscape. In general, each ecoregion has a distinctive composition and pattern of plant and animal species distribution. Abiotic factors, such as climate, landform, soil, and hydrology are important in the development of ecosystems, and thus help define ecoregions. Within an individual ecoregion, the ecological relationships between species and their physical environment are essentially similar. Washington State is generally considered to encompass nine ecoregions.
http://www.landscope.org/washington/natural_geography/ecoregions/

ecoPRO SUSTAINABLE BEST PRACTICES
(Revised 12/2018)

This section outlines Sustainable Best Practices for landscape design, construction, and maintenance. The best practices are organized around **eight key principles**:
- Protect and Conserve Soils
- Conserve Water
- Protect Water and Air Quality
- Protect and Create Wildlife Habitat
- Conserve Energy
- Sustain Healthy Plants
- Use Sustainable Methods and Materials
- Protect and Enhance Human Health and Well-being*

   Human Health and Well-being BMPs are blended into all the BMP sections.

HOW TO USE

The tables of best practices on the following pages present choices for sustainable landscaping that a professional may apply to each site, as appropriate. The understanding is that every site and situation is unique.

Best practices designated with a *diamond (♦)* indicate a "core" best practice that ecoPRO certified professionals should employ on all sites, where applicable. Since many practices conform to multiple principles, the right-hand columns cross-link the practices to the applicable principles. There is some duplication of best practices.

Underlined terms are defined in the Glossary located at the back of the book.

PROTECT AND CONSERVE SOIL

Key concepts: soil protection zones, soil management plans, amending soils, mulching, mulch-mowing, composting, managing stormwater runoff and erosion, minimize soil disturbance, closed system management

Protect & Conserve Soil

DESIGN

		Protect and Conserve Soil	Conserve Water	Protect Water and Air Quality	Protect and Create Wildlife Habitat	Conserve Energy	Sustain Healthy Plants	Use Sustainable Methods/Materials	Protect/Enhance Human Health/Well-being
1.	**Identify and map soil characteristics of landscape site**								
☐	♦Perform a soil test and analysis to inform design and management decisions	X	X				X		
☐	♦Designate soil protection, disturbance, and other construction management areas on a Soil Management Plan (See requirements in Washington State Stormwater Management Manual in "Sources" at end of this document)	X					X		
☐	Test soil drainage in several locations	X	X				X		
☐	Define the location and boundaries of all vegetation and soil protection zones	X					X		
☐	Design the landscape with designated onsite recycling areas	X						X	X X
2.	**Review site grading specifications for accuracy**								
☐	♦Limit overall cut and fill through efficient design and layout	X		X	X			X	X
☐	♦Limit vegetation clearing to avoid soil erosion and compaction	X		X	X				
☐	Retain natural topographic features that slow and store stormwater flows and limit steep, continuous slopes	X	X						

CONSTRUCTION

		Protect and Conserve Soil	Conserve Water	Protect Water and Air Quality	Protect and Create Wildlife Habitat	Conserve Energy	Sustain Healthy Plants	Use Sustainable Methods/Materials	Protect/Enhance Human Health/Well-being
1.	**Use the least invasive construction methods and tools and site sensitive construction methods**								
☐	♦Protect soil from compaction, wherever possible	X	X				X		X X
☐	♦Minimize major grading, soil disturbance, and compaction	X						X	X
☐	♦Avoid creating soil interfaces when preparing soils for planting	X						X	
☐	♦Prevent loss of onsite and stockpiled soils from stormwater runoff and wind erosion	X						X	
☐	♦Restore disturbed/compacted soil with compost amendment	X						X	
☐	Perform grading operations during the low rainfall seasons	X	X						X
☐	Avoid handling and installing saturated soils, especially during wet weather	X						X	
☐	Use heavy equipment fitted with flotation tires or wide tracks that distribute heavy loads	X	X				X	X	

Protect & Conserve Soil

		Protect and Conserve Soil	Conserve Water	Protect Water and Air Quality	Protect and Create Wildlife Habitat	Conserve Energy	Sustain Healthy Plants	Use Sustainable Methods/Materials	Protect/Enhance Human Health/Well-being
	Prevent concrete waste and materials washout into adjacent properties and waterways	X	X					X	X
2.	**Protect tree root zones**								
	◆Define and fence off the tree root protection zone. If access is necessary cover zone with 4-6 inches of coarse wood chips, crushed rock, or with metal plates (See ANSI 300 tree protection standards and "Tree Protection on Construction and Developments Sites" in the "Sources" at end of this document)	X	X				X	X	
3.	**Reduce import and export of earth materials**								
	◆Remove and stockpile existing topsoil before grading, for reuse onsite	X						X	
	◆Improve existing soil as an alternative to importing topsoil	X					X	X	X	X
	◆Inspect imported topsoils and soil amendments to verify specifications are met	X						X	
	Identify an area to store topsoil during construction	X						X	
	Reuse organic debris onsite, or recycle at a composting facility	X					X		X	X
4.	**Prepare or amend soil to maximize water holding capacity and drainage**								
	◆Amend soils over entire planting area with 2-4 inches of compost tilled to a depth of 8-12"	X	X	X			X	X	X
	◆Install topsoils properly by ripping in the first lift (layer) to mix into existing native soil	X	X	X			X	X	X

MAINTENANCE

1.	**Build healthy soils**									
	◆Perform a soil test and analysis when analyzing problems or when renovating landscapes	X					X	X	
	◆Maintain 2-4 inches of large particle size organic mulch over the surface of soil	X	X	X			X	X	X
	◆Apply organic mulches a few inches from the base of trees and plants and extending at least to the dripline	X	X	X			X	X	X
	◆Use compost, compost tea, or other amendments to establish beneficial soil organisms and release nutrients over the long term	X	X	X			X	X	X
	◆Use organic recycled materials onsite by mulching, mulch-mowing, and composting	X					X	X	X	X
	Sow nitrogen fixing or deeply rooted cover crops to improve soils and limit erosion, then till these in before seed set.	X	X	X			X	X	X
	Allow fallen leaves to remain as mulch in landscaped beds and natural areas	X					X	X	X	X
	Assess and apply compost and/or mulch to landscaped beds annually or as needed	X	X	X			X	X	X
	Avoid practices that degrade soil fertility and biodiversity	X	X	X			X		X
	Avoid synthetic barriers or mulches that prevent or inhibit natural biodegradation of organic matter	X		X			X	X	X	X

Protect & Conserve Soil

		Protect and Conserve Soil	Conserve Water	Protect Water and Air Quality	Protect and Create Wildlife Habitat	Conserve Energy	Sustain Healthy Plants	Use Sustainable Methods /Materials	Protect/Enhance Human Health/Well-being
2.	**Address problem drainage areas with appropriate drainage solutions**								
☐	Keep debris and leaves away from storm drains	X	X						X
☐	Replant with plants adapted to wet conditions	X	X				X	X	
☐	Mechanically aerate and top dress turf soils as needed	X	X				X		X
☐	Use power augers, water jets, or air spades to create holes in compacted tree and shrub root zones and fill with compost	X	X				X	X	X
3.	**Create a sustainable plant nutrient management program**								
☐	♦Base nutrient management programs for turf, trees, and shrubs on soil tests, tissue analysis, and clear indication of need	X		X	X	X	X		X
☐	♦Base any application of phosphorus on soil test indicating plant need	X	X				X	X	X
☐	♦Use naturally derived fertilizers from organic sources such as blood or bone meal, alfalfa, fishmeal, kelp, and natural minerals that slowly release nutrients over a 1-to-4 month timeframe	X	X	X	X	X	X	X	
☐	Schedule fertilization for site conditions, plant needs, and dry weather	X	X				X		X
☐	Select fertilizers that contain 30% or more of the nitrogen in slow release form	X	X				X	X	X
☐	Follow fertilizer label rates and schedule recommendations	X					X		
☐	Apply mycorrhizal inoculants, as appropriate	X	X				X		

CONSERVE WATER

Key concepts: irrigation water conservation, irrigation system/design/maintenance efficiency, certified designers, sustainable irrigation materials, water budget, conservation/weather-based irrigation management, water use monitoring and auditing

Conserve Water

	Protect and Conserve Soil	Conserve Water	Protect Water and Air Quality	Protect and Create Wildlife Habitat	Conserve Energy	Sustain Healthy Plants	Use Sustainable Methods/Materials	Protect/Enhance Human Health/Well-being
DESIGN								
1. Map and assess site <u>hydrology</u>								
◆ Map <u>hydrozones</u>, existing plantings, and soil types	X	X	X			X		X
◆ Map topography and drainage		X	X			X		X
2. Design high-efficiency irrigation systems								
◆ Design watering systems with zones to match plant water needs		X	X			X		X
◆ Specify <u>smart controllers</u> that are weather-based or add soil moisture sensors		X	X			X	X	X
◆ Include irrigation system controller and maintenance instructions in a <u>Landscape Management Plan</u>		X				X	X	X
Specify <u>rain shut-off sensors</u>		X	X			X	X	X
Specify system monitoring features such as flow meters		X				X	X	X
Specify that irrigation designs be prepared or reviewed by an <u>Irrigation Association</u> certified irrigation designer		X					X	X
Specify non-PVC pipe such as <u>PEX</u> or HDPE for irrigation systems		X	X		X		X	X
3. Maximize use of onsite water conservation options								
◆ Specify water supply systems for the period of planting establishment		X				X		
◆ Design with drought tolerant and low water use plants that require no or minimal irrigation		X				X	X	
Collect rainwater for onsite <u>graywater</u> use (check with local regulatory agencies)		X	X				X	X
Design recycling water features		X						
Design <u>drip irrigation</u> systems for maximum efficiency		X	X			X	X	X
CONSTRUCTION								
1. Install automatic irrigation systems as designed								
◆ Follow industry best practices for installation		X				X		
◆ Audit system at installation to ensure uniform coverage and verify application rates		X	X			X		X

Conserve Water

	Soil	Water	Air	Wildlife	Energy	Plants	Materials	Human
☐ Pressure test lines and test controllers		X					X	

MAINTENANCE

1. Develop a <u>water budget</u> and multi-year watering plan to guide irrigation scheduling

	Soil	Water	Air	Wildlife	Energy	Plants	Materials	Human
☐ ♦Plan to adjust watering after plant establishment period (1-3 years)		X				X	X	
☐ ♦Test and repair irrigation systems at start of each season and by draining at end of season		X					X	
☐ ♦Set and adjust irrigation schedules as needed to minimize evaporation and overwatering		X	X			X		X
☐ ♦Set and adjust irrigation schedules for seasonal weather conditions, site characteristics, edible crops and vegetation water needs		X	X			X		X

2. Monitor and maintain systems for best performance and efficiency

	Soil	Water	Air	Wildlife	Energy	Plants	Materials	Human
☐ ♦Monitor irrigation regularly for broken heads, leaks, runoff, and uniform distribution, and repair irrigation problems promptly		X	X				X	X
☐ Maintain and analyze irrigation water consumption records to find leaks and to maximize opportunities for efficiencies		X	X				X	X

3. Improve system efficiency with conservation features

	Soil	Water	Air	Wildlife	Energy	Plants	Materials	Human
☐ Add <u>smart controllers</u>		X					X	X
☐ Add <u>rain shut-off sensors</u>		X					X	X
☐ Add flow sensors or flow management detection devices		X					X	X
☐ Use Pressure regulation devices		X					X	X

4. Manage plantings with irrigation

	Soil	Water	Air	Wildlife	Energy	Plants	Materials	Human
☐ ♦Manage water use for plant health and best root development		X				X		
☐ ♦Group plants into <u>hydrozones</u> by water needs and drought tolerance		X				X		
☐ ♦Apply organic <u>mulches</u> a few inches from the base of trees and plants and extending at least to the dripline	X	X				X	X	
☐ Irrigate turf to deeper depths while watering less frequently		X	X			X	X	X
☐ Maintain low-traffic turf areas for no/minimal irrigation, allowing them to go dormant in summer		X	X			X	X	X
☐ Reduce turf area where possible, to reduce water, fertilizer, and maintenance inputs	X	X	X				X	X
☐ Use soaker hoses or inline drip irrigation under mulches, where appropriate		X	X				X	X

5. Manage irrigation for edible crops

	Soil	Water	Air	Wildlife	Energy	Plants	Materials	Human
☐ Exercise caution with using unfiltered, harvested rainwater for irrigating edible food crops		X					X	X

PROTECT WATER AND AIR QUALITY

Key concepts: Green Stormwater Infrastructure (GSI), Low Impact Development (LID), onsite water infiltration/dispersion, prevent erosion, air movement, sound absorption, carbon cycle

Protect Water and Air Quality

		Protect and Conserve Soil	Conserve Water	Protect Water and Air Quality	Protect and Create Wildlife Habitat	Conserve Energy	Sustain Healthy Plants	Use Sustainable Methods/Materials	Protect/Enhance Human Health/Well-being

DESIGN

1. Minimize water runoff

☐	♦Design Green Stormwater Infrastructure (GSI) features that direct runoff into compost-amended soil/vegetated areas, swales, rain gardens and bioretention cells, pervious paving, cisterns, rain barrels, and vegetated roofs – check with regulatory agencies (See "LID -Low Impact Development Technical Guidance Manual" in "Sources" at end of this document.0	X	X	X				X	
☐	♦Minimize impervious surface area	X		X		X		X	
☐	Avoid materials specifications for roofs and other impervious surfaces that contain toxins or release pollutants, including treated wood, copper, or zinc anti-moss strips	X		X				X	X
☐	Specify bio-engineering and other "soft" methods to manage stream bank and slope erosion	X		X	X			X	X
☐	Avoid use of concrete bulkheads or other hardscape solutions to manage erosion	X		X				X	X

2. Improve air quality and sound absorption and reduce fuel use

☐	♦Specify paints, sealants, and coatings that emit low levels of volatile organic compounds (VOCs)	X		X	X			X	X
☐	♦Source local materials to reduce transportation			X		X		X	X
☐	Design with consideration for existing and desirable air flow patterns			X		X			X
☐	Select and locate plants and hardscape features to encourage air flow and sound absorption			X		X			X
☐	Specify existing site materials to reduce transportation			X		X		X	X
☐	Design for minimal power tool use in construction and maintenance			X		X		X	X

CONSTRUCTION

1. Prevent erosion before and during construction

☐	♦Avoid draining, disturbing, or filling wetlands	X	X	X		X			X
☐	♦Cover bare soils and maintain throughout construction with tarps, wood chip mulch, compost blankets, and/or compost filter socks	X	X	X				X	X
☐	Maintain all soil covers during construction	X	X	X				X	X

2. Maximize on-site water infiltration and detention capacity

☐	♦Prepare and/or amend soil to maximize water-holding capacity and drainage	X	X	X			X		

Protect Water and Air Quality

		Soil	Water	Water/Air	Wildlife	Energy	Plants	Materials	Health
☐	◆Install Low Impact Development (LID) and Green Stormwater Infrastructure (GSI) features	X	X	X	X		X	X	
☐	◆Ensure final grades direct rainfall runoff to spread and disperse into soil, swales, and other Green Stormwater Infrastructure (GSI)			X					
☐	Avoid creating drainage to neighboring properties	X	X	X			X		X
3.	**Reduce fuel use and noise pollution**								
☐	◆Use energy-efficient equipment and power tools		X	X		X		X	X
☐	◆Maintain all equipment and tools in optimal working condition		X	X		X		X	X
☐	Use hand tools as appropriate		X	X		X		X	X
☐	Reduce the need for landscape supplies and materials that require factory processing and transportation		X	X		X		X	X

MAINTENANCE

1. Use closed system management

		Soil	Water	Water/Air	Wildlife	Energy	Plants	Materials	Health
☐	◆Recycle and compost organic waste and reuse landscape materials on site			X		X	X	X	X
☐	◆Maintain all onsite stormwater infiltration, Low Impact Development (LID), and other Green Stormwater Infrastructure (GSI) to WA Dept of Ecology standards (See "LID Manual")	X		X			X	X	X
☐	Maintain pervious paving by keeping it free of debris and vacuuming at least once per year			X				X	X
☐	Improve/enhance a plant's ability to process CO2 and pollutants on site	X		X			X	X	X

2. Minimize point source pollution into stormwater

		Soil	Water	Water/Air	Wildlife	Energy	Plants	Materials	Health
☐	◆Base nutrient management inputs for turf trees, and shrubs on soil tests, tissue analysis, and clear indication of need			X			X	X	X
☐	◆Minimize or eliminate use of chemical pesticides	X		X			X	X	X
☐	◆Minimize use of synthetic fertilizers	X		X			X	X	X
☐	Avoid contaminating water with soluble landscape chemicals, oil, cleaners, etc.			X				X	X

3. Minimize air and noise pollution

		Soil	Water	Water/Air	Wildlife	Energy	Plants	Materials	Health
☐	◆Maintain vehicles, equipment and power tools in optimal working condition to prevent fuel, hydraulic fluids and oil drips, leaks, and spills	X		X		X		X	X
☐	◆Use energy-efficient equipment and power tools	X		X		X		X	X
☐	Use 4-cycle power gasoline powered equipment	X		X		X		X	X
☐	Avoid use of 2-cycle gasoline-powered equipment	X		X		X		X	X
☐	Use electric, propane, or natural gas-powered equipment	X		X		X		X	X
☐	Choose cultural maintenance strategies and hand tools	X	X	X		X	X	X	X

Protect Water and Air Quality

		Protect and Conserve Soil	Conserve Water	**Protect Water and Air Quality**	Protect and Create Wildlife Habitat	Conserve Energy	Sustain Healthy Plants	Use Sustainable Methods / Materials	Protect/Enhance Human Health/Well-being
☐	Avoid burning piles of organic waste material	X		X				X	X
☐	Maintain appropriate air movement and circulation in the landscape			X			X		X
☐	Prune to optimize air flow for plant and human health			X			X		X
☐	Implement management practices based on an understanding of the carbon cycle	X	X	X			X		X

PROTECT AND CREATE WILDLIFE HABITAT

Key concepts: protect/conserve/build/enhance biodiversity and wildlife habitats

Protect and Create Wildlife Habitat

			Protect and Conserve Soil	Conserve Water	Protect Water and Air Quality	Protect and Create Wildlife Habitat	Conserve Energy	Sustain Healthy Plants	Use Sustainable Methods/Materials	Protect/Enhance Human Health/Well-being
DESIGN										
1.	**Prioritize designs that improve or create healthy habitats for native wildlife**									
	♦Survey, conserve, and protect existing native wildlife and their habitats		X		X	X		X		X
	♦Design landscape to provide food, water, and shelter for native wildlife					X				
	Minimize high-maintenance landscapes with less habitat for native wildlife		X	X	X	X	X	X	X	
	Preserve existing mature trees and other vegetation that provides functional wildlife habitat		X		X	X		X		X
	Retain wetlands and existing natural areas		X		X	X		X		X
2.	**Use local native <u>plant communities</u> as models to support biodiversity**									
	Plan for natural evolution of the landscape and habitat changes					X				
	Plan for adaptive management in response to wildlife impacts and modification of landscapes					X				
CONSTRUCTION										
1.	**Protect onsite wildlife habitat**									
	♦Protect existing habitat including wetland areas and landscape features		X	X	X	X		X		X
	♦Minimize impacts to existing desirable vegetation during construction activities					X		X		
	Create and manage refuge areas for wildlife during construction					X				
2.	**Construct wildlife habitat**									
	Create shelter sources, such as brush and rock piles from landscape waste					X	X		X	
	Create water sources					X				
	Plant vegetation food sources for specific native wildlife					X				
MAINTENANCE										
1.	**Maintain and enhance sources of food, water, and shelter for native wildlife**									
	♦Survey, conserve, and protect existing habitat for native wildlife					X				
	♦Schedule maintenance tasks to avoid disturbing native wildlife and their habitats					X				
	♦Preserve and plant native vegetation to enhance native wildlife diversity		X		X	X		X		
	Avoid cultivation of landscaped areas to retain soil organisms and soil habitat					X				

Protect and Create Wildlife Habitat

		Protect and Conserve Soil	Conserve Water	Protect Water and Air Quality	Protect and Create Wildlife Habitat	Conserve Energy	Sustain Healthy Plants	Use Sustainable Methods/Materials	Protect/Enhance Human Health/Well-being
	Avoid disturbing wildlife habitat during critical times in the wildlife cycle (e.g. nesting seasons)				X				
	Minimize pruning to enhance habitat				X				
	Create brush and rock piles from landscape waste				X	X		X	
	Maintain water sources				X				
	Maintain shelter sources, such as brush and rock piles				X				
	Avoid premature removal of flowers, stems, and seed heads that provide a food source or habitat for wildlife				X				
2.	**Look for opportunities to create habitat**								
	◆Allow decomposition of organic matter on the surface of garden beds as natural mulch to protect and build habitats for amphibians, insects and arachnids	X	X	X			X	X	
	◆Maintain habitat for <u>pollinators</u> and biological predators				X		X	X	X
	Convert dead or declining trees to habitat snags for cavity-nesting birds and other wildlife				X	X			
3.	**Practice <u>Integrate Pest Management (IPM)</u> and <u>Plant Health Care (PHC)</u>**								
	◆Eliminate or reduce the use of pesticides harmful to wildlife	X	X	X	X	X	X	X	X
	◆Create diversity in landscapes to encourage natural, biological pest control processes				X	X	X		X

CONSERVE ENERGY

Key concepts: embodied-energy, low energy use materials/features, fuel efficient equipment/power tools, vehicle fuel reduction, manual tools and methods

Conserve Energy

	Protect and Conserve Soil	Conserve Water	Protect Water and Air Quality	Protect and Create Wildlife Habitat	Conserve Energy	Sustain Healthy Plants	Use Sustainable Methods/Materials	Protect/Enhance Human Health/Well-being
DESIGN								
1. Design low-energy use landscapes								
♦ Select site-appropriate turf and plants to minimize power tool use for mowing, shearing and pruning maintenance	X	X	X	X	X	X	X	X
♦ Design with plants and hardscape materials that minimize adjacent buildings energy consumption (heating, cooling, natural lighting)					X		X	X
♦ Consider the sustainability of manufacturing and transportation when specifying plants and hardscape materials		X			X		X	X
♦ Specify efficient lighting systems by using solar, low-voltage and LED fixtures, photo cells, and timers					X		X	X
Purchase plants and landscape materials from manufacturers whose practices increase energy efficiency					X		X	X
Specify features designed to mitigate the Heat Island Effect in urban areas		X		X	X		X	X
Specify low embodied-energy materials					X	X	X	X
Design for minimal use of energy in landscape construction					X		X	X
CONSTRUCTION								
1. Use energy-efficient vehicles, power tools, and heavy equipment								
♦ Maintain all vehicles and equipment in optimum working condition	X		X		X		X	X
Select battery-powered, electric, propane, or other alternative energy power tools	X		X		X		X	X
2. Use hand tools								
Choose hand tools when practical for construction tasks	X		X		X		X	X
MAINTENANCE								
1. Allow minimal use of equipment and power tools								
Choose and use hand and mechanical tools	X		X		X		X	X
2. Minimize energy and fuel use and optimize fuel efficiency								
♦ Optimize landscape contribution to adjacent building energy conservation (heating, cooling,					X			X

Conserve Energy

	Protect and Conserve Soil	Conserve Water	Protect Water and Air Quality	Protect and Create Wildlife Habitat	Conserve Energy	Sustain Healthy Plants	Use Sustainable Methods/Materials	Protect/Enhance Human Health/Well-being
natural lighting)								
♦ Schedule landscape maintenance and related activities to minimize miles driven		X	X		X		X	X
Purchase plants and landscape materials from manufacturers whose practices increase energy efficiency		X	X		X		X	X
Choose low-emissions equipment, such as electric, propane, or natural gas		X	X		X		X	X
Choose and use four-cycle gasoline-powered equipment		X	X		X		X	X
Choose vehicles and equipment that prevent air pollution		X	X		X		X	X
Avoid use of two-cycle gasoline-powered equipment		X	X		X		X	X

SUSTAIN HEALTHY PLANTS

Key concepts: Right plant/right place, low input landscapes, no pesticide use, Integrated Pest Management, Plant Health Care, Human health issues

Sustain Healthy Plants

DESIGN

		Protect and Conserve Soil	Conserve Water	Protect Water and Air Quality	Protect and Create Wildlife Habitat	Conserve Energy	Sustain Healthy Plants	Use Sustainable Methods/Materials	Protect/Enhance Human Health/Well-being
1.	**Use sustainable selection and purchasing practices**								
☐	♦Specify locally produced, propagated, and sourced plant material and seed						X	X	X	X
☐	♦Purchase plants/seed when possible from sources that certify sustainable production and business practices	X	X	X	X	X	X	X	X
☐	Specify organic seed and plant stock when possible	X	X	X	X	X	X	X	X
2.	**Design landscape plantings appropriate for the site, climate, and <u>ecoregion</u>**								
☐	♦Incorporate and protect existing thriving plants and trees where possible and desirable	X	X	X	X		X		X
☐	♦Design plantings to encourage maximum soil coverage	X	X				X		
☐	♦Specify plants needing minimum inputs for water, fertilizer, pruning, and other maintenance needs	X	X	X	X	X	X	X	X
☐	♦Specify native, climate-adapted, or other low water use plants that require no or minimal irrigation		X		X		X	X	X
☐	Use natural communities as a guide to group plants by cultural needs		X		X		X		
☐	Reduce turf area where possible, to reduce water, fertilizer, and maintenance inputs	X	X				X	X	X
☐	Select turf varieties labeled by the Turfgrass Water Conservation Alliance (See "Sources")		X	X			X		X
3.	**Design landscape plantings appropriate for the site and climate**								
☐	♦Place plants in the proper location to prevent poor performance		X				X		
☐	♦Regularly consult the local <u>Noxious Weed List</u> for plants to avoid in the landscape design	X	X	X	X	X	X	X	X
☐	♦Specify disease and pest-resistant plants		X		X		X	X	X
☐	Avoid use of non-native plants in natural areas or areas directly adjacent to high quality natural areas				X		X		
☐	Specify weed-free nursery stock	X		X	X		X	X	X
☐	Specify locally produced, propagated, and sourced plant material and seed						X	X	X	X

Sustain Healthy Plants

		Protect and Conserve Soil	Conserve Water	Protect Water and Air Quality	Protect and Create Wildlife Habitat	Conserve Energy	Sustain Healthy Plants	Use Sustainable Methods/Materials	Protect/Enhance Human Health/Well-being
4.	**Develop a Landscape Management Plan, including Plant Health Care (PHC) and Integrated Pest Management (IPM), to guide annual and future maintenance**								
☐	♦Develop a Landscape Management Plan to guide maintenance activities	X	X	X	X	X	X	X	X
☐	♦Design and plan for plant growth, species longevity, and succession during the life of the landscape	X	X	X	X	X	X	X	X
☐	Encourage plant biodiversity, especially plants native to an ecoregion, and use plants that attract beneficials and biological pest predators				X		X		
☐	Survey for known pests, noxious weeds, and invasive species on site	X		X	X		X		X

CONSTRUCTION

1.	**Protect existing trees and vegetation**								
☐	♦Follow best management practices to protect existing trees and other plants during construction (see Tree Protection Handbook at http://pnwisa.org)	X	X	X	X		X		X
2.	**Select and install healthy plants**								
☐	♦Inspect all vegetation for health, pests, and diseases						X	X	
☐	♦Install plants properly (ecoPRO Required Reading, Version 2, Chapter 8 "Managing Trees, Shrubs, and Beds Sustainably", pages 157-160, "The Planting Hole")							X	
☐	♦Use local, reputable nurseries as sources for plants				X		X	X	X
☐	♦Monitor, water and protect plant material until installation						X	X	X
☐	♦Make planting adjustments in the field based on actual site conditions				X		X		
☐	♦Remove and replace non-site-adapted, pest-susceptible plants and noxious weeds	X	X	X	X	X	X	X	X
☐	Inspect plants that are field-grown and container grown for proper root mass and development appropriate to the size of the plant (See ANSI Z60 – American Standard for Nursery Stock in "Sources" at end of this document)						X		
☐	Use the most appropriate materials to create ideal habitat for chosen trees and plants						X	X	
☐	Avoid placing edible plants in contact with known toxic materials, such as treated wood						X		X
☐	Avoid using non-organic seeds and plants if organic choices are available					X	X	X	X

MAINTENANCE

1.	**Maintain and update a Landscape Management Plan to guide annual and future maintenance practices**								
☐	♦Maintain and update a Landscape Management Plan to guide annual and future maintenance practices	X	X	X	X	X	X	X	X

Sustain Healthy Plants

		Protect and Conserve Soil	Conserve Water	Protect Water and Air Quality	Protect and Create Wildlife Habitat	Conserve Energy	Sustain Healthy Plants	Use Sustainable Methods/Materials	Protect/Enhance Human Health/Well-being
2.	**Manage all landscapes to be healthy and functioning ecosystems that maximize plant health and diversity**								
☐	♦Practice <u>Plant Health Care (PHC)</u>	X	X	X	X	X	X	X	X
☐	♦Avoid use of <u>synthetic fertilizers</u>	X	X	X	X	X	X	X	X
☐	♦Encourage plant establishment and continuing health by appropriate watering and mulching	X	X		X		X	X	X
☐	♦Remove and replace diseased or failing plants with resilient or more site-appropriate selections		X	X		X	X	X	X
☐	♦Avoid use of combination pesticide and fertilizer products	X	X	X	X	X	X	X	X
☐	♦Avoid use of synthetic mulches, such as rubber	X	X	X	X	X	X	X	X
☐	♦Prune properly to maintain the natural form of the plant					X			
☐	♦Apply organic mulches a few inches from the base of trees and plants and extending at least to the dripline	X	X		X		X	X	
☐	Manage water use for plant health and deepest root development	X	X	X			X		X
☐	Minimize disturbance of naturally occurring <u>beneficials</u>, such as biological predators and other natural control mechanisms					X	X		
☐	Fertilize plants with natural, organic products for healthy growth and flower/fruit production	X	X	X	X	X	X	X	X
☐	Thin or transplant overplanted material as needed to allow room for growth and air circulation						X		
☐	Avoid shearing plants	X	X	X	X	X	X	X	X
☐	Avoid off-target impacts to plants, animals, birds, fish and humans while applying pesticides	X	X	X	X	X	X	X	X
3.	**Use sustainable lawn care practices**								
☐	♦Use mowing practices, fertilization, aeration, topdressing, and over seeding to control weeds and sustain dense turf	X	X	X	X	X	X	X	X
☐	♦Promote nutrient cycling and deep rooting by <u>mulch mowing</u> at 2-4 inches or as appropriate for grass species		X	X	X	X	X		X
4.	**Practice <u>Integrated Pest Management (IPM)</u>**								
☐	♦Maintain healthy plants						X		
☐	♦Choose plants that are pest- and disease-resistant						X		
☐	♦Monitor for, remove/contain/control, and properly dispose of invasive plants found on the local <u>Noxious Weed List</u> for the local county area	X	X	X	X	X	X	X	X
☐	♦Monitor the worksite often to detect and identify potentially damaging pests and diseases					X	X		
☐	♦Identify all pest insects, weeds, and diseases and understand their lifecycle					X	X		
☐	♦Tolerate a few insects, weeds and diseases						X		

Sustain Healthy Plants

	Protect and Conserve Soil	Conserve Water	Protect Water and Air Quality	Protect and Create Wildlife Habitat	Conserve Energy	Sustain Healthy Plants	Use Sustainable Methods/Materials	Protect/Enhance Human Health/Well-being
♦ Replace plants that attract damaging pests and diseases				X		X		
♦ Establish action thresholds for actively managing pests						X		
♦ Manage pests and diseases most susceptible lifecycle stage, when management is easier, less costly, and more likely to succeed						X		
♦ Utilize IPM strategies and methods that reduce or eliminate the need for chemical pesticides	X	X	X	X	X	X	X	X
♦ Minimize or eliminate the use of chemical pesticides	X	X	X	X	X	X	X	X
♦ Use 2-4 inches of organic mulches to suppress weeds, such as cardboard, arborist wood chips, and bark	X	X				X	X	X
♦ Use ground covers to shade soil for weed control	X	X			X	X	X	X
♦ Evaluate how IPM strategies work, modify and adapt new strategies						X		
♦ Recognize and protect common beneficials	X		X	X		X		X

USE SUSTAINABLE METHODS AND MATERIALS

Key concepts: sustainable materials, salvage landscape plants and materials, recycled content, composting, closed system management

Use Sustainable Methods and Materials

DESIGN

		Protect and Conserve Soil	Conserve Water	Protect Water and Air Quality	Protect and Create Wildlife Habitat	Conserve Energy	Sustain Healthy Plants	Use Sustainable Methods / Materials	Protect/Enhance Human Health/Well-being
1.	**Design with existing and local materials from sustainable businesses**								
☐	◆Specify renewable, biodegradable, and recycled materials	X	X	X		X		X	X
☐	◆Specify new materials with recycled content		X	X		X		X	X
☐	◆Specify locally sourced materials			X		X		X	X
☐	Design with sustainable materials that can be later re-purposed, reused and recycled		X	X		X		X	X
☐	Specify Forest Stewardship Council (FSC) certified wood products	X		X	X	X	X	X	X
☐	Specify recycled compost and mulch	X			X		X	X	X
☐	Reuse on-site structures, hardscapes, and landscape amenities			X		X		X	X
☐	Avoid use of polyvinyl chloride (PVC) and non-biodegradable materials as weed barriers	X	X	X	X	X	X	X	X
☐	Purchase materials from manufacturers whose process reduce resource consumption and waste	X	X			X		X	X
2.	**Avoid specifying toxic products or materials**								
☐	◆Specify paints, sealants, and coatings that emit low levels of volatile organic compounds (VOCs)	X	X	X	X	X		X	X
3.	**Consider human health issues in plant selection**								
☐	Use edible plants in planting design							X	X
☐	Avoid use of noxious weeds or genetically modified organisms (GMOs)	X		X	X	X	X	X	X
☐	Avoid specifying known allergenic plants or materials			X				X	X
☐	Avoid specifying poisonous plants, especially for clients with children							X	X
4.	**Design to maximize use of water and energy conservation options**								
☐	◆Design to maximize water and energy conservation options		X			X		X	X

CONSTRUCTION

1.	**Use closed system management**								
☐	◆Salvage, reuse, compost and recycle materials from site, demolition, and construction	X	X	X	X	X		X	X
☐	◆Dispose of waste material in the most environmentally sound manner available	X	X	X		X		X	X

Use Sustainable Methods and Materials

		Protect and Conserve Soil	Conserve Water	Protect Water and Air Quality	Protect and Create Wildlife Habitat	Conserve Energy	Sustain Healthy Plants	Use Sustainable Methods/Materials	Protect/Enhance Human Health/Well-being
	♦ Use landscape materials that are salvaged or have recycled content	X	X	X	X	X		X	X
	Salvage existing plants for reuse				X		X	X	X
	Reuse plants salvaged from an alternate, local site				X		X	X	X
	Recycle used plant containers			X	X			X	X
2.	**Manage stormwater onsite**								
	♦ Manage erosion through Temporary Erosion and Sediment Control (TESC) practices	X		X	X			X	
	♦ Install <u>low impact development (LID)</u> and <u>green stormwater infrastructure (GSI)</u> features	X		X	X		X	X	X

MAINTENANCE

1.	**Minimize fuel use, air and noise pollution**									
	♦ Use energy-efficient vehicles, equipment and power tools			X		X		X	X	
	♦ Maintain vehicles, equipment and power tools in optimal working condition to prevent fuel, hydraulic fluids and oil drips, leaks, and spills	X		X	X	X	X	X	X	
2.	**Use <u>closed system management</u>**									
	♦ Recycle or reuse organic matter generated during site operations and maintenance	X	X	X	X	X	X	X	X	
	♦ Provide plant nutrition from renewable materials such as compost and mulches	X	X	X	X	X	X	X	X	
	♦ Reuse salvaged materials on site						X	X	X	
	Apply organic mulches a few inches from the base of trees and plants and extending at least to the dripline	X	X		X			X		
	Compost organic waste and materials on site				X		X	X	X	
	Reduce the need for offsite sources of landscape materials and supplies	X	X	X	X	X		X	X	
3.	**Support sustainable business practices**									
	♦ Send organic debris and materials that cannot be used onsite to an offsite composting or recycling facility	X		X	X	X		X	X	
	Provide plant nutrition from renewable materials that are sustainably harvested	X	X	X	X	X	X	X	X	
	Purchase materials from manufacturers whose process reduce resource consumption and waste	X	X	X	X	X		X	X	
4.	**Practice <u>Plant Health Care (PHC)</u>**									
	♦ Know your plants	X	X	X	X	X	X	X	X	
	♦ Determine key problems: biotic and abiotic	X	X	X	X	X	X	X	X	
	♦ Optimize plant health	X	X	X	X	X	X	X	X	
	♦ Study the landscape ecosystem	X	X	X	X	X	X	X	X	

Use Sustainable Methods and Materials

		Protect and Conserve Soil	Conserve Water	Protect Water and Air Quality	Protect and Create Wildlife Habitat	Conserve Energy	Sustain Healthy Plants	Use Sustainable Methods/Materials	Protect/Enhance Human Health/Well-being
	◆ Employ <u>Integrated Pest Management (IPM)</u> strategies	X	X	X	X	X	X	X	X
5.	**Practice Integrated Pest Management (IPM)**								
	◆ Create an IPM plan to produce a long-term, sustainable suppression and prevention of pests and diseases	X	X	X	X	X	X	X	X
	◆ Avoid using toxic products or materials	X	X	X	X	X	X	X	X
	◆ Establish action thresholds for actively managing pests							X	
	◆ Use cultural, mechanical and biological IPM strategies	X		X	X		X	X	X
	◆ Create diversity in landscapes to encourage natural, biological pest control processes	X		X	X	X	X	X	X
	◆ If pesticides are necessary, choose the least toxic products	X		X	X	X	X	X	X
	Choose manual pest management methods such as hand pulling weeds	X		X			X	X	X
	Remove non-site-adapted, pest-susceptible plants and noxious weeds	X	X	X	X		X	X	X
6.	**Be aware of human health and safety issues in landscapes**								
	Avoid using toxic landscape products or materials	X		X	X		X	X	X
	Exercise caution with using unfiltered, harvested rainwater for irrigating edible food crops							X	X
7.	**Provide regular training for staff**								
	◆ Train staff in <u>green stormwater infrastructure (GSI)</u> feature function, repair, and maintenance							X	
	◆ Train staff to use and maintain irrigation systems for maximum efficiency and plant health							X	
	◆ Train staff in wildlife identification, biology, and habitat design management							X	
	◆ Train staff in proper pruning practices							X	
	◆ Train staff in <u>PHC practices,</u> strategies and methods							X	
	◆ Train staff in <u>IPM practices,</u> strategies and methods							X	

Note: Human Health and Well-being BMPs are blended into all the BMP sections.

SOURCES

ANSI A300 Tree Care Standards, https://www.tcia.org/TCIA/BUSINESS/ANSI_A300_Standards_/TCIA/BUSINESS/A300_Standards/A300_Standards.aspx

ANSI Z60 American Nursery Stock Standards, https://www.americanhort.org/page/standards

Bay-Friendly Landscape Guidelines: Sustainable Practices for the Landscape Professional, Stopwaste.org (Alameda County, CA program). www.BayFriendly.org

EnviroStars Application/Worksheet: Landscapers & Nurseries, EnviroStars Program, www.envirostars.com

Guidance for Federal Agencies on Sustainable Practices for Designed Landscapes, October 2011. https://www.sustainability.gov/pdfs/sustainable_landscaping_practices.pdf

Link, Russell. Living with Wildlife in the Pacific Northwest. University of Washington Press, 2004.

LID -Low Impact Development Technical Guidance Manual, revised December 2012, WSU and Puget Sound Partnership, http://www.psp.wa.gov/downloads/LID/20121221_LIDmanual_FINAL_secure.pdf

Matheny, Nelda and James R. Clark. Trees and Development: A Technical Guide to Preservation of Trees During Land Development, International Society of Arboriculture, 1998.

McDonald, David. Ecologically Sound Lawn Care for the Pacific Northwest, December 1999, Seattle Public Utilities. See "Lawns" at www.seattle.gov/util/LandscapeProfessionals or

Organic Land Care Standard, 4th Edition, Society for Urban Land Care (SOUL), 2007. www.organiclandcare.org

Oregon Tilth Organic Land Care Policies & Standards, 1st edition, 2009. Oregon Tilth Accredited Organic Land Care Program, Oregon Tilth. https://tilth.org/education/resources/organic-land-care-accredited-practitioners/

Resource-efficient Natural Landscaping: Design, Build, Maintain, May 2007. Seattle Public Utilities, See www.seattle.gov/util/LandscapeProfessionals or

Soils for Salmon (soil best practices), Washington Organic Recycling Council, www.soilsforsalmon.org or for builders www.buildingsoil.org

Sonoma State College Sustainable Landscape Certificate program, http://www.sonoma.edu/

Standards for Organic Land Care: Practices for the Design and Maintenance of Ecological Landscapes, 5th edition, January 2011. Northeast Organic Farming Association (NOFA), www.organiclandcare.net

The Sustainable Sites Initiative: Guidelines and Performance Benchmarks, 2009. American Society of Landscape Architects, Lady Bird Johnson Wildflower Center at The University of Texas at Austin, United States Botanic Garden. http://www.sustainablesites.org/

Tree Protection classes and information, http://pnwisa.org

Tree Protection on Construction and Development Sites Guidebook http://file.dnr.wa.gov/publications/rp_urban_treeprtctnguidbk.pdf

Turf and Landscape Irrigation Best Management Practices, 2010. Irrigation Association, http://www.irrigation.org

WSU Extension Master Gardener Program, http://mastergardener.wsu.edu/

Turfgrass Water Conservation Alliance, https://www.tgwca.org/

Washington State Stormwater Management Manuals, for Western and Eastern WA, www.ecy.wa.gov/programs/wq/stormwater/manual.html

SECTION I: Sustainable Landscape Management

IN THIS SECTION	PAGE
Introduction to Sustainability *Source: Chapter 1 of Sustainable Landscape Management:* *Design, Construction, and Maintenance*	33
Sustainable Lanscape Construction: **Process, Irrigation Systams, and Hardscape Materials** *Source: Chapter 3 of Sustainable Landscape Management:* *Design, Construction, and Maintenance*	47
Retrofitting Existing Landscapes for Sustainability *Source: Chapter 4 of Sustainable Landscape Management:* *Design, Construction, and Maintenance*	69
Ecosystem Development & Management **in the Context of Sustainable Landscapes** *Source: Chapter 5 of Sustainable Landscape Management:* *Design, Construction, and Maintenance*	89
Building a Sustainable Future *Source: Chapter 1 of Designing the Sustainable Site: Integrated* *Design Strategies for Small Scale Sites & Residential Landscapes*	109
The Sustainable Sites Initiative: **The Case for Sustainable Landscapes** *Source: American Society of Landscape Architects, Lady Bird* *Johnson Wildflower Center at The University of Texas at Austin,* *and United States Botanic Garden*	125

chapter 1
Introduction to Sustainability

INTRODUCTION

Sustainable landscape management is a philosophical approach to creating and maintaining landscapes that are ecologically more stable and require fewer inputs than conventional landscapes. They are still artificial landscapes inserted into highly disturbed site environments and maintained to meet the expectations of owners and occupants. Sustainability is a relative concept and more a goal to strive for rather than a well-defined end point. There will never be truly self-sustaining constructed landscapes, only landscapes that are more or less sustainable than our current efforts. To better understand sustainability, it is useful to review the historical origins of the movement. This will shed light on why there is so much interest in the topic.

HISTORICAL PERSPECTIVE

The sustainability movement started shortly after the industrial revolution, beginning in the 18th century. As cities became more industrialized and the ability to extract and use resources increased, it was not long before cities grew to an unprecedented scale and the population began to explode. This transformation changed everything and quickly brought out detractors. It was 1798 when Thomas Malthus, an English country parson, penned his *Essay on Population*. In this writing, he questioned whether the earth could support geometric population growth (Malthus 1798). He feared the poor (the laboring classes) would reproduce faster than the world could provide for them, resulting in a total collapse of society. Malthus's essay sparked reaction and has been debated almost continually since it was published. The heart of the debate is whether nations can keep finding and extracting enough resources to support a constantly increasing population without running out.

The philosophical discussion deals with political and economic theory. Many of the major figures in the sustainable development movement have been economists. While industrialists were busy exploiting resources, there was always a skeptical economist who would raise his or her hand and say, "Wait a minute. I think we may have a problem." In 1865, William Jevons wrote *The Coal Question* (Jevons 1865). In Jevons's time, coal was the only functional source of energy. He hypothesized that as population (and demand for coal) increased, Britain would exhaust its reserves and the economy would fail. He proposed that the British economy would slowly decline and be displaced by other countries with more natural resources. In terms of coal, he was essentially correct. It never occurred to him that other energy sources would ever be economically feasible (which was a big mistake). Two things can be learned from Jevons: first, hard-and-fast predictions will probably be wrong; and, second, technology will attempt to solve any problem caused by misuse of resources.

The idea that there is a technological fix for every problem is debated among those interested in sustainability. Even though humankind has been incredibly resourceful in finding new technological solutions for energy resources, there is a nascent feeling among proponents of sustainability that the world cannot indefinitely rely on innovation to find ways to exploit the earth's resources. In their view, it is time to find ways to avoid depleting those resources and (perhaps) even enhance them.

Prior to today's sustainability movement, countries supported ever-increasing populations by extracting resources to produce food and other staples without regard for the environmental consequences. What these efforts were doing to the earth or how they might affect its capacity to provide for future generations did not factor into the equation. For example, the basic strategy for obtaining oil has always been to find new places to drill and to drill deeper. Oil companies have scoured the earth using an incredible array of technologies in search of more oil. Drilling occurs in climates and locations that would have been impossible a hundred years ago. As such, each new source seems to increase the potential for environmental catastrophes (e.g., the *Exxon Valdez* in 1989 and Gulf of Mexico in 2010).

EMERGENCE OF THE SUSTAINABILITY MOVEMENT

There is no verifiable starting point for the current sustainability movement. It seems to have converged from several different broad ideas concerning our relationship with the natural world. Some of the key figures who have contributed to the discussion include Frederick Law Olmsted and Calvert Vaux, John Muir, Theodore Roosevelt and Gifford Pinchot, Aldo Leopold, Rachel Carson, and Ian McHarg. Their history provides a better understanding of how the sustainability movement has evolved to the present. This discussion will consider the landscape management perspective.

Olmsted and Vaux

In the mid-1800s, Frederick Law Olmsted and Calvert Vaux partnered to develop the Greensward Plan for an urban park, now known as Central Park, in New York City. Even though the park was built on largely derelict land and required massive efforts to reconfigure the topography, these two artists produced a relatively wild and natural landscape that provided a welcome natural experience for the public. This came at a time when New York City was becoming increasingly industrialized and home to a huge labor force living in squalid tenement buildings. Population density was high, and workers were unable to escape the summer cholera epidemics. There were virtually no recreational options available to the working class. Life was hard for all but the wealthy.

Olmsted, the more dominant and vocal of the two, stood out as a passionate advocate for natural spaces in the city that would provide passive recreational activities for city dwellers. He viewed landscapes in the same manner as a naturalist would view a forest or prairie (Figure 1-1). Olmsted and Vaux's designs created apparent natural landscapes that were, in fact, manufactured. Interestingly, though Olmsted obsessed over plant materials, he felt constrained by his lack of knowledge of plants and their appropriate niches in the landscape.

Olmsted's and Vaux's careers (and those of Olmsted's sons) spanned a period of major public park development throughout the United States. Their efforts enhanced the public's awareness of the value of beautiful and natural-looking landscapes. During his 50-year career, Olmsted was involved in designing some of the most outstanding

Figure 1-1 The designs of Frederick Law Olmsted and Calvert Vaux often mimicked nature. These natural landscapes are typical of scenes created in their work: (a) mountain meadow, (b) lake surrounded by forest, and (c) towering trees in a forest.

and enduring public parks in the world. He was well ahead of his competition and today is widely regarded as the father of landscape architecture in the United States.

Preservation versus Conservation

Coming from a completely different perspective and emerging as a major voice during the last half of Olmsted's career was John Muir. Muir was a self-taught naturalist who devoted much of his life to extolling the virtues of the natural world and who lamented the defiling of the wilderness by humans. Muir felt wilderness should be preserved for its own sake (Figure 1-2).

A visit to Yosemite in California in 1868 fueled Muir's love of wilderness and nature. He spent much of his time exploring this region and quickly began

Figure 1-2 John Muir's view was to preserve wilderness by making it off-limits to all commercial interests.

to understand the negative impact of cattle and sheep grazing on fragile ecosystems. During this time, the nation was rapidly expanding, and opportunists were quick to exploit all natural areas as they sought their fortunes. This new breed of entrepreneurs disregarded the intrinsic value of natural areas and how resource extraction threatened to destroy nature.

Muir's efforts eventually led to the preservation of several wilderness areas, notably Yosemite Valley in California. Muir founded the Sierra Club in 1892, long considered one of the most powerful voices for preservation of wilderness. A split developed between preservationists like Muir, who believed wilderness should be left alone and appreciated for its beauty and spiritual values, and conservationists such as Gifford Pinchot and President Theodore Roosevelt, who believed that forests and wilderness areas should be preserved but also be profitably used for grazing, timber harvest, and other commercial activities (Figure 1-3). This difference in opinion continues today and is reignited whenever plans are announced for logging in old-growth forests or when areas containing endangered species are targeted for development.

Figure 1-3 Theodore Roosevelt and Gifford Pinchot believed wilderness should be conserved but still used for commercial resource extraction, such as the logging shown in this photo.

Emergence of the Land Ethic

In the 1940s, Aldo Leopold expressed a more philosophical view of the relationship between nature and humans. Trained as a forester, Leopold spent much of his career working with wildlife in the arid Southwest and later in the Midwest of the United States. Although he held strong opinions about how the earth should be treated, he was not entirely opposed to using natural resources for hunting and fishing or even mining. His opinion was different from the opinions of other environmentalists and his message less extreme than that of the preservationists.

In 1949, shortly after his death, Leopold's *A Sand County Almanac* was published. This collection of essays starts with the naturalist's year in Sand County, Wisconsin, followed by his experiences in the western states, where he observed human successes and failures in understanding ecosystems in a diverse array of climates. The text concludes with an elaboration of his philosophy about wilderness, conservation, and, ultimately, what he called "the land ethic." The land ethic is best explained in his own words:

> All ethics so far evolved rest upon a single premise: that the individual is a member of a community of interdependent parts. His instincts prompt him to compete for his place in that community, but his ethics prompt him also to co-operate (perhaps in order that there may be a place to compete for). (Leopold 1949)

> The land ethic simply enlarges the boundaries of the community to include soils, waters, plants, and animals, or collectively: the land. (Leopold 1949)

He goes into more detail in later passages:

> A land ethic of course cannot prevent the alteration, management, and use of these "resources," but it does affirm their right to continued existence in a natural state. (Leopold 1949)

> In short, a land ethic changes the role of *Homo sapiens* from conqueror of the land-community to plain member and citizen of it. It implies respect for his fellow-members, and also respect for the community as such. (Leopold 1949)

Leopold believed that people need to view the natural world in terms of a biotic pyramid (what today is known as an ecosystem), defined by interconnected webs of relationships among soil, plants, and animals. How humans impact the land affects, often profoundly, the relationships among all participants, and they need to be mindful of everything they do managing the "land." Even though Leopold's emphasis was on wild lands, his message is just as powerful when considering constructed landscapes (Figure 1-4).

Post–World War II

Reflecting on the times, it is interesting to consider that when Leopold was working, there were only about 125 million people in the United States. The nation had just emerged from the Great Depression and the Dust Bowl and had yet to develop the fertilizer and chemical industries of modern times. The dawn of the chemical age began just after World War II and had profound impacts on every facet of our relationship with the earth and all of its inhabitants. It is hard to imagine the sense of optimism that defined the postwar period from 1945 through the 1950s. In his description of this era in *The Life and Times of the Thunderbolt Kid*, Bill Bryson summarizes the period perfectly:

> Happily we were indestructible. We didn't need seatbelts, air bags, smoke detectors, bottled water, or the Heimlich maneuver. We didn't require child-safety caps on our medicines. We didn't need helmets when we rode our bikes or pads for our knees and elbows when we went skating. We knew without a written reminder that bleach was not a refreshing drink and

Figure 1-4 Aldo Leopold's land ethic promoted the idea that humans should be part of nature rather than in control of it. (a) Natural area accessible to people and (b) wildlife area in the middle of an urban development.

that gasoline when exposed to a match had a tendency to combust. We didn't have to worry about what we ate because nearly all foods were good for us: sugar gave us energy, red meat made us strong, ice cream gave us healthy bones, coffee kept us alert and purring productively. (Bryson 2006)

In the midst of the euphoric optimism of the 1950s, the world embraced nearly all technological marvels. One of the biggest marvels was synthetic pesticides, or, more specifically, fungicides, herbicides, and insecticides. Having been developed during World War II, many products had just recently been released for public use. Significant among these was dichlorodiphenyltrichloroethane (DDT), an insecticide that promised to eliminate nearly every insect pest that affected humans and crops. At the time, it was considered safe for people, which meant that it could be used indiscriminately—and it was. By 1960, it was becoming apparent that users did not understand all of the implications of DDT, as well as other pesticides that were rapidly coming into the market. For one person in particular, widespread use of insecticides posed a real threat to the natural world that was without precedent.

Rachel Carson

Rachel Carson was a naturalist, marine biologist, and author. Starting in 1941, she produced a trilogy of "sea" books: *Under the Sea Wind*, *The Sea around Us* (1951), and *The Edge of the Sea* (1955). *The Sea around Us*, the most successful of the three, explores nearly every facet of the sea. Carson's ability to blend science with the awe and wonder of the natural world made the life aquatic come alive. The book demonstrated her vast scientific knowledge and her love of nature and ecology. It was after her sea trilogy that she began work on her last, and by far most influential, book. In 1962, just two years before she died of cancer, Carson completed *Silent Spring*. *Silent Spring* was a different kind of book than the public had grown to expect from her. Rather than awe and wonder, it was filled with anger and frustration as she took to task "man's assaults upon the environment" (Carson 1962). Specifically, she singled out "contamination of air, earth, rivers, and sea with dangerous and even lethal materials" (Carson 1962).

Carson focused primarily on indiscriminate use of insecticides (DDT, endrin, dieldrin, and chlordane, among others). She was fully aware of the problems insects posed to humans and crops and made this clear early when she wrote:

> All this is not to say there is no insect problem and no need for control. I am saying, rather, that control must be geared to realities, not to mythical situations, and that the methods employed must be such that they do not destroy us along with the insects. (Carson 1962)

She expanded on this later:

> It is not my contention that chemical insecticides must never be used. I do contend that we have put poisonous and biologically potent chemicals indiscriminately into the hands of persons largely or wholly ignorant of their potentials for harm. (Carson 1962)

She then went on to detail numerous examples of environmental catastrophes and human tragedies resulting from poor judgment and plain misuse of insecticides in the quest for cheap and effective insect control. Although she does profile problems associated with other pesticides, insecticides are the primary focus.

This iconic book was controversial when it was published and remains so today. It split the world into two distinct camps: those who valued the benefits of pesticides and those who believed pesticides caused more problems than they solved. In the nearly 50 years since it was first published, copious resources have been spent looking for evidence to support either view. Many magazine articles and several books have followed *Silent Spring*, challenging Carson's viewpoint (Bailey 2002; Makson 2003; Marco, Hollingworth, and Durham 1987; Whitten 1966).

The impact of *Silent Spring* has been immense. It was influential in banning the use of DDT and numerous other chlorinated hydrocarbon insecticides, in creating the U.S. Environmental Protection Agency, and in providing a blueprint for modern environmentalism. Along the way, Carson has been lauded for producing one of the most influential books of the century, cursed as a radical environmentalist who was wrong about many of the questions she raised, and blamed for the death from insect-borne illnesses of millions of people worldwide who otherwise might have lived if DDT had been available. Given her background in science, her distinguished career as a marine biologist, and her success as a nature writer, Rachel Carson cannot be dismissed as a mindless crank spreading doom and gloom without regard for the consequences.

It is remarkable how accurate she was in her analysis of how humans can create problems because of their failure to fully study the ramifications of their decisions. Her descriptions of fish kills as a result of widespread application of insecticides to control gypsy moths (*Lymantria dispar*) in forests stand out as systematic failures of public policy. Her book demonstrates the importance of studying problems thoroughly before acting and exercising healthy skepticism about new technology before it is adequately tested.

Design with Nature

In 1969, Ian McHarg, an urban planner at the University of Pennsylvania, wrote *Design with Nature* (McHarg 1969), which addressed many of the same issues raised by Rachel Carson. His discussion was in the context of our approach to the built environment. At intervals in his thesis, McHarg outlined in great detail various catastrophes of failed planning, which included a study of the New Jersey shore where lack of intelligent planning resulted in indiscriminate building of vacation homes on fragile dune areas. A major storm in March 1962 resulted in serious destruction of homes and roads throughout the development. McHarg's study explained the inevitability of this failure and showed that careful analysis of a site could enable us to develop areas mindfully, avoid destroying ecosystems, provide desired

Figure 1-5 This freeway interchange demonstrates our ability to impose our will on the land. Ian McHarg believed it was possible to design the built environment in harmony with the natural environment and avoid the problems associated with thoughtless development.

recreational opportunities, and facilitate a sustainable tourist industry.

McHarg's analysis demonstrates the power of careful investigation and the value of producing win-win solutions to solve problems, ranging from determining the least intrusive location for highways to developing metropolitan areas without spoiling watershed ecosystems or eliminating local agriculture (Figure 1-5). His approach required study of multiple factors such as historic features, scenic values, social values, geology, ecological associations, stream quality, forests, marshes, beaches, and wildlife. By creating a series of overlapping transparent maps, he was able to delineate areas suited to development and areas to be held "off-limits" to development. His efforts demonstrated that, in virtually all situations, it is possible to identify the most effective and least destructive way to develop an area.

McHarg was remarkably philosophical about the issues facing humankind. His writing is infused with lofty visions of the role of humans in protecting the natural world. One of his themes involves the concept of entropy, which, in simple terms, is an increasing state of disorder. Negentropy is the opposite; it refers to an increasing state of order. In his view, entropy is synonymous with destruction, and negentropy is synonymous with creation. According to McHarg, our goal, as participants in the world around us, is to create diverse landscapes appropriately sited and constructed in a way that fosters biological diversity and builds from native plant palettes. In other words, we should strive for negentropy. The common process of removing all existing features of a site and imposing an artificial structure and landscape complete with imported soils and plants chosen without regard to the environment to which they are adapted simply increases entropy. In today's terminology, landscapes imposed on a site rather than fitted to it would not be considered sustainable.

Earth Day

Concerns about the world and our ability to sustain life on earth became increasingly focused on our treatment of the environment during the 1960s. In

1970, Senator Gaylord Nelson of Wisconsin called for an Earth Day celebration on April 22. Earth Day was a national alert that promoted the idea that all was not well with the earth and change was needed. Predictions of doom were abundant and focused on the effects of overpopulation and impending starvation. The predictions included the loss of 65 million Americans by 1989 due to starvation; a loss of more than 80 percent of the world's species within 25 years; a 50 percent reduction in the amount of light reaching the earth; a severe reduction in the earth's temperature, leading to an ice age; and exhaustion of world crude oil supplies by the year 2000 (Bailey 2000). Although none of these scenarios came true (think back to William Jevons's predictions), they did awaken the public from its complacency and served as a warning of what might happen to the earth if no one is paying attention to its needs.

Our Common Future

An awareness of sustainability continued to evolve through the efforts of concerned environmentalists, scientists, and governments. In 1983, the United Nations created the World Commission on Environment and Development. Led by the former prime minister of Norway, Gro Harlem Brundtland, the commission produced a report, titled *Our Common Future*, in 1987. Among other accomplishments of the report, the commission defined sustainable development as "meeting the needs of the present without compromising the ability of future generations to meet their own needs" (World Commission on Environment and Development 1987). This definition, simple and vague as it is, reinforces the reality that if resources are overused or misused, there will be fewer resources for future generations to draw on.

In a follow-up book, *Signs of Hope*, Brundtland writes in the foreword:

> Our Common Future is a hard-won consensus of policy principles forming the basis for sound and responsible management of the Earth's resources and the common future of all its creatures. (Starke 1990)

Sustainable development has since become the banner for creating a world where everyone can live now and into the future. The concept was further detailed in a report titled the *World Conservation Strategy: Living Resource Conservation for Sustainable Development*, published by the International Union for Conservation of Nature and Natural Resources, the World Wildlife Fund, and the United Nations Environment Programme.

According to the report:

> For development to be sustainable it must take account of social and ecological factors, as well as economic ones; of the living and non-living resource base; and of the long term as well as the short term advantages and disadvantages of alternative actions. (*World Conservation Strategy* 1980)

This echoes the methods espoused by Ian McHarg and demonstrates that principles of sustainability apply not only to buildings, roads, and natural resources but to all aspects of our world, including our approach to landscape management.

SUSTAINABLE LANDSCAPES

Now that more people are taking the idea of sustainability seriously, there is a need to define specific practices and approaches that will move us in the direction of more sustainable landscapes. Much of this book will address the difficulties in balancing our desire to produce truly sustainable landscapes with the realities of designing, building, and maintaining landscapes. It will also address the issue of what to do with existing landscapes to make them more sustainable (Figure 1-6).

Efforts are currently under way throughout the industry to develop sustainable landscape practices.

Figure 1-6 Which landscape is more sustainable: (a) this totally sheared and mulched bed; (b) this beautiful arrangement of herbaceous perennials; or (c) this urban park with water features, natural grass plantings, and a modest lawn area?

Several organizations have (or are currently developing) standards. Opportunities to move landscaping practices toward sustainability are outlined in Figure 1-7.

Leadership in Energy and Environmental Design

The Leadership in Energy and Environmental Design (LEED) Green Building Rating System was first developed in 1998 by the U.S. Green Building Council. The rating system sets certification standards for building construction and, to a limited degree, landscape development associated with the building. LEED certification is awarded on a point system and addresses six basic categories (LEED 2009):

- Sustainable sites
- Water efficiency
- Energy and atmosphere
- Materials and atmosphere
- Indoor environmental quality
- Innovation and design process

Landscapes are addressed primarily under the "water efficiency" category with rating points allowed for reducing water use by 20 to 50 percent, using no potable water (or no water at all), and using innovative wastewater management technology. Points are also available under the "sustainable sites" category for reducing site disturbance through protection or restoration of open space, storm water management, and reducing heat islands associated with hard surfaces and roofs.

LEED certification recognizes landscapes as a component of the overall development of a building site but assigns somewhat arbitrary point values for landscape design strategies, leading to a "paint by

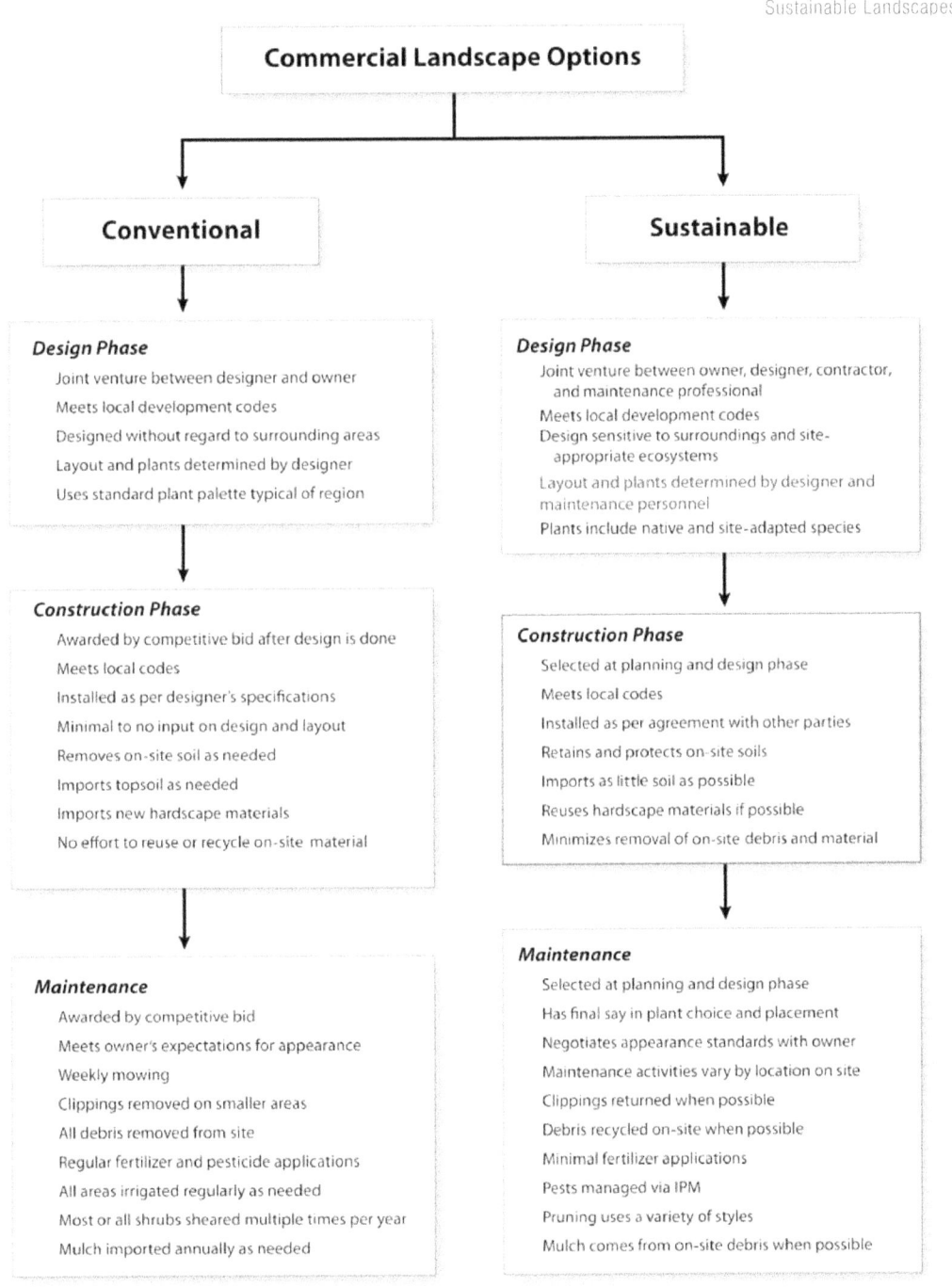

Figure 7 General comparison between conventional landscapes and sustainable landscapes.

numbers" approach to achieving the points necessary to earn specific certifications. It also involves only the designers in the certification process. Although it may be easy at the design stage to specify there will be no irrigation in the landscape, it may create numerous problems later for construction, establishment, and maintenance of the landscape. A more comprehensive and collaborative approach is needed to produce truly sustainable landscapes.

Sustainable Sites Initiative

In 2005, the American Society of Landscape Architects, the Lady Bird Johnson Wildflower Center, the University of Texas at Austin, and the United States Botanic Garden joined forces to develop sustainability guidelines for encouraging sustainable landscape development. The Sustainable Sites Initiative (SSI) interpreted the Brundtland report definition of sustainability as "design, construction, operations, and maintenance practices that meet the needs of the present without compromising the ability of future generations to meet their own needs" (Sustainable Sites Initiative 2009a). The intention of the initiative is to produce guidelines that "enable built landscapes to support natural ecological functions by protecting existing ecosystems and regenerating ecological capacity where it has been lost" (Sustainable Sites Initiative 2009b). As elaborated in Chapter 1 of the 2009 draft, the "Initiative's guidelines and benchmarks are designed to preserve or restore a site's sustainability within the context of ecosystem services—the idea that healthy ecosystems provide goods and services of benefit to humans and other organisms" (Sustainable Sites Initiative 2009b).

The guidelines and performance benchmarks identify five basic areas as criteria for determining whether sites are sustainable: soils, vegetation, hydrology, materials selection, and human health and well-being (Sustainable Sites Initiative 2009b). In attempting to elaborate on these areas, the SSI has opted for delineating desired outcomes rather than detailing prescriptive measures. Recognizing the lack of standardized practices that define sustainability, the SSI's hope is that the industry will innovate and develop its own strategies for sustainable practices.

Ultimately, the U.S. Green Building Council anticipates incorporating SSI benchmarks into the LEED Green Building Rating System. In its present form, the SSI focuses strongly on the design, construction, establishment, operations and maintenance, and monitoring and innovation phases of new developments. The need for ongoing evaluation is recognized due to the dynamic nature of landscapes. The SSI makes it clear that the initiative is a work in progress and will likely evolve over time.

Sustainable Maintenance

There are many facets of sustainable landscape management. In recent years, sustainable criteria for design and construction have become well defined, but what makes for sustainable maintenance practices is less clear. Currently, there is no blueprint for what constitutes sustainable maintenance. Further, maintenance is currently ongoing on the 99 percent of all existing landscapes that were neither designed with sustainability in mind nor constructed using sustainable methods.

Maintenance contractors historically have been out of the decision-making process until the landscape is completed. They have no input in design from a maintenance perspective and often are not involved in construction. They have no say regarding where new sites are located. They enter into the process after a significant amount of time, money, and resources have been spent to create the landscape and often when considerably less money is available for ongoing maintenance. They inherit all of the underlying problems associated with the site, including soil quality and quantity deficiencies, irrigation system design and installation deficiencies, and plant material issues. They also have to contend with the owner's expectations, which may differ from the design intent.

Figure 1-8 Current designs often include large water features and large lawn areas all kept green and neat and tidy. The corporate world embraces this look. Will their standards change any time soon?

Because aesthetic appearance is the criterion by which most judge a landscape, there is a premium on neat and tidy looking landscapes that distinguish themselves in this manner (Figure 1-8). The image projected by the building and grounds of a corporate headquarters is important to corporate stakeholders because, as the saying goes, "Image is everything." Over time, as owners come and go, maintenance contractors have to adapt to changing attitudes and trends. In short, maintenance contractors are forced to find ways to efficiently maintain sites that may have many built-in deficiencies from a sustainable perspective. Clearly, the challenges of maintaining existing landscapes are immense if the goal is to achieve sustainability.

Greenwashing

As the age of sustainability dawns, it brings with it those who claim to use sustainable practices or products when, in fact, they do not. The common term for this is "greenwashing," which is defined as "the act of misleading consumers regarding the environmental practices of a company or the environmental benefits of a product or service" (TerraChoice Environmental Marketing 2009). According to TerraChoice Environmental Marketing, the vast majority of products offered in a range of markets are guilty of greenwashing by committing one or more of the "seven sins" of greenwashing. The most common sins include:

Hidden trade-offs. Pointing out one positive attribute while ignoring other negative attributes

Vague claims. Claims that are so broad or ill-defined that they mislead consumers

No proof to support claims. Offering no proof that claims are substantiated by research

These sins can be used to promote services as "natural," "green," or "organic" when they are no different from conventional landscape maintenance practices. A healthy dose of realism is needed as the industry pursues the goal of sustainable landscape management. It may be that on many sites contractors are already practicing sustainable maintenance while others who claim to be sustainable are only greenwashing.

SUMMARY

To succeed, sustainability has to be more than just a fad. In this chapter, the historical glimpse of how sustainable ideas have developed over time demonstrates that interest in sustainability has been a relevant topic for a long time. In all segments of society, there are opportunities to develop sustainable approaches, which include constructed landscapes. At this point, there are few rules and many ideas. The search for sustainable landscape management strategies is just beginning and will continue for some time. Techniques will evolve over time as a result of both successes and failures. This book aspires to offer practical ideas and techniques, based on current knowledge, to begin the process of creating sustainable landscapes.

STUDY QUESTIONS

1. Define sustainability as it relates to landscapes. Are any constructed landscapes truly sustainable? Explain.
2. Thomas Malthus and William Jevons were both pessimistic about the future. How have their predictions played out so far?
3. How did Frederick Law Olmsted and Calvert Vaux view the role of landscapes (parks) in the context of the urban environment? What did they strive for in designing their parks?
4. John Muir and Gifford Pinchot were both intimately involved with the wilderness areas in the western United States. How did their views differ from each other? What was Muir's lasting legacy?
5. Aldo Leopold developed the land ethic. Exactly what is the land ethic and what does it have to do with sustainability? How did Leopold's ideas differ from Muir's?
6. What changes occurred after World War II that led to the current nonsustainable approach to landscape maintenance? Is conventional maintenance really unsustainable? Explain.
7. What did Rachel Carson do that has affected today's sustainability movement?
8. Explain Carson's attitude toward chemical pest control. In her view, what was wrong with pest control strategies in the DDT era?
9. What did Ian McHarg prove through his approach to landscape planning? Explain what McHarg meant by entropy and negentropy.
10. How did *Our Common Future* explain the concept of sustainability? How can that be interpreted in constructed landscapes?
11. What is LEED and what does it have to do with sustainability?
12. What is the Sustainable Sites Initiative trying to accomplish? What are the five areas it has designated to determine the sustainability of landscapes?
13. What challenges does the landscape maintenance industry face in attempting to develop more sustainable landscapes?
14. What is greenwashing? How does it threaten the sustainable landscape movement?

SUGGESTED READING

Background

Edwards, A. R. 2005. *The sustainability revolution: Portrait of a paradigm shift*. Gabriola Island, BC: New Society Publishers.
Leopold, A. 1949. *A Sand County almanac: And sketches here and there*. Oxford: Oxford Univ. Press.
McDonough, W., and M. Braungart. 2002. *Cradle to cradle: Remaking the way we make things*. New York: North Point Press.
McHarg, I. L. 1969. *Design with nature*. Garden City, NY: Doubleday/Natural History Press.

The Environmentalist Perspective

Bormann, F. H., D. Balmori, and G. T. Geballe. 2001. *Redesigning the American lawn: A search for environmental harmony*. 2nd ed. New Haven, CT: Yale Univ. Press.
Carson, R. 1962. *Silent spring*. New York: Houghton Mifflin.

The Skeptic Perspective

Bailey, R. 2000. Earthday, then and now. *Reason Online* (May), http://www.reason.com/news/show/27702.html (accessed June 8, 2009).
Lomborg, B. 2001. The skeptical environmentalist: Measuring the real state of the world. Cambridge: Cambridge Univ. Press.
Sacks, D. 2008. Green guru gone wrong. *Fast Company* (November 1), http://www.fastcompany.com/magazine/130/the-mortal-messiah.html (accessed June 8, 2009).

chapter 3
Sustainable Landscape Construction: Process, Irrigation Systems, and Hardscape Materials

INTRODUCTION

Landscape design and landscape construction cannot truly be separated because issues that affect one segment affect the other segment. Because the design and construction processes involve multiple phases and often multiple personnel, good communication between parties is imperative in order to achieve design goals and the long-term success of the landscape. Ideally, the designer, the landscape contractor, and the landscape maintenance professional will communicate during the design development and installation phases to ensure project goals are achieved. In some cases, changes to the original design may be warranted to make the landscape more sustainable. Establishing a shared vision and a set of clearly stated goals that the entire team understands is critical to a successful landscape.

Sustainable landscape construction includes modifying conventional construction processes so existing vegetation and soil are considered a site resource and managed appropriately. It also includes properly designed and installed irrigation systems and integration of sustainable hardscape materials.

This chapter will discuss the following topics:

The conventional landscape construction process

A sustainable landscape construction process alternative

Sustainable irrigation design and installation strategies

Sustainable hardscape materials

THE CONVENTIONAL LANDSCAPE CONSTRUCTION PROCESS

The landscape construction process consists of multiple phases and varies depending on the size of the project, the location of the project, and the landscape contractor's preferences. Figure 3-1 illustrates the most common phases of a landscape construction project. As the focus of this text is sustainable landscape management, only the grading phase of the construction process will be discussed here. See the suggested reading at the end of this chapter for detailed information on the entire construction process.

Rough Grading

During the rough grading phase, the site is manipulated into the desired landform, which facilitates site drainage. In many cases, erosion control features are temporarily installed to limit on-site

Step 1
Preconstruction activities and site preparation

Step 2
Rough grading, drainage, site utilities, irrigation, and distribution lines installed

Step 3
Retaining walls, stairs, and any paving completed

Step 4
Site structures finished

Step 5
Finish grading, fencing, and freestanding walls

Step 6
Site amenities, plant material, and turf

Figure 3-1 Diagram showing the most common phases of a typical commercial landscape construction project.

erosion and prevent erosion from impacting areas outside of the construction site (Figure 3-2). Once erosion control measures are in place, existing site vegetation, including turf, ground covers, shrubs, or other nonprotected vegetation, are removed. In this conventional approach, these materials are usually disposed of off-site. The next step is to scrape the existing topsoil and stockpile it either on-site or nearby for use later when the site is brought back to final grade. What remains is the subgrade soil, which may have poor structure, poor permeability, nonoptimal pH, or low nutrient content (Color Plate 3-1). Using heavy equipment, the subgrade is cut and filled to create the overall shape and contours of the site. This often entails grading to create

Figure 3-2 An erosion control fence can be an effective way to minimize on-site and off-site erosion during construction.

a relatively flat area for the building (Figure 3-3). The grade that is created at the end of this phase is called the "rough grade." The rough grade is usually 5 inches (410 centimeters) below the final or finished grade to account for the addition of topsoil for planting areas or the installation of paving materials (Figure 3-4). Additional erosion control measures may need to be installed at the completion of rough grading to provide further protection against on-site and off-site erosion.

In some cases, gravel is spread over the subsoil after the rough grading is completed to make it easier for construction vehicles to maneuver around the site. Although this prevents vehicles from getting stuck in muddy conditions, it also makes for very difficult planting conditions once the construction is complete.

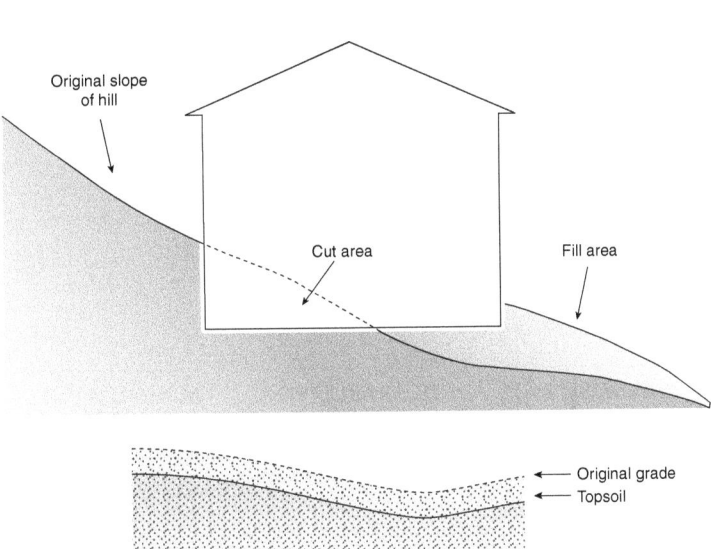

Figure 3-3 During the grading process, some areas of the existing topography are cut (removed), while others are filled with additional soil to change the overall site contours to accommodate the building and landscape.

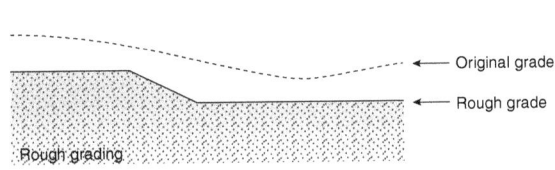

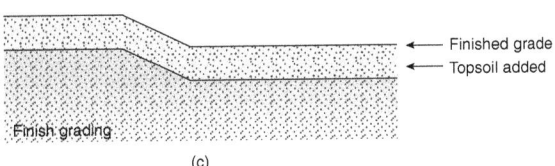

Figure 3-4 Site grading is a sequential process as illustrated in steps (a), (b) and (c). Once the rough grade is established, the last step is to bring the site to final grade by adding topsoil.

SLOPE TERMINOLOGY AND CALCULATIONS

The outcome of site grading is a change in the site's topography, in particular, the slopes found on the site. Slopes are measured as a mathematical ratio between a vertical distance and a specified horizontal distance (Figure 3-5). Slopes are generally referenced as a ratio or percentage. In either case, slope represents a change in elevation over a specified distance. Table 3-1 provides basic slope guidelines for a variety of landscape settings. These guidelines must be considered during the grading phase of the construction project to ensure the site has maximum functionality and meets accessibility requirements.

Ratio
- H/V (horizontal distance/vertical distance)
- 20:1

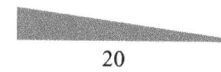

Percent slope: 20:1 = 1/20 = 0.05 = 5%

Figure 3-5 Diagram illustrating how to calculate the slope based on changes in vertical and horizontal distances.

TABLE 3-1 Slope Guidelines Relative to How the Landscape Space Will Be Used

AREA	MAXIMUM (%)	DESIRABLE (%)	MINIMUM (%)
Street	17	1–8	0.5
Parking	6	1–4	0.5
Service area	4	1–3	0.5
Walks			
Building approach	4	2–3	1
Major walkway	5	2–4	0.5
Ramp	8.33	6–8	0.5
Paved pedestrian areas (seating, plazas)	2	1.5	1
Lawn (mowed)	25	4–10	2
Lawn (mowed, adjacent to building)	25	4–10	2 (absolute minimum)
Unmowed bank	50	33	—
Swales	5–6	1–4	0.5
Playing field	4	3	2

Accessibility issues for the disabled:
- Maximum slope of 8 percent.
- 1.5 m long level landing provided for every 0.75 m of vertical climb (30 horizontal feet of ramp at 8 percent slope).
- Maximum cross-slope of 2 percent.
- Railing needed on both sides if slope is greater than 5 percent.
- Handicapped parking space access 2 percent or less in both directions.

Finish Grading

Once the site utilities (sewer, gas, electric, etc.), irrigation distribution lines, retaining walls, stairs, driveways, walkways, and outdoor seating areas have been installed, the finish grade is started. The finish grade is achieved by spreading topsoil, from the stockpile that was created during the rough grading phase, over the areas where turf and planting beds will be installed. The topsoil is carefully raked to the finish grade.

The Impact of Grading on Existing Soil

The techniques used to modify drainage patterns and create structurally sound foundations for buildings and hardscapes often result in planting areas that are not well suited for plant growth. As a result of completing general site work, the soil layers on a site are layered differently than if the soil were in its native state. As described previously, the topsoil is scraped off the building site; heavy equipment moves across the area during construction, causing soil compaction; and generally before the new landscape is installed, a layer of topsoil is brought in and spread across the area. Generally, this layer of new topsoil is not tilled into the compacted layer below, creating an interface between the two disparate soil types (Figure 3-6). The term "sandwich soil" is used to describe many urban soils where new construction has been completed because of the layering effect that is created.

Soil Compaction

Soil becomes compacted when aggregates and individual soil particles are pressed together with force. Compacted soils have higher bulk density, fewer large pores, decreased infiltration and percolation rates, and increased resistance to root penetration (Day and Bassuk 1994). This combination can be deadly to plants. Some plants are more tolerant of such growing conditions, but all plants will ultimately suffer from extended time in this type of growing environment.

Figure 3-6 Topsoil (the dark soil in this image) has a much different composition from subgrade soil and should be tilled into the existing site soil to prevent a soil interface problem.

In addition to being a poor growing environment, compacted soils also have the problem of precipitation (rain or irrigation) accumulating on the soil surface. This causes a crust to form on the surface as the soil dries out (Color Plate 3-2). Susceptibility to compaction is highly correlated to the textural composition of soil. (For a better understanding of textural categories, see http://soils.usda.gov/technical/manual/contents/chapter3_index.htm.)

Cleanup

Once the landscape installation is complete, site cleanup can begin. Typically, this involves removing any remaining construction debris, including temporary erosion control measures; any remaining vegetation that was removed when the site was cleared; and extra construction materials such as pavers, rock, or stone. These materials are generally transported and disposed of off-site. After the debris is removed and final touch-ups to the construction are complete, the walkways, driveways, and other hardscape areas are swept or washed to remove soil, mulch, or other

TOPSOIL

Many construction plans call for placement of topsoil after site construction is complete and prior to plant installation. But what constitutes topsoil is broadly defined. Sometimes the topsoil originally stockpiled from the site is used. This soil tends to be in fair shape and serves the necessary functions of topsoil. In other instances, topsoil is imported. Imported topsoil may be very different from the native soil on the site. Often it is a sandy loam or a compost/soil mix that is very high in organic matter. In both cases, it creates a shallow and nonfunctional growing environment. Another common practice is to use excavation spoils as topsoil. Although these spoils are a cheap alternative, they often contain subsoil, rocks, and soil parent material, none of which provides a suitable growing environment for plant roots. Ideally, the topsoil that is used has good aeration and drainage, contains adequate organic matter, and is free of weed seeds.

Figure 3-7 The soil erosion that has occurred on this construction site has ended up in the street and adjacent to the curbs. It will be hard to avoid polluting the storm sewers as this site is cleaned up.

organic matter. When the areas are cleaned using a hose or power washer, the wastewater often runs into storm sewers either on the site or adjacent to the site, or into nearby waterways (Figure 3-7). The sediment in this water can cause a significant increase in nonpoint source pollution for affected streams and rivers.

Conventional landscape construction processes do not account for the environmental impact that results from the site work. Removing native soils and existing vegetation significantly disrupts and damages the pre-existing ecosystems on the site. Often this type of damage is difficult and costly, if not impossible, to repair. Conventional cleanup strategies at the end of the project can cause further environmental damage to the site and surrounding areas. Wastewater from the cleanup phase typically ends up in streams, rivers, and storm sewers. These systems are particularly vulnerable to pollution from sediment runoff and chemical waste from the construction process. Relatively minor modifications to how the construction process unfolds can result in significant reductions in environmental damage to the site. A number of these modifications are encompassed in the term "sustainable development."

A SUSTAINABLE LANDSCAPE CONSTRUCTION PROCESS ALTERNATIVE

Low-impact development (LID), also called "sustainable development" or "green development," implements practices and strategies that allow site development while minimizing the impact on the environment. A major component of LID for landscapes is to use site-appropriate designs and environmentally sensitive construction practices that minimize the impact on the site.

Just as with the design process, the Sustainable Sites Initiative (2009) has created a matrix to evaluate sustainability of the landscape construction process. The overriding goal outlined in the matrix is to "minimize effects of construction-related activities" (Sustainable Sites Initiative 2009). Table 3-2 lists each goal and the outcome that is achieved when

TABLE 3-2 Environmentally Sensitive Construction Practices as Outlined in the Sustainable Sites Initiative (2009)

Goal	Purpose
Control and retain construction pollutants.	Prevent and minimize discharge of construction site pollutants and materials to protect receiving waters (including surface water, groundwater, and combined sewers or storm water systems), air quality, and public safety.
Restore soils disturbed during construction.	Restore soils disturbed during construction in all areas that will be revegetated (all areas that will not be built upon) to rebuild soils' ability to support healthy plants, biological communities, water storage, and infiltration.
Restore soils disturbed by previous development.	Restore soil function in areas of previously disturbed topsoils and subsoils to rebuild the site's ability to support healthy plants, biological communities, water storage, and infiltration.
Divert construction and demolition materials from disposal.	Divert construction and demolition (C&D) materials generated by site development from disposal in landfills and combustion in incinerators. Recycle and/or reuse C&D materials on-site when possible or redirect these materials back to the manufacturing process, other construction sites, or building materials reuse markets to support a net zero-waste site and minimize down-cycling of materials.
Reuse or recycle vegetation, rocks, and soil generated during construction.	Divert from disposal vegetation, soils, and mineral/rock waste generated during construction to achieve a net zero-waste site.
Minimize generation of greenhouse gas emissions and exposure to localized air pollutants during construction.	Use construction equipment that reduces emissions of localized air pollutants and greenhouse gas emissions.

the goal is met. Three of these goals are directly related to the construction process and include the following:

- Control and retain construction pollutants.
- Divert construction and demolition materials from disposal.
- Reuse or recycle vegetation, rocks, and soil generated during construction.

These three goals are described below, and all of the goals are outlined in detail in the Sustainable Sites Initiative (2009).

Control and Retain Construction Pollutants

A frequent consequence of standard construction practices is soil compaction, and compacted soils are directly related to reduced infiltration rates and subsequent increased runoff. Recently, federal and state regulations mandating management of on-site and off-site erosion during the construction phase have been implemented (National Pollutant Discharge Elimination System 2009; U.S. Environmental Protection Agency 2009).

Retaining pollutants and sediments on-site prevents off-site contamination of waterways used for drinking water and recreation such as swimming and fishing. Creating and implementing an erosion, sedimentation, and pollutant control plan, commonly referred to as a Stormwater Pollution Prevention Plan (SWPPP) or an Erosion and Sedimentation Control (ESC) Plan, can provide the framework to accomplish this goal. Examples of strategies often outlined in the plan include the following:

- Prevent the loss of soil during construction by storm water runoff or wind erosion by protecting stockpiled topsoil.

- Prevent runoff and infiltration of other pollutants from the construction site (i.e., concrete wash, fuels, solvents, hazardous chemical runoff, and pavement sealants) and ensure proper disposal (Sustainable Sites Initiative 2009).

Divert Construction and Demolition Materials from Disposal

Implementing sustainable design approaches can reduce waste generated from the landscape site as a result of demolition and construction processes. Retaining and reusing these materials reduces landfill disposal costs and also reduces the costs for new construction materials because fewer materials are needed.

Reuse or Recycle Vegetation, Rocks, and Soil Generated during Construction

During the typical landscape construction process, vegetation, boulders, and, in some cases, soil are removed and disposed of off-site after the clearing and grading phases have been completed. A sustainable construction approach involves incorporating these existing resources in the landscape design and using them during the construction phase. For example, boulders from the site can be used to create retaining walls or to add aesthetic interest to the design (Figure 3-8). Soil that was removed due to grading can be used on a different location at the site. If vegetation must be removed during site clearing, it should be stockpiled as mulch or composted on-site. Compost can be used as an organic amendment to the soil, and mulch can be applied to new planting beds or used as an erosion protection measure. By using these strategies, less demolition and construction debris will end up in landfills or incinerators, thereby reducing the waste stream and enhancing the sustainability of the construction process.

Figure 3-8 Boulders that were uncovered during excavation on this site were used to create a series of retaining walls.

Preserving and Incorporating Existing Vegetation

In addition to managing soil during the construction process, LID also includes preserving and incorporating existing vegetation when possible. Wooded building sites often command a premium purchase price. Yet all too frequently, the existing trees and shrubs that make the site attractive and valuable are damaged during the construction process. Construction damage to existing plants occurs from physical injury or changes to the environment around the plants. Examples of physical injury include broken limbs, gouged trunks or root collars, and severed roots. Environmental changes include increased light exposure, soil compaction, decreased root zone aeration due to excessive fill soil depth, and changes in drainage patterns that result in a significant increase or decrease in soil moisture and oxygen available to the roots. Not all species are equally sensitive to soil-related construction injury, and younger, smaller trees can withstand more root injury than large mature trees. Table 3-3 lists tree species that are tolerant to some construction damage. Conifers, oaks, redbud, and sugar maple are sensitive to soil condition changes, whereas other species such as poplar, willow, basswood, and river birch tend to tolerate these changes (Elmendorf, Gerhold, and Kuhns 2005). In general, many shrubs can withstand construction damage, because they are multistemmed, smaller than trees, and able to regenerate new root systems rapidly.

Arborists and skilled landscape contractors should work collaboratively with general contractors during initial site development to implement environmentally sensitive construction protocols.

TABLE 3-3 Common Landscape Tree Species and Their Relative Tolerance to Construction Damage

Scientific Name	Common Name	Root Severance	Soil Compaction and Flooding
Evergreen Trees			
Abies balsamea	Balsam fir	Tolerant	Tolerant
Abies concolor	White fir	Tolerant	Sensitive
Juniperus viginiana	Eastern red cedar	Tolerant	Sensitive
Picea abies	Norway spruce	Tolerant	Tolerant
Picea mariana	Black spruce	Tolerant	Tolerant
Picea pungens	Colorado spruce	Intermediate	Tolerant
Pinus banksiana	Jack pine	Tolerant	Sensitive
Pinus resinosa	Red pine	Tolerant	Sensitive
Pinus strobus	White pine	Tolerant	Sensitive
Pinus sylvestris	Scotch pine	Tolerant	Sensitive
Thuja spp.	Arborvitae	Tolerant	Tolerant
Tsuga canadensis	Eastern hemlock	Sensitive	Sensitive
Deciduous Trees			
Acer rubrum	Red maple	Tolerant	Tolerant
Acer saccharinum	Silver maple	Tolerant	Tolerant
Acer saccharum	Sugar maple	Tolerant	Sensitive
Amelanchier alnifolia	Serviceberry	Intermediate	Intermediate
Betula nigra	River birch	Tolerant	Tolerant
Betula papyrifera	Paper birch	Intermediate	Sensitive
Carpinus caroliniana	Ironwood	Sensitive	Sensitive

(Continued)

TABLE 3-3 (Continued)

Scientific Name	Common Name	Root Severance	Soil Compaction and Flooding
Celtis occidentalis	Hackberry	Tolerant	Intermediate
Cercis canadensis	Eastern redbud	Intermediate	Intermediate
Cornus spp.	Dogwood	Intermediate	Intermediate
Crataegus spp.	Hawthorn	Tolerant	Tolerant
Fagus grandifolia	American beech	Sensitive	Sensitive
Fraxinus nigra	Black ash	Tolerant	Tolerant
Ginkgo biloba	Ginkgo	Tolerant	Tolerant
Gleditsia triacanthos	Honey locust	Tolerant	Tolerant
Gymnocladus dioicus	Kentucky coffee tree	Intermediate	Intermediate
Liriodendron tulipifera	Tulip tree	Sensitive	Intermediate
Malus spp.	Crab apple	Tolerant	Tolerant
Nyssa sylvatica	Black gum	Tolerant	Tolerant
Prunus serotina	Black cherry	Intermediate	Sensitive
Quercus alba	White oak	Sensitive	Sensitive
Quercus bicolor	Swam white oak	Intermediate	Intermediate
Quercus macrocarpa	Bur oak	Tolerant	Tolerant
Quercus palustris	Pin oak	Sensitive	Tolerant
Quercus rubra	Red oak	Tolerant	Sensitive
Tilia americana	American basswood	Sensitive	Sensitive
Ulmus fulva	Slippery elm	Tolerant	Intermediate

For example, they can determine how the site will be cleared and what trees should be protected and preserved. These professionals prioritize which trees to retain based on the tree's location, overall health, species, and structural soundness. The next step is determining what type of protection, such as a root protection zone, is necessary to preserve the tree during the construction process (Figure 3-9). When the site allows, landscape contractors can plan construction traffic patterns that minimize root damage and soil compaction. They can also designate appropriate locations for on-site soil storage to minimize the likelihood of suffocating roots. If plant materials are damaged, qualified arborists and landscape contractors will be able to make correct pruning cuts if necessary to limbs and roots to ensure wound closure and to minimize the opportunity for disease or insect attack.

It takes three to seven years for construction damage to appear on most tree species. If property

Figure 3-9 (a) Root zone protection is essential to prevent damage to existing trees during construction. (b) In many cases, however, roots are not protected, and construction occurs adjacent to large trees, causing irreparable damage.

managers implement an annual tree care program, even trees moderately affected by construction damage often recover. Preserving existing plant material and incorporating it into newly constructed landscapes is a valuable part of sustainable design. If plants are protected appropriately and withstand minimal construction damage, the amount of new plant material required can be significantly reduced.

SUSTAINABLE IRRIGATION DESIGN AND INSTALLATION STRATEGIES

In the quest for sustainability, it may be easy to conclude that irrigation systems should be left out of the plan entirely because proper plant selection for the site should alleviate the need for supplemental water. Perhaps this would make sense in situations where natural landscapes evolve slowly over centuries, but it is shortsighted in the context of constructed landscapes. Constructed landscapes present a number of challenges to plant establishment and growth, including major soil disturbance, the fact that a majority of new plantings use large nursery-grown stock with compromised root systems, and the reality that planting is sometimes done during undesirable times of the year. The result of these challenges is drought-induced plant mortality, which delays development of the landscape and costs everyone involved time and money. Ultimately, client expectations and the designer's knowledge of plant materials and the local climate should guide the decision on whether or not irrigation should be installed.

Irrigation Design

Assuming irrigation is necessary, the goal is to produce a system that accomplishes two things. First, the system must meet the needs of the developing landscape by providing adequate moisture during the establishment phase. Second, the system must be designed for long-term efficiency and effectiveness. Chapter 2 described the importance of designing an irrigation system in parallel with the lawn and planting bed areas to accomplish these two goals.

IRRIGATION SYSTEMS: SHORT- AND LONG-TERM BENEFITS

Forgoing an irrigation system strictly on the principle that it is an unnecessary addition to the landscape is shortsighted. From a short-term perspective, a well-designed and well-managed irrigation system can provide the necessary assurance that plants will survive during the establishment phase. From a long-term perspective, an irrigation system allows for multiple options for replanting a landscape should the function of the landscape change. Retrofitting a landscape to add irrigation is more expensive than installing a system during the initial construction phase of the project.

Figure 3-10 This pop-up head is watering a shrub, ground cover, and turfgrass, all of which have different watering needs.

Creating Irrigation Zones

The size of individual irrigation zones is largely determined by the hydraulic capabilities of the local water supply or the pumping capacity of wells. When designing irrigation zones, there are two key rules to follow: minimize the number of zones and create separate lawn and shrub bed zones wherever possible. Using fewer zones minimizes the number of zone valves and reduces installation costs. A consideration with this approach, however, is that, as zones become larger, the chance of dissimilar areas being watered together increases (Figure 3-10) because those areas requiring more irrigation will determine run times and areas requiring less water will get too much.

The design of an irrigation system must take into account the current size of the plantings, the size of the plantings at maturity, and the relative location of irrigation zones. For example, a new lawn oriented in a north–south layout may be in full sun at installation. The north–south irrigation zones will ensure each end receives the same amount of water (Figure 3-11a). Such an arrangement is adequate at the outset while the surrounding landscape is still small and trees and shrubs have not matured to large canopies. However, as the trees grow and the grouping planted at the southern end of the lawn begins to provide summer shade, this portion of the lawn will require less water (Figure 3-11b). In this future scheme, when the necessary amount of water is applied to the exposed northern part of the lawn, the shaded southern end will be overwatered (likewise, if the system applies only the amount of water required by the southern end—the northern end of the lawn will be too dry). Had the irrigation zones been arranged differently during the design phase (i.e., east–west orientation), this variation in the future water requirements of the different turf areas would have been addressed (Figure 3-11c).

Creating separate zones for planting beds and lawns makes sense only if precipitation rates are considered and run times are adjusted to deliver the appropriate amount of water to the ornamental plants and the lawn.

Irrigating at the Plant and Hardscape Interface

Common sense suggests that any irrigation water that goes beyond the boundary of the lawn or planting bed is wasteful and inefficient. In egregious cases of water overspray, this is true. But, in reality,

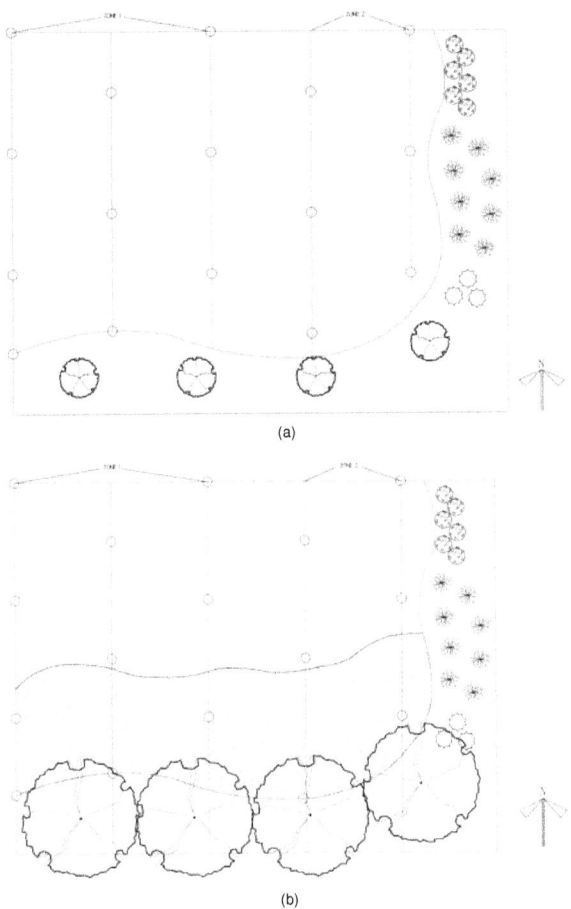
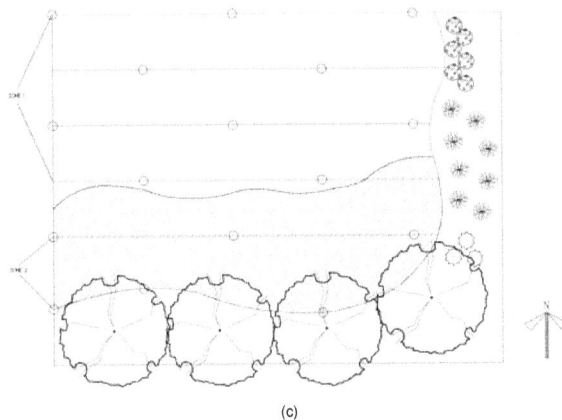

Figure 3-11 (a) When the landscape is immature and the tree canopies are small, the irrigation zoning shown here will work fine. (b) As the landscape matures and the canopy size increases, however, the current zoning will be ineffective. The turf shaded by the trees will be overwatered compared to the turf in full sun. (c) This is an example of an irrigation system that is zoned correctly to account for the maturing landscape and increased canopy size, which will shade the lawn.

the only way to water edges is to apply water to an area slightly larger than the target area. Some water needs to spray onto sidewalks or other hardscapes in order to get enough water on the lawn or adjacent bed. In large lawn areas crisscrossed by sidewalks, it makes more sense to irrigate without respect to the hardscape so a more uniform distribution of water is achieved across the entire area.

Irrigation Installation

The irrigation installation process is largely governed by local regulatory codes, but there are several practical issues that should be negotiated with designers or used by installers. Examples of these include the height of the rotor head relative to the lawn surface (stem length), installing an appropriate system for the planting beds, the head spacing, and the nozzle size. All of these have a major impact on how well the irrigation system functions.

Height of the Rotor Head Relative to the Lawn Surface (Stem Length)

Pop-up rotor heads are the irrigation method of choice for irrigating lawns. Part of this system includes a stem at the base of the head (Figure 3-12),

Figure 3-12 Pop-up rotor heads on stems of different lengths allow for effective and efficient irrigation.

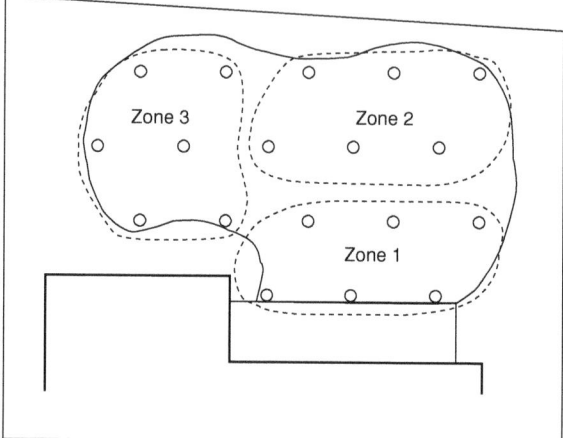

Figure 3-13 This well-designed irrigation system has multiple zones with proper head spacing in each zone to achieve optimum coverage.

which varies in length. In most instances, a longer [6 inches (15 cm)] pop-up stem is a better choice than a shorter [4 inches (10 cm)] stem. Longer stems are less likely to be obscured by grass as the system settles over time and will also compensate for the eventual buildup of thatch, allowing the head to rise high enough to ensure uniform distribution.

Installing an Appropriate System for Planting Beds

Planting beds can create a unique challenge when selecting an irrigation system. Because the perennials, shrubs, and trees in these beds will grow and mature over time, both the initial size and the mature size need to be considered when selecting and installing the system. Depending on the situation, tall pop-up heads or tall fixed heads will be most effective in bed interiors. Pop-up and fixed heads should be fitted with high-arc nozzles designed to shoot over shrubs where necessary. When berms or slopes are being irrigated, low-precipitation-rate stream rotor nozzles are a good choice and will reduce runoff potential.

Head Spacing

After initial placement of the heads, it is important to remeasure the distance between heads to ensure that the spacing is correct and optimum coverage is achieved. Where the dimensions of the area do not allow for optimum placement, heads should be positioned so the distance between them is uniform instead of some being too close and others being too far apart (Figure 3-13). Faulty measurement and poor head placement will result in uneven spacing and inadequate coverage. It is much easier to adjust head spacing during construction than after the system is installed.

Nozzle Size

Like head spacing, another critical irrigation system design consideration is nozzle size. In zones with both full- and partial-circle heads, the only way to achieve matched precipitation for the zone is to use different-sized nozzles. For instance, if a full-circle head delivers 4 gallons/minute (gpm) (16 liters/minute), half-circle heads should deliver 2 gpm (8 lpm), and quarter-circle heads should deliver 1 gpm (4 lpm). There is a tendency among some installers to use prenozzled heads. This often results in all irrigation heads, whether full- or part-circle, applying the same amount of water and leads to poor application uniformity.

SUSTAINABLE HARDSCAPE MATERIALS

Most landscapes include a combination of hardscapes (entrance areas, driveways, walkways, and outdoor seating areas), turf areas, and ornamental plants. In commercial and public spaces, hardscapes can be a significant part of the overall landscape. The diverse products available on the market today make it possible to select from a wide variety of hardscape materials, many of which will enhance the overall sustainability of the landscape. For example, permeable pavements create more efficient land use by eliminating the need for retention ponds, swales, and other storm water management devices. As a result, these products have the ability to lower overall project costs.

Figure 3-14 Limestone salvaged from a demolished retaining wall was used to create a functional patio for this seating area.

Reduce, Reuse, Recycle

Sustainability can be achieved by using fewer virgin materials in the landscape, reusing existing materials when possible, and selecting recycled products. Recycling existing materials and using products created from recycled materials also result in using fewer virgin materials.

It is possible to reuse existing materials such as wood, glass, brick, and concrete in landscapes without the materials first going through the resource-intensive industrial recycling process. Examples include reusing limestone boulders or slabs for retaining walls; using broken pieces of concrete for an outdoor seating area or walkway; or using crushed, tumbled glass as an alternative material in asphalt, concrete, or other paving mixes or as an inorganic mulch (Thompson and Sorvig 2008) (Figure 3-14). Another example of reusing existing materials is the practice of using some types of construction debris to create ballast for berms or other artificial landforms on the site.

In other cases, new hardscape products are made when materials do go through an industrial recycling process. Composite wood products, manufactured by combining recycled plastics with wood by-products,

Figure 3-15 Composite wood products are available in a range of colors, textures, and dimensional sizes.

are an example of this type of hardscape material (Figure 3-15). Consulting local, regional, and national organizations affiliated with the recycling industry can be a good way to learn about recycled products available in your area.

Environmental Impact after Installation

Hardscape materials vary in their effect on the environment. For example, concrete prevents water from soaking into the soil, thus increasing runoff, which can carry contaminants into streams and other water sources. Porous materials such as permeable interlocking concrete pavers, porous asphalt, and pervious concrete allow water to soak into the soil. Limestone is a material that will slowly break down over time and alter the pH of the adjacent soil. Chemically treated wood can be used for a number of landscape applications, but there is significant concern about the leaching properties of some of these products. Much of this concern is unfounded, yet public perception persists that these products will release harmful amounts of chemical preservatives into the soil (American Wood Preservers Institute 2004). New wood-based products have come on the market, which use more environmentally sensitive chemicals to preserve the wood or use no chemical preservatives at all.

TREATED WOOD

After being used for more than 70 years as a wood preservative, chromated copper arsenate (CCA) was removed from the nonindustrial wood preservative market on December 31, 2003. CCA is still used for products with an industrial end use such as highway construction, utility poles, and pilings (American Wood Preservers Institute 2004). Removal of CCA from the market was due in part to new policy standards and a safety review of potential health hazards from arsenic. In place of CCA, three new generations of wood-preserving products have come on the market: ammoniacal copper quat (ACQ), copper boron azole (CBA), and copper azole (CA-B). These products are marketed as ACQ Preserve, NatureWood, and Wolmanized Natural Select wood (American Wood Preservers Institute 2004). As with CCA, the new preservatives have gone through rigorous health and safety testing and have been approved for use by the U.S. Environmental Protection Agency (American Wood Preservers Institute 2004; Wilson 2002). These wood preservative products can extend the useful life of natural wood products from just a few years to more than 20 years.

EVALUATING HARDSCAPE SUSTAINABILITY

Before selecting any hardscape material, evaluate it on a variety of criteria, including:

- What virgin materials were used in manufacturing the product?
- Does the product incorporate recycled or reused materials?
- Is the surface water permeable?
- Is the material aesthetically pleasing and appropriate for the landscape design?
- Does the product have adequate structural strength for its intended use?
- How long will the product last?
- How much maintenance will the product require based on the environment where it will be installed?
- What are the initial product and installation costs?
- What tools and additional materials are needed for installation?
- Is the product readily available in your area?
- Is the product allowed for use in your area by regulatory (municipal) codes?

Maintenance Requirements

The long-term maintenance costs of some hardscape materials can be significant. Examples of maintenance include power washing composite wood, occasional vacuuming of pervious concrete, resanding concrete paver joints, resetting pavers due to settling, and reseeding turf blocks. Maintenance needs vary by product and the environment where it is used. For specific information, consult a landscape construction reference (see the Suggested Reading at the end of this chapter) or a local landscape contractor who has experience with the specific material.

Sustainable Hardscape Products for Entrance Areas, Driveways, Walkways, and Outdoor Seating Areas

Because hardscapes can account for a significant portion of commercial landscapes, it is important to choose materials that can enhance the overall sustainability of the site. The combination of increased land prices and the need to meet new storm water management requirements have led to interest in using materials other than impervious materials such as concrete (Figure 3-16).

Impervious hardscapes have a significant effect on the need for storm water management strategies. If storm water is not managed on-site, then it becomes an off-site issue that still needs to be

Figure 3-16 This public fountain in Chicago, Illinois, was surrounded with permeable interlocking concrete pavers. The result is a beautiful outdoor space and a large hardscape area that does not have runoff.
Courtesy of Unilock, Inc.

> **DISCUSSION POINTS**
>
> A 12-acre (5 ha) commercial project, which included 7 acres (3 ha) of parking, was recently developed. The development plan originally called for 1-½ acres (0.5 ha) to be set aside as a storm water detention basin. The developer opted to use pervious concrete instead of standard concrete. As a result, the developer was able to eliminate the storm water retention pond, which resulted in an overall net savings of $400,000. Why was the developer able to eliminate the storm water retention pond? What could have accounted for the net savings?

addressed. One way to manage storm water on-site is to use permeable pavements. Significant research has demonstrated the ability of permeable pavements to substantially reduce urban runoff (Interlocking Concrete Pavement Institute 2008; D. A. Smith, pers. comm.). Further, permeable pavements are recognized as a best management practice (BMP) by the U.S. Environmental Protection Agency and many local and regional storm water management agencies (Interlocking Concrete Pavement Institute 2008). Low-impact development (LID), which was discussed earlier in this chapter, includes permeable pavements as a cornerstone of its regulations, and the Leadership in Energy and Environmental Design (LEED) program offers credit for site designs that include permeable pavements (Burak and Smith 2008; U.S. Green Building Council 2009).

Permeable pavements are characterized by having high initial surface infiltration rates. These surfaces can immediately infiltrate and store rainfall and, in many cases, runoff is completely eliminated. If contaminants (oil, landscape chemicals, etc.) are on the surface of these paving materials at the time of a rainfall event, the contaminants are moved along with the rainfall through the stone subbase where they are then subjected to the natural processes that cleanse water (Bean et al. 2004; D. A. Smith, pers. comm.). When these products are used around or adjacent to plantings, they will allow water and oxygen to infiltrate into the soil, which is necessary for plant growth and development.

In commercial landscape situations, the primary technologies used to make vehicular and pedestrian pavement permeable are pervious concrete, porous asphalt, and permeable interlocking concrete pavement (Interlocking Concrete Pavement Institute 2008). Each technology has advantages and disadvantages, but all are viable alternatives to impervious hardscapes, which can result in storm water runoff. Table 3-4 compares these three products in regard to color choices, installation issues, surface cleaning requirements, winter durability, ease and effectiveness of repairs, the recycled content included in the products and if the materials themselves can be reused, and the product costs.

Pervious Concrete

Although pervious concrete has been used throughout Europe for decades, it has only been used in the United States in the past decade. It is a durable, high-porosity concrete that allows water and air to pass through it (Figure 3-17). The products function by moving water through the concrete to a 10 to 12 inch (25 to 30 cm) thick subgrade aggregate base, which holds the water until it can soak into the soil or flow to the sides (or into tiling) and into a storm water system (Figure 3-18). Pervious concrete is produced by mixing carefully controlled amounts of water and cementitious materials to create a paste, which is then mixed with aggregate particles, resulting in a thick coating around the individual particles. This results in a series of interconnected voids that allow water to drain quickly (National Ready Mixed Concrete Association 2009).

Porous Asphalt Pavement

Porous asphalt pavements are fast and easy to construct. With the proper information, most asphalt manufacturers can easily prepare the mix, and general paving contractors can install it (Asphalt

TABLE 3-4 Comparison of Characteristics of Pervious Concrete Pavement, Permeable Interlocking Concrete Pavement, and Porous Asphalt

	Color	Installation	Maintenance: Surface Cleaning	Maintenance: Winter Durability	Maintenance: Repairs	Recycled Content and Reuse	Cost
Pervious concrete pavement	Limited range of colors and textures	Cast in place; requires formwork; requires seven-day curing period	Vacuum-sweep and pressure-wash to remove sediment and surface debris	Deicing chemicals not recommended; saturation when frozen may damage concrete; snow melts and immediately drains, reducing ice hazard	Damaged or highly clogged areas can be cut out and replaced; repaired area needs to cure before use; repaired area will not match original material	Generally not manufactured with recycled aggregate or cement substitutes; concrete can be crushed and recycled	Competitive with permeable interlocking concrete pavement
Permeable interlocking concrete pavement	Wide range of colors and textures	Manufactured units of uniform size; no formwork required; can be mechanically installed; can be used immediately after installation	Vacuum-sweep to remove sediment and surface debris	Deicing salt resistant; saturation when frozen will not damage pavement; snow melts and immediately drains, reducing ice hazard	Units and aggregate can be removed, repaired, and replaced; repaired area will match surrounding area	Manufactured units can accommodate cement substitutes (e.g., fly ash, slag, etc.); pavers can be crushed and recycled	Competitive with pervious concrete pavement and porous asphalt; life cycle costs may be lower than these two products in some markets
Porous asphalt	Black or shades of gray	Requires no formwork; temperature of the mix is critical to project success; requires 24-hour curing period	Vacuum-sweep and pressure-wash to remove sediment and surface debris	Liquid deicing materials recommended; saturation when frozen may damage asphalt; snow melts and immediately drains, reducing ice hazard	Limited repair potential; can patch with impervious material; repair will not match original area	Generally not manufactured with recycled asphalt or recycled aggregate; pavement can be recycled	Less expensive than permeable interlocking concrete and pervious concrete pavement

Source: Table adapted from Interlocking Concrete Pavement Institute (2008).

Figure 3-17 Pervious concrete is a sustainable hardscape alternative. The large pores allow water to quickly flow through the paving material to the base below.

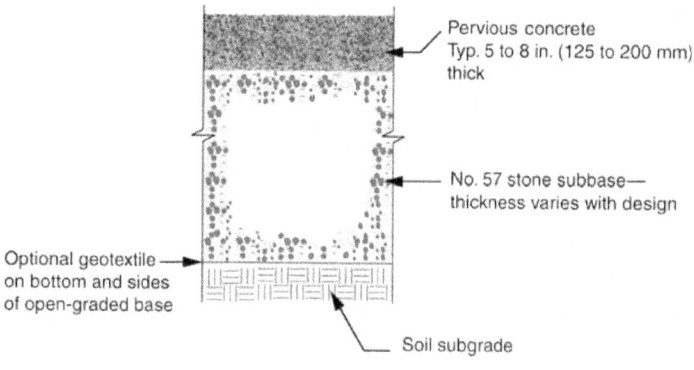

Figure 3-18 Cross section of a pervious concrete installation.

Courtesy of Interlocking Concrete Pavement Institute.

Pavement Alliance 2009). Similar to pervious concrete, water drains through the porous asphalt and into the stone subbase and then infiltrates into the soil. In contrast to pervious concrete, however, the stone subbase for porous asphalt is often 18 to 36 inches (45 to 90 cm) deep (Figure 3-19).

Permeable Interlocking Concrete Pavement

Permeable interlocking concrete pavement (PICP) is similar to both pervious concrete and porous asphalt in infiltration rate, but differs in that the pavement surface is composed of concrete pavers separated by ⅛ to ½ inch (0.3 to 1.25 cm) wide joints filled

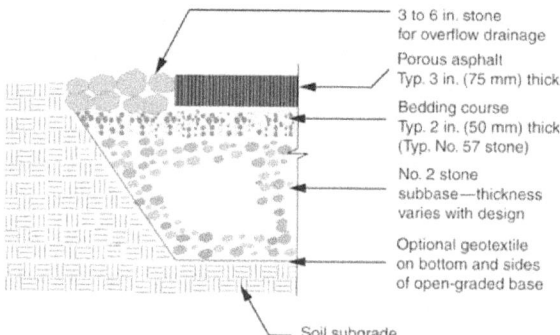

Figure 3-19 Cross section of a porous asphalt installation.
Courtesy of Interlocking Concrete Pavement Institute.

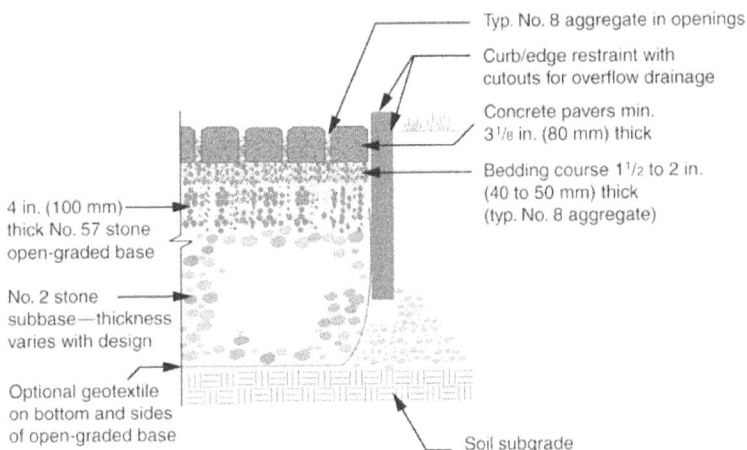

Figure 3-20 Cross section of a permeable interlocking concrete pavement installation. Courtesy of Interlocking Concrete Pavement Institute.

with aggregate (Figure 3-20). The pavers themselves are not pervious, but the joints between the pavers are, which accounts for the high infiltration rates. The pavers are installed on top of a 1½ to 2 inch (4 to 5 cm) thick bedding course of small aggregate, which sits on top of a stone subbase that is 8 to 12 inches (20 to 30 cm) thick. This stone subbase serves as a reservoir for water that has filtered through the aggregate-filled joints.

Other Sustainable Hardscape Products

In addition to the hardscape materials described earlier for entrances, walkways, driveways, and parking lots, other sustainable hardscape materials are available for other landscape uses. One such product is composite wood. Composite wood is made from a combination of recycled plastic, wood products, and glue (resin) (Color Plate 3-3). Occasionally, a small amount of virgin material, compared to the volume of recycled plastic and wood, is added to increase strength and wear resistance. The plastic and wood combination resists ultraviolet light (sunlight) damage and does not warp, bow, or fade over time and is moisture and insect resistant. It also does not require sealing, painting, or staining.

Composite wood is available in the same sizes as other dimensional lumber (i.e., 1 × 4, 2 × 4, etc.). It is also milled into prefabricated decorative elements such as balusters, handrails, rail posts, and post caps and is available in a range of colors and textures. This product can be used for outdoor seating such as benches or retaining wall caps and for large planters. Although the initial cost of composite wood products is slightly higher than that of products made from wood, the long-term cost savings can be substantial. The composite products do not require frequent maintenance such as painting or staining, and most products have a 25-year replacement warranty for cracking, warping, and splintering.

SUMMARY

Landscape construction is a multiphase process, and successful installation projects benefit from having good communication between the designer and the landscape contractor. This chapter compared the traditional landscape construction process to a low-impact development (LID) alternative that focuses on maintaining as much of the initial site integrity as possible with a specific focus on soils and existing vegetation. Additional ways to enhance the sustainability of a construction project discussed in this chapter include designing and installing an efficient irrigation system for lawns and planting beds, managing storm water runoff by choosing permeable pavement options over traditional impervious products, and selecting site amenities made from recycled materials.

STUDY QUESTIONS

1. Describe site grading, including the sequential steps, end result, and ways to make it a more sustainable process.
2. Define "rough grade."
3. Define "finish grade."
4. List the acceptable slope percentages for the following landscape features:
   a. Major walkway
   b. Parking area
   c. Lawn (mowed)
   d. Unmowed bank
5. Describe the impacts of soil compaction on plant establishment and growth.
6. List and describe three ways to make site development more sustainable.
7. Describe the benefits and drawbacks of incorporating existing site vegetation into a design.
8. List four strategies that can be used to prevent construction damage to existing site vegetation.
9. Describe the concept of irrigation zones. Why are they important? How can their design make a landscape more sustainable?
10. Describe treated wood and the controversy associated with its use.
11. What types of questions should be asked when evaluating the sustainability of a hardscape material?
12. What is permeable pavement?
13. Define and differentiate:
    a. Pervious concrete
    b. Porous asphalt
    c. Permeable interlocking concrete pavement

SUGGESTED READING

Sauter, D. 2005. *Landscape construction*. 2nd ed. Clifton Park, NY: Thompson Delmar.

chapter 4
Retrofitting Existing Landscapes for Sustainability

INTRODUCTION

By their very nature, landscapes evolve over time. As a result, many landscapes grow and mature into a space different from that originally intended or are no longer maintained as originally planned. When this happens, the landscape should be redesigned to integrate resource efficiency (sustainability), site functionality, and aesthetics. Through careful planning and execution, existing landscapes can be retrofitted to improve sustainability. The goal of this modification is to minimize the landscape's environmental impact and maximize the value received from the dollars expended. This chapter will focus on design and management strategies and will explore options to change existing landscapes so they are more sustainable. In large measure, this chapter is about taking a critical look at existing landscapes and finding ways to eliminate problem areas to make the site more sustainable. Specific landscape design, installation, and management strategies are described in the other chapters of this text.

This chapter will discuss the following topics:

Site analysis for retrofitting

Identifying opportunities to improve landscape sustainability

SITE ANALYSIS FOR RETROFITTING

Site analysis of an existing landscape is different from site analysis for a new landscape design. However, one common element between the two is the need to understand the design intent. Working with the original landscape designer for the site can be a valuable first step in analyzing the existing landscape. The other specific elements to evaluate during the site analysis can be summed up by addressing three main questions:

Does the landscape design still work aesthetically?

Are there landscape maintenance issues?

Are there problems with the infrastructure elements (sidewalks, driveways, parking areas, lighting elements, etc.)?

Does the Landscape Design Still Work Aesthetically?

Because ornamental plants and lawns account for a significant portion of landscapes, it is important to determine how well the plants are functioning in the existing landscape. What follows is a list of specific plant-related questions that should be asked to determine if the design needs to be modified. Each question is followed by possible reasons why the issue developed and potential retrofit solutions.

Are Key Plants Serving Their Purpose in the Landscape?

Plants have a number of functional and aesthetic roles in the landscape. Functional roles include defining spaces, framing desirable views or screening undesirable views, impacting circulation patterns, controlling erosion, and deflecting light. When plants are used for functional purposes such as screening or hedging, it is important to allow the plants to mature into those functional roles. Plants that are serving a purely aesthetic role should be allowed to mature into their natural size and form. Sometimes careless and unnecessary pruning leads to oddly shaped and grotesquely distorted plant forms that do not enhance the aesthetic of the planting composition (Figure 4-1a).

SOLUTION

Appropriate plant selection combined with appropriate management strategies allows plants to fulfill their intended functional or aesthetic purpose in the landscape. In the example shown in Figure 4-1a of a parking lot planting, the overall aesthetic of the design would be greatly enhanced if the shrubs were allowed to develop into their natural form (Figure 4-1b). The planting composition would be improved further by including ground covers to reduce the inputs (labor and/or chemicals) needed for weed control.

Are Plant Sizes in the Right Proportion to Each Other?

Plants have variable growth rates, and, over time, these differences may become quite pronounced. One way to alleviate this problem initially is to combine larger sizes [5-gallon (20 l)] container or balled-and-burlapped stock of slow-growing plants with smaller sizes [4-inch or 1-gallon (10 cm or 4 l) container] of fast-growing plants. This should help the planting composition stay in the correct proportion throughout the early years of the landscape's life span.

SOLUTION

If, over time, the proportions have changed significantly, and some plants are just too large relative to others, plants can be selectively replaced. This is a

(a)

(b)

Figure 4-1 (a) These shrubs have been sheared into unnatural plant forms that detract from the aesthetic of this planting and result in a lot of bare ground suitable for weed germination. (b) Allowing the plants to develop into their natural form and adding ground cover to the bed will make the design more attractive and reduce the need for herbicides and labor to control weeds.

more sustainable option to replacing the entire landscape. It may also be a better long-term solution than having to constantly prune large plants to keep them in scale. This type of pruning is not sustainable as it requires substantial labor inputs and it creates a large amount of green waste.

Has There Been Significant Attrition, Inappropriate Additions, or Invasion of Volunteer Plants over Time? Does Order to the Overall Composition Need to Be Restored?

As microclimates on a site change due to a maturing landscape, so, too, will the plant species that are best suited to the site. Loss of original plants due to attrition can be a major problem in older landscapes. In addition to these losses, the original planting composition can change significantly because new plants are added or volunteer plants have colonized the site. All three of these combine to create a very different-looking design than what was originally intended.

SOLUTION
The landscape may require major redesign and the inclusion of a very different plant palette than that of the original design. The new plants should be selected based on the current site conditions with an eye toward additional microclimate changes that are expected due to continued growth and development of the landscape.

Are There Too Many or Too Few Annual Flower Beds?

Flower beds filled with annuals are a beautiful addition to the landscape. They are a great way to accentuate a driveway or a building entrance. But these plantings are resource (labor, plants, water, and fertilizer) intensive. Thoughtful design and incorporation of these beds in key locations can be an effective way to visually enhance the landscape.

SOLUTION
Consider how to maximize the impact gained from these planting beds. Locate them only in high-visibility areas; select plants that thrive with minimal inputs of water, fertilizer, and deadheading; and use mass plantings to maximize visual impact (Color Plate 4-1).

Are Lawns Used Inappropriately Such as on Steep Slopes, Areas That Are Difficult to Mow, or Areas with Poor Drainage?

Often lawn areas are used as "filler" in commercial designs. They are relatively inexpensive to install, grow in quickly, and give an instant visual appeal. Unfortunately, it seems that little thought is given to the long-term maintenance needs of lawns, including watering, fertilizing, and mowing. Odd-shaped lawn areas make it difficult to do these tasks.

SOLUTION
In some cases, a similar design aesthetic can be achieved by substituting ground covers for lawn areas (Figure 4-2). Consider replacing narrow medians, parking lot strips, and other areas that do not have high foot traffic with a low-growing ground cover such as common periwinkle (*Vinca minor*) in full-sun areas or bugleweed (*Ajuga reptans*) in shady locations. Once established, the ground covers will

Figure 4-2 Japanese pachysandra (*Pachysandra terminalis*) makes a dense ground cover in this narrow planting bed. It is a sustainable alternative to turf, which would be hard to mow and difficult to water effectively because of the shape and slope on the site.

require fewer inputs of water, fertilizer, and labor, making them an attractive and sustainable choice.

Are There Landscape Maintenance Issues?

Landscape management practices must evolve as the landscape evolves. Yet, in many cases, these practices don't change much from year to year. Ultimately, although the landscape has changed, the maintenance strategies have not. It is important for landscape managers to evaluate their maintenance program at least annually, if not more frequently, depending on the growing climate. Following are a series of landscape maintenance questions to ask when evaluating sustainability, along with reasons the maintenance problems may have developed and potential solutions.

Are the Plants Vigorous and Healthy?

Not matching plants to the growing conditions of the landscape site can lead to reduced plant vigor and poor health. These problems can be exacerbated as a result of changing microclimates (sun exposure, moisture availability, reduced air circulation) on the site over time (Figure 4-3a).

SOLUTION
A retrofit option includes removing plants that are not performing well and replacing them with species better adapted to the site. For example, a rhododendron (*Rhododendron* spp.) growing in a relatively high pH, full-sun parking lot planting island will never thrive (Figure 4-4). It should be replaced with a tough shrub able to handle the soil conditions as well as the high levels of reflected light and heat. In other

(a)

(b)

Figure 4-3 (a) As the evergreen tree on this site has developed, the shade it creates has caused the lawn under it to thin out. (b) A sustainable design alternative is to modify the existing planting bed and replace the turf with a shade-tolerant ground cover.

Figure 4-4 Most rhododendrons (*Rhododendron* spp.) are not well suited to the harsh growing conditions of parking lot planting islands. This one should be replaced with a species that is better adapted to the site conditions.

Figure 4-5 The extensive inputs required to edge the unique shape of this hardscape do not reflect sustainable practices.

cases, the retrofit may require a major redesign of the landscape. Lawn and bed areas may need to change in size and shape to accommodate new species added to the design or to account for new microclimates that have developed since the original design was installed (Figure 4-3b).

Do Odd-Shaped Lawns and Awkward Bed Lines Need to Be Streamlined to Make Maintenance Easier?

The designer's intent to develop a visually pleasing landscape can result in difficult maintenance situations. Just because something looks good on paper, doesn't necessarily mean it can be maintained in an efficient and cost-effective way (Figure 4-5). Balancing aesthetic goals with maintenance realities will result in a more sustainable landscape and should be a primary consideration during the design phase.

SOLUTION
Some maintenance problems will be easier to address than others. The hardscapes in Figure 4-5 will make the design difficult to retrofit. One option is to replace the turf with a slow-growing ground cover that will only need edging once or twice a growing season, rather than the biweekly edging that the lawn requires. Figure 4-6 illustrates a design/maintenance problem that can easily be alleviated by extending the mow strip around the base of the wall to the sidewalk. It may not be the most attractive solution, but it works.

Figure 4-6 This maintenance problem is easily fixed by enlarging the unmowed area adjacent to the wall.

Is the Current Maintenance Program Appropriate for All Parts of the Landscape?

All areas of a landscape do not need to be maintained at the same level. Obviously, high-visibility areas will need more inputs, but in other areas, a lower visual quality of the landscape may be acceptable. Maintenance contractors should work closely with property managers and owners to determine their goals for the landscape.

Solution
Providing property managers and owners with landscape management alternatives, such as less frequent lawn mowing, irrigation, or pruning to allow plants to develop into their natural shape, is an important role for landscape managers. Explaining how these changes can enhance the site's sustainability and translate into cost savings will be appreciated by most clients.

Are There Opportunities to Replace High-Maintenance Plants with Lower-Maintenance Plants?

High-maintenance plants can require significant amounts of water, fertilizer, and labor. Sometimes species are considered high maintenance because they are susceptible to disease and insect infestations. These infestations must be managed or the plants will perform poorly or even die. Hybrid tea roses are a prime example of such plants. Landscapes that have even just a few of these high-maintenance species can require a lot more inputs than landscapes that only contain low-maintenance species.

Solution
This solution is straightforward: replace high-maintenance species with low-maintenance species. For example, hybrid tea roses can be replaced with low-maintenance, disease-resistant shrub roses such as Carefree Wonder (*Rosa* 'MEIpitac') or Knock Out (*Rosa* 'RADrazz') (Color Plate 4-2). Both provide great color throughout the summer, and both require minimal inputs.

Have Pruning Practices Improved or Detracted from the Landscape's Appearance?

Allowing plants to develop into their natural form greatly enhances the landscape's aesthetic. The landscape design and subsequent maintenance program should allow for this to occur. When the plants selected are too large, they will require constant pruning to keep them in bounds. Often this indiscriminate pruning results in ugly and misshapen specimens. Sometimes regular pruning isn't done because the plants are too large for the site but rather to shape the plants into neat and tidy looking forms (Figure 4-7). In either case, this type of pruning detracts from the landscape's appearance.

Solution
Replace plants that have been severely pruned to the point of deformity with other species that will work in that location. Consider the role of the plants in the design, functional or aesthetic, and select them based on this. Choose species that are slow growing and space them according to their mature height and spread.

Figure 4-7 The small shrubs under this bank of windows should be allowed to mature into a natural hedge.

Are There Competition Problems between Shrubs and Ground Covers?

Shrubs and ground covers growing in a planting bed are competing for the same water and fertilizer resources. Because many ground covers are fast growing, they can quickly cover the soil and outcompete shrubs that may be slower to establish. If this competition isn't managed, especially during the establishment phase, the shrubs may struggle to grow.

SOLUTION

Removing an area of ground cover adjacent to the shrub trunk and extending it to the shrub's drip line will allow the shrub roots to effectively absorb water and nutrients without competing with the ground cover (Figure 4-8). Landscape managers may need to manage this competition annually depending on the growth rate of the ground cover.

Does the Landscape Require Excessive Use of Herbicides to Manage Weeds?

A relatively dense canopy of plants prevents light from reaching the soil, thereby limiting the germination potential for many weed species. Landscape designs that are not planted densely enough to provide significant coverage of plant material often result in major weed problems. The exposed soil, or mulch, is a prime location for weed seeds to germinate and spread (Figure 4-9a). In established beds, the loss of plants through attrition can result in vast expanses of mulch with a few shrubs. The result is the same as an underplanted bed: the area becomes quickly infested with weeds. In both cases, excessive herbicides and/or hand labor are required to manage the weed population. Neither of these options is sustainable over the long term.

SOLUTION

Landscapes that have adequate canopy density generally have fewer weed problems and require fewer herbicides (Figure 4-9b). This density can be created by arranging plants so they overlap just slightly at maturity. It can also be achieved by using ground covers. Once established, ground covers are often able to outcompete many weeds. They also make it difficult for weed seeds to reach the soil surface, which prevents them from germinating.

Does the Site Generate Significant Landscape Waste? If So, How Is Landscape Waste Managed?

Excessive pruning due to poor plant selection can result in a significant amount of green waste. Coupled with high irrigation and fertilizer applications, this can have a dramatic impact on the amount of landscape waste generated at the site. Often this waste must be managed by removing it from the site. Although historically the waste would end up in landfills, much of it now goes to municipal or private composting facilities. The end product created from the composting process is then sold back to landscape companies to be reapplied to the landscape.

SOLUTION

Replacing plants that require excessive pruning with species that are better suited is a good first step. Table 4-1 provides examples of dwarf, compact, or slow-growing cultivars of some common landscape plants. A second strategy is to limit irrigation and fertilizer applications to the minimum point needed to maintain an acceptable level of plant quality. Combining the plant replacement strategy with the reduced irrigation and fertilizer concept should result in selecting low-input species that generate minimal landscape waste.

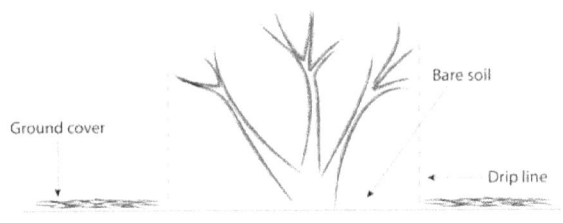

Figure 4-8 This illustration shows how an open area can be created by removing ground cover from the base of a shrub to its drip line. This will eliminate competition.

Figure 4-9 (a) The open ground in this bed makes it easy for weed seeds to germinate. (b) In contrast, the ground in this planting is covered by ground cover and shrubs, which prevent weed growth.

TABLE 4-1 Examples of Dwarf, Compact, or Slow-Growing Cultivars of Some Common Ornamental Plant Species

Plant Species and Cultivar	Height (feet)	Spread (feet)
Deciduous Trees		
Malus spp.		
'Lanzam' (Lancelot)	8–10	8
'Louisa'	15	15
'Select A' (Firebird)	5	8
'Snowdrift'	15–20	20–25
'Tina'	5	10
Evergreen Shrubs		
Buxus microphylla		
var. *koreana* × *sempervirens* 'Glencoe' (Chicagoland Green)	2–3	2–3
var. *koreana* × *sempervirens* 'Green Velvet'	2–3	3
Juniperus chinensis		
'Kallays Compacta'	2–3	6
'Saybrook Gold'	2–3	6
Juniperus communis var. *depressa*	2–5	8–12
'AmiDak' (Blueberry Delight)	1	4–5
Juniperus procumbens		
'Nana'	6–10	3–5
Picea abies		
'Little Gem'	2–3	2–3
'Nidiformis'	3	2–3
Picea glauca		
'Conica'	5	2–3
Pinus mugo	3–5	3–6
Pinus strobus		
'Blue Shag'	3–5	3–5
'Nana'	4	7
Taxus × *media*		
'Tauntonii'	3–4	4–6
Thuja occidentalis		
'Hetz Midget'	2	2–3
'Holmstrup'	4	2
'Rheingold'	4–5	3–4

Plant Species and Cultivar	Height (feet)	Spread (feet)
Deciduous Shrubs		
Acer tataricum ssp. *ginnala*		
'Bailey Compact'	10–12	10–12
'Emerald Elf'	5–6	5–6
Berberis thunbergii		
var. *atropurpurea* 'Bailone' (Ruby Carousel)	3–4	3
var. *atropurpurea* 'Bailtwo' (Burgundy Carousel)	3	4–5
Caragana frutex		
'Globosa'	2–3	2–3
Cornus alba		
'Bailhalo' (Ivory Halo)	5–6	5–6
Deutzia gracilis		
'Nikko'	2	5
Euonymus alatus		
'Compactus'	6–8	6–8
'Rudy Haag'	4–5	4–5
Ilex verticillata		
'Afterglow'	4–6	4–6
Lonicera tatarica		
'Honeyrose'	10	8–10
Lonicera xylosteum		
'Miniglobe'	3–4	3–4
Physocarpus opulifolius		
'Dart's Gold'	4–5	4–5
Rhamnus frangula		
'Columnaris'	12	3
Ribes alpinum		
'Green Mound'	2–3	2–3
Spiraea × *bumalda*		

Plant Species and Cultivar	Height (feet)	Spread (feet)
'Anthony Waterer'	3–4	4–5
Stephanandra incisa		
'Crispa'	1–3	3–6
Syringa × 'Bailsugar'	4–5	4–5
Syringa meyeri		
'Palibin'	4–5	5–7
Syringa patula		
'Miss Kim'	4–8	4–8
Viburnum dentatum		
'Christom' (Blue Muffin)	5–7	4–6
'Synnestvedt' (Chicago Lustre)	10	10

Is the Irrigation System Functional and Updated with Current Controllers and Heads?

Inefficient irrigation systems result in a number of landscape maintenance problems, including a reduced aesthetic and poor plant performance from either overwatering or underwatering.

SOLUTION
Annual maintenance of the irrigation system will ensure the system is fully functional. Updating the system with current equipment and technology will further enhance its effectiveness. See Chapters 8 and 9 for more information on irrigation system management.

Are There Problems with Infrastructure Elements (Sidewalks, Driveways, Parking Areas, Lighting Elements, etc.)?

The infrastructure of a landscape, including hardscapes, lighting, and other site amenities, are essential to the functionality of the landscape. If walkways and driveways are in poor repair or are not functional, circulation and access on the site will be limited. When lighting components are obscured because of plant growth, their functionality is lost. Although these elements tend to be more expensive to retrofit than some of the other examples discussed previously, their impact on the landscape is substantial. Following are a few questions related to landscape infrastructure elements, along with reasons why the problems may have developed and potential solutions.

Are Sidewalks and Other Hard-Surface Features in Working Order?

The functionality of sidewalks, driveways, parking lots, and other hardscapes can decline over time. Often this decline is due to wear and tear, harsh weather conditions impacting the material, or improper installation. Ensuring a uniformly level walking surface is important for both accessibility and safety. Parking areas should be easy to access without interference from plant materials in island beds.

SOLUTION

Damaged hardscapes should be replaced. Particular attention should be given to walkways and other areas in the landscape that have significant pedestrian traffic (Figure 4-10). Replacing damaged materials with more durable and sustainable products where appropriate and ensuring the materials are installed properly will reduce the need for future repairs.

Have Access and Circulation Declined over Time?

Maturing trees and shrubs can significantly reduce access and circulation patterns on a site (Figure 4-11). Accounting for mature size is essential when selecting plants for a design, particularly those that will be adjacent to walkways, driveways, parking lots, and buildings.

SOLUTION

Although selective pruning may restore accessibility and circulation in some cases, in other situations the

Figure 4-10 Concrete unit pavers are easy to install, fix, and replace if necessary.

Figure 4-11 Evergreens planted on this site are adjacent to the sidewalk and are already maturing to the point where they are impeding circulation.

plants may need to be removed and replaced with more appropriately sized species. Generally, removing and replacing plants is a cheaper alternative to altering a hardscape.

Can Impervious Surfaces Be Converted to Permeable Surfaces?

Managing storm water on-site continues to be an important design and management component of many landscapes. For commercial sites, this is a particular challenge because the large hardscape areas are often constructed from mostly impervious materials. Finding ways to contain the water on-site, rather than moving it off-site, is a key component of the Sustainable Sites Initiative (2009).

SOLUTION

Chapter 3 describes a number of permeable hardscape alternatives, including pervious concrete, porous asphalt, and permeable interlocking concrete pavement. Retrofitting hardscape areas by replacing existing nonpermeable surfaces with one of these permeable alternatives can greatly reduce storm water runoff and significantly enhance the site's sustainability (Figure 4-12).

Are Lighting Elements Functioning at Their Optimum Level?

Loss of functional lighting on a site can be a result of poor design, maturing plants, and poor product quality. Poor design results in lights being placed too close to trees or in turf areas where it is difficult to mow around them (Figures 4-13 and 4-14). As the trees mature, they will partly or completely obscure the lighting element. Designers must account for this tree growth, and installation contractors must work with designers during the installation phase when there is an obvious placement conflict between these two elements. Installing inferior lighting products can also reduce their functionality over the long term.

SOLUTION

Some landscape architecture companies specialize in outdoor lighting design. If this phase of a project is contracted out, then it must be reviewed in the

Figure 4-12 This parking lot area at Morton Arboretum was converted to permeable interlocking concrete pavement to eliminate storm water runoff.
Courtesy of Unilock, Inc.

Figure 4-13 Clearly, the light (on the right) is too close to the tree to be functional. This layout should never have been installed.

Figure 4-14 Uplighting is an effective way to highlight certain plants, but the location of these lights in lawn areas makes maintenance difficult and time consuming.

context of the entire landscape design before it is installed. Once a lighting system is installed, it can be costly to retrofit. Examples of retrofitting might include either removing a plant that is obscuring a light (easy enough to do for small shrubs) or removing the lighting element and relocating it (which might be a better alternative when large trees are involved). Lights that are placed in lawn areas should have mow circles installed around them to protect the fixtures. Poor-quality lighting elements should be replaced with high-quality sustainable products.

IDENTIFYING OPPORTUNITIES TO IMPROVE LANDSCAPE SUSTAINABILITY

The property manager and landscape maintenance contractor are important resources to consult when retrofitting an existing landscape. Their familiarity with the property will provide important information regarding problem areas such as sections of a walkway that have standing water after a rain or steep slopes that are difficult and dangerous to mow. These professionals can provide further information on areas of poor site functionality due to things like inadequately sized entrances or overgrown plant materials. Their input can also highlight aesthetic features of the landscape that should be maintained or accentuated, like views from inside the office building that are particularly attractive. All of this information can then be used to address problems on the site and create a landscape that is sustainable as well as aesthetically pleasing.

Once the retrofitting needs have been determined, the first step is to prioritize which areas to address. First on the list are problem areas, followed by high-visibility areas such as entrances, areas used by employees, and distant areas of the landscape that are not regularly used. After the areas have been prioritized, the next step is to determine the types of retrofitting that needs to be done. In the case of many mature landscapes, addressing five main issues can increase sustainability. These issues include:

Eliminating problem areas

Improving access and circulation

Improving maintenance efficiencies

Improving irrigation effectiveness

Managing water on-site

Eliminating Problem Areas

Many landscape issues can fit into the category of "problem area" when a landscape is being evaluated for ways to improve sustainability. Some examples, such as walkway sections with standing water, steep slopes where the lawn is dangerous or hard to mow, or poor site functionality, have already been listed. Each landscape will have its own unique set of problem areas. Walking the site, completing a site analysis, and conducting detailed interviews with the property manager and landscape maintenance contractor are the best place to start when determining what areas need to be fixed. Often these problem areas are related to a few specific issues such as ineffective access and circulation, maintenance inefficiencies, and irrigation inefficiencies.

Improving Access and Circulation

Landscape functionality requires having appropriately sized spaces for both foot and vehicular traffic and the ability to easily gain access to these areas. As the landscape grows and matures, it may become difficult to access spaces (i.e., entrances, driveways, and sidewalks) within the landscape and to move within those spaces due to overgrown plants. In other cases, the hardscape materials in that area may have failed completely or be in disrepair.

In cases where access and circulation are limited because plant material has outgrown the allotted space, judicious pruning may alleviate the problem. Pruning should be limited to that which maintains natural growth patterns. Hedging, topping, and shearing of landscape plants to keep them at a desired size and shape encourages excessive new growth and generates considerable landscape waste. If substantial and regular (monthly, bimonthly, or even annual) pruning is required, a better alternative is to remove the plant and replace it with a more suitable alternative. In some cases, that alternative may be a dwarf or compact cultivar of the species, while, in other cases, a completely different species may be a better choice (Table 4-1).

Hardscapes used for driveways, walkways, and parking lots may fail and need repair after years of use. In addition to replacing the materials used in the driveway, walkway, or parking lot, these areas may need to be redesigned to account for increased traffic load or even different-sized vehicles than the spaces were originally designed to accommodate. Chapter 3 describes a number of sustainable hardscape material options. The combination of redesigning the area to make it more functional and using sustainable hardscapes will have a positive impact on the functionality and sustainability of the site.

Improving Maintenance Efficiencies

Maintaining a landscape consists of balancing three related goals: keeping the living part of the landscape healthy, keeping the constructed parts in good repair, and balancing the first two goals against human uses of the space (Thompson and Sorvig 2008). Regular and appropriate maintenance is a critical factor in the long-term success of a landscape and is described in detail in Chapters 8 and 9. When maintenance efficiencies are evaluated when retrofitting a landscape, the focus should be on design modifications, paying particular attention to the size and shape of planting beds and lawns. The ornamental plant materials on the site should also be evaluated regarding their suitability to the site and the overall design.

Good Design Results in Easier Maintenance

Good design is the first place to start with improving maintenance efficiencies. Retrofitting a landscape to improve sustainability provides a great opportunity to analyze the existing design and make necessary modifications. These design changes should focus on creating maintainable spaces. An obvious place to start is designing bed and lawn shapes to facilitate easy mowing and edging and to minimize obstacles that increase hand work (Figure 4-15).

As part of this redesign, it is important to consider the type of equipment used to maintain the site. Examples include adequately sized gates that allow equipment to pass through, turf areas that allow mowers to turn easily, and hedges that can be trimmed without needing to reach over a fence or other obstacle. Consulting with the landscape maintenance contractor will provide essential information on the types of equipment that are used on the site and any current maintenance problems he or she is facing. Once equipment needs are addressed in

74 Retrofitting Existing Landscapes for Sustainability

Figure 4-15 In this design, extending the planting bed to the sidewalk is a good design alternative and would eliminate the odd-shaped lawn area and the need to mow around the fire hydrant.

the design, the focus can shift to the plants and the aesthetics associated with their arrangement.

Modifying Planting Beds

When a landscape designer does not account for the changes in size and shape of maturing trees, shrubs, and ground covers, the design often fails. Sometimes selective removal of a few plants can rectify the problem, but other times the entire planting may need to be removed and the area redesigned and then replanted. The redesign process should account for both the types of plants to be included and the type of irrigation system to be used. Both of these may have a significant impact on the size and shape of the new planting bed.

Completely redesigning existing planting beds provides another opportunity to improve the site's sustainability. Sustainable landscape plantings should be composed mainly of low-input plants such as native or site-adapted species. Proper plant selection, as described in Chapter 2, has a major impact on the amount of resources needed to maintain the plants. Appropriate plant selection coupled with integrated pest management (IPM) strategies reduces the need for insecticide, herbicide, and fungicide applications and supports minimal use of fertilizers.

Figure 4-16 shows two alternative landscape designs. Figure 4-16a was not designed with sustainability in mind. The layout would be difficult to maintain because of overplanted shrub beds and odd-shaped lawn areas that are hard to access. The design also includes many high-input species that need regular applications of fertilizers or pesticides to maintain their appearance. Figure 4-16b was designed with sustainability in mind, which is reflected in the overall site layout, how the plants are arranged in the beds, and the inclusion of low-input and disease- and insect-resistant species.

In cases where major renovations are required, soil testing and improvement prior to planting should be done. Based on the soil test, necessary modifications can be made to the planting area, which should ensure the long-term success of the plantings. For example, incorporating organic matter before planting can improve otherwise poor soils into a growing medium that supports healthy plant growth while reducing water and fertilizer requirements (Figure 4-17). Once the soil has been improved, attention can then be focused on the functionality and aesthetic roles of the planting beds.

Modifying Lawn Areas

Before replanting lawns, the functionality of that area within the landscape should be evaluated, as should the existing irrigation system and potential turfgrass cultivars. If the lawn plays an important design role in the landscape, then it may warrant inclusion in its previous size and shape. However, if it was used as more of a "filler" in the overall design concept, then the space should be redesigned to fill a more functional need. Examples of functional roles include a collection space for on-site storm water management, an outdoor gathering space for building occupants, an open vista to the rest of the landscape, or a natural area attractive to wildlife. In some cases,

Identifying Opportunities to Improve Landscape Sustainability   75

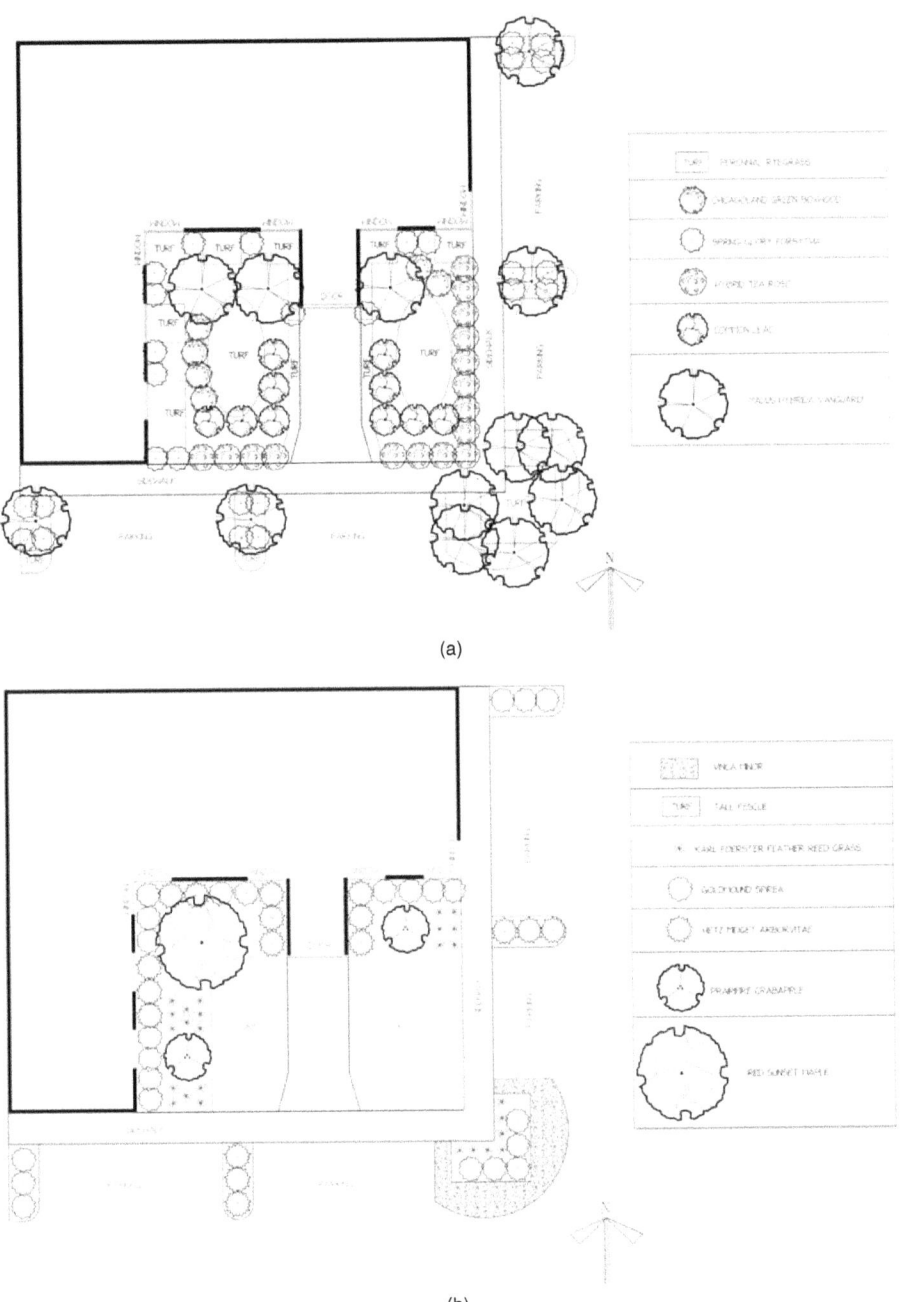

Figure 4-16 (a) This landscape design is an example of a high-maintenance, low-sustainability landscape. (b) The increase in sustainability comes from redesigning the planting beds and lawn areas and selecting low-input plant species.

Figure 4-17 This planting bed was renovated and new organic matter added and incorporated into the soil. The site is now ready to plant.

Figure 4-18 Low-volume drip irrigation systems are an effective way to irrigate planting beds.

a new design element could be added to the site by converting irrigated lawns to meadow areas or tree groves (Color Plate 4-3).

Sometimes lawns are not maintained in a sustainable way because the shape of the area makes it difficult to operate standard landscape equipment. Prior to replanting, the shape of the space should be evaluated and redesigned if necessary to accommodate standard mowing equipment. Consulting the current landscape maintenance contractor about this issue can lead to beneficial changes that improve the sustainability of the lawn area.

Improving Irrigation Effectiveness

In tandem with changes to the landscape design, the irrigation system should be evaluated. The system will need to be modified to address changes to the size and shape of the planting beds and lawn areas, as well as the new plants themselves. A retrofit of the system might also include connecting it to a weather station–based controller and using nonpotable water sources. Both of these will further the landscape's sustainability.

Planting Beds

The shape and size of a planting bed directly impacts the type of irrigation system that should be used. Although standard pop-up heads can be used, other alternatives are to use low-volume heads, which deliver significantly less water to the planting area than traditional heads, and low-volume drip systems (Figure 4-18). And, as mentioned in Chapter 2, grouping plants within a planting bed based on water use requirements prevents low-water-use plants from being overwatered, and their neighboring higher-water-use plants from being underwatered.

Lawns

Improving the irrigation effectiveness of lawn areas involves two choices: redesigning the size and shape of the lawn area to fit the irrigation system or redesigning the irrigation system to fit the lawn area. Another option is to remove lawns from areas that are difficult to irrigate with sprinklers such as parking strips and other areas bordering hard surfaces (Figure 4-19). The lawn in these areas can be replaced with other plants such as ground covers and

Identifying Opportunities to Improve Landscape Sustainability

Figure 4-19 This small planting bed filled with mowing obstacles should have been planted with a ground cover.

low-growing shrubs that can be watered effectively with drip systems. This will reduce water waste due to sprinkler overthrow. Chapter 9 describes numerous strategies to ensure irrigation systems effectively water lawn areas, including design strategies, components, and maintenance programs.

Connecting the Irrigation Controller to a Weather Station

Overwatering is something property managers try to avoid. Increasing water scarcity in recent years, together with extended droughts in some regions of the United States, has made efficient water management essential. The best way to apply the correct amount of water to a landscape is to tie the irrigation system to the local weather conditions through a "smart controller." Smart controllers work by delivering the right amount of water to plants at the right time, thereby creating healthier growing conditions. The end result is efficient water management combined with improved plant performance.

Many irrigation companies manufacture some type of smart controller. Most also manufacture some type of weather station that can be connected to virtually any existing irrigation controller. The companies also provide the software necessary for an existing controller to access a weather station unit.

Retrofitting an irrigation system with a smart controller is a relatively inexpensive investment that will yield significant savings in irrigation water use.

Irrigating with Nonpotable Water Sources

Potable water is water that is safe to drink. Because potable water is a valuable natural resource, finding alternative water sources for landscape irrigation is an important step toward achieving a more sustainable landscape. Irrigation alternatives to potable water include recycled gray water; captured rainwater, including water from rooftops (Figure 4-20); storm

Figure 4-20 A rain barrel attached to a downspout is an effective way to capture rainwater so it can be used for irrigation. This concept is applicable to commercial buildings and landscapes as well.

ecoPRO Handbook

water basins; air conditioner condensate; or any other source of water that is treated and conveyed by a public agency specifically for nonpotable uses. Gray water is wastewater generated from domestic activities such as dish washing, laundry, and bathing. Gray water comprises 50 to 80 percent of wastewater generated from residential sanitation equipment except for toilets (Wikipedia 2010a). In some urban areas, gray water is collected from commercial buildings and repurposed for other uses on-site such as irrigation or ornamental water features. The Sustainable Sites Initiative (2009) lists a 50 percent reduction in potable water used for irrigation as a prerequisite in the site design section in order to achieve a sustainable landscape.

Managing Water On-Site

Many cities in the United States were built years before passage of the Clean Water Act in 1972. As a result, systems are in place that treat rainfall as wastewater to be disposed of rather than as a resource to be captured and reused. This is an unfortunate approach, since water is a precious commodity. In the United States alone, demand for water has increased by over 200 percent since 1950 (U.S. Environmental Protection Agency 2007a). Part of this increase is due to landscape irrigation, which accounts for more than a third of residential water use [or more than 7 billion gallons per day nationwide (26.5 billion liters)] (U.S. Environmental Protection Agency 2007b). A sustainable approach is to find ways to capture the water on-site and then reuse it for other purposes such as irrigation, or allow it to filtrate into the groundwater and provide recharge to the natural hydrologic cycle (Figure 4-21).

In 2000, the European Union adopted the Water Framework Directive, which commits European

Figure 4-21 Interest in rain gardens continues as municipalities, landscape managers, and others look for sustainable ways to manage storm water. This rain garden is an effective way to prevent runoff into the nearby river.

Figure 4-22 The concept for this bioswale is good. However, the block retaining wall makes it difficult to maintain. A better alternative is to remove the wall and plant the area with species that can handle periodic flooding.

Union member states to take steps to improve and preserve water quality for all water bodies by 2015 (Wikipedia 2010b). Over time, this legislation will likely achieve results similar to those gained from the Clean Water Act in the United States.

When retrofitting an existing landscape, aboveground retention ponds or bioswales can be created to capture and hold the water from a heavy rain event until it is reused or has time to filter into the soil (Figure 4-22). Another option is to install belowground cisterns. Water can be captured from impermeable surfaces such as rooftops and then funneled via a gravity-fed system to the cistern. In both of these cases, the water can then be redistributed throughout the landscape for irrigation when necessary.

SUMMARY

Evaluating existing landscapes to determine their overall sustainability is an important role for landscape managers. The evaluation should determine ways to improve the efficiency of the resources used to maintain the space, as well as to improve the overall site functionality and aesthetics. To frame this evaluation, three questions should be asked: Does the landscape design still work aesthetically? Are there landscape maintenance issues? Are there problems with the infrastructure elements? Based on the answers to these questions, the retrofitting priorities can be established and should start with addressing problem areas first. Much of the retrofitting will focus on redesigning areas to improve access and circulation and redesigning planting beds and lawn areas to make irrigation and maintenance more efficient. The equipment used to maintain the landscape should be considered when redesigning the site. Both the planting beds and the lawn areas should be modified to accommodate the irrigation needs of the landscape. The irrigation system should be updated to improve efficiency. As part of planting bed renovation, site-appropriate plants should be selected. Finally, addressing water management on the site will lead to successful retrofits that enhance the overall sustainability of the landscape site.

STUDY QUESTIONS

1. Describe the concept of retrofitting an existing landscape to improve sustainability.
2. List 10 examples of landscape issues or situations that would benefit from retrofitting. For each of these, outline a process that could be followed to accomplish a successful retrofit.
3. Describe four strategies to retrofit a lawn area to make it more sustainable.
4. Describe four strategies to retrofit a planting bed to make it more sustainable.
5. What is the recommended process for prioritizing landscape areas to retrofit?
6. Assume you have been hired as the new maintenance contractor for a 15-acre (6 ha) corporate park. The company CEO wants to improve the site's sustainability and has asked you to develop a proposal to accomplish this. Describe how you would develop the proposal and what it would include.

chapter 5
Ecosystem Development and Management in the Context of Sustainable Landscapes

INTRODUCTION

Ecological landscape design focuses on the development of landscapes as ecosystems. An ecosystem is a complex set of relationships among the living resources, habitats, and residents of an area (U.S. Forest Service 2010). It includes plants and animals, environmental elements such as water and soil, and people. Though ecosystems vary in size, all share the common feature that each element that contributes to the ecosystem is a self-contained, functioning unit. If one part of the ecosystem is damaged or disappears, it has an impact on everything else. Ecosystems are critical to human well-being, including our health, prosperity, security, and social and cultural identity (Millennium Ecosystem Assessment 2007).

A healthy ecosystem is sustainable, and all of the system elements live in balance, or in a state of natural equilibrium (U.S. Forest Service 2010). A sustainable ecosystem also includes biodiversity. Ahern, Leduc, and York (2006) suggest the National Biological Information Infrastructure (NBII) definition of biodiversity is inclusive of many concepts agreed on by governmental, nongovernmental, academic, and industry stakeholders. This multidisciplinary organization defines biodiversity as "the sum total of the variety of life and its interactions and can be subdivided into (1) genetic diversity, (2) species diversity, and (3) ecological or ecosystem diversity."

By taking into account the complex and interrelated features that constitute an ecosystem, ecological landscape design considers landscapes as ecosystems. This design approach addresses how to establish a new planting as well as what happens to

THE CLIMAX STAGE OF AN ECOSYSTEM

Ecosystems evolve over time by passing through a serial progression of phases. Ecologists originally believed that a climax phase was the end point of this progression and was a long-term steady state of the landscape. However, more recent research has shown that the climax phase is neither completely stable nor necessarily long term and self-perpetuating. Today, ecologists realize that the periodic disturbance of natural events such as fire, flooding, and damage by insects plays a critical role in maintaining the diversity of species and habitats in a region. These events are now considered essential to creating ecosystems in different succession stages, which include different vegetation types and result in different habitats. For more information on ecosystem progression, see Lee (2009).

the landscape over time as it matures and how environmental factors affect its growth, development, and function.

This chapter will discuss the following:

Sustainable landscapes and ecosystem services

Historical review of ecological design

How landscapes function as ecosystems

Considerations in designing a new landscape ecosystem

Establishment strategies for a new landscape ecosystem

Management strategies for a landscape ecosystem

SUSTAINABLE LANDSCAPES AND ECOSYSTEM SERVICES

In the context of creating a sustainable landscape, where a landscape is representative of an ecosystem, it is important for the landscape designer, landscape contractor, and landscape manager to work toward a holistic approach to the landscape's function. This approach will require selecting plant material for more than just functional (i.e., screening and recreation) or aesthetic purposes. The ability of these plants to provide ecosystem services, such as air and water cleansing, pollination, and habitat, is equally important.

Ecosystem services are goods and services of direct or indirect benefit to humans that are produced by ecosystem processes involving the interaction of living elements and nonliving elements (Sustainable Sites Initiative 2009a). A less cumbersome way to describe ecosystem services is to imagine how our lives are improved as a result of what happens in the ecosystem. For example, carefully managing a wetland area and keeping it intact allows the plants to filter out excess nitrogen from fertilizer that ended up in the street when it was improperly applied to a landscape and then carried via storm water to the wetland area. The result is clean water entering into an adjacent stream or percolating down into the water table. Because the nitrogen has been removed, the water is now of a higher quality and may be suitable for drinking water or as a suitable habitat for fish. This is just one of the many examples of ecosystem services described in the Sustainable Sites Initiative (2009a).

Table 5-1 describes the 12 broad classifications of ecosystem services defined by the Sustainable Sites Initiative (2009a). For a detailed description of these ecosystem services and additional background information about how these services were selected and the value of sustainable landscapes, refer to the "Case for Sustainable Landscapes" (Sustainable Sites Initiative 2009b). This publication provides a thorough discussion of each ecosystem service; their interrelatedness; and their impacts on local, regional, and global scales.

Along with identifying these 12 key ecosystem services, the Sustainable Sites Initiative (2009a) has also developed a detailed evaluation matrix that measures how the multiple steps in the landscape design, construction, and operations and maintenance processes can be measured against their capacity to achieve one or more of the ecosystem services. The Sustainable Sites Initiative's goal in identifying ecosystem services and developing the evaluation matrix is to help landscape professionals develop sustainable sites. According to its work, "a sustainable site protects, restores and enhances ecosystem services wherever possible through sustainable land development and management practices" (Sustainable Sites Initiative 2009a).

HISTORICAL REVIEW OF ECOLOGICAL DESIGN

Since the 1960s, ecology has increasingly influenced the design professions, resulting in a more inclusive outlook on nature, the environment, and the landscape. Makhzoumi and Pungetti (1999) argue that

TABLE 5-1 Twelve Ecosystem Services Described by the Sustainable Sites Initiative

Ecosystem Service	Description
Global climate regulation	Maintaining balance of atmospheric gases at historic levels, creating breathable air, and sequestering greenhouse gases
Local climate regulation	Regulating local temperature, precipitation, and humidity through shading, evapotranspiration, and windbreaks
Air and water cleansing	Removing and reducing pollutants in air and water
Water supply and regulation	Storing and providing water within watersheds and aquifers
Erosion and sediment control	Retaining soil within an ecosystem and preventing damage from erosion and siltation
Hazard mitigation	Reducing vulnerability to damage from flooding, storm surge, wildfire, and drought
Pollination	Providing pollinator species for reproduction of crops and other plants
Habitat functions	Providing refuge and reproduction habitat to plants and animals, thereby contributing to conservation of biological and genetic diversity and evolutionary processes
Waste decomposition and treatment	Breaking down waste and cycling nutrients
Human health and well-being benefits	Enhancing physical, mental, and social well-being as a result of interaction with nature
Food and renewable nonfood products	Producing food, fuel, energy, medicine, or other products for human use
Cultural benefits	Enhancing cultural, educational, aesthetic, and spiritual experiences as a result of interaction with nature

Source: Adapted from Sustainable Sites Initiative (2009a).

the launch of ecological design came as a result of dissatisfaction with traditional design approaches:

> Enthusiasm for ecological landscapes was prompted by the failure of contemporary landscape architecture to find a convincing theoretical and practical basis for dealing with urban landscape problems. Some argue the urban landscape has an aesthetic viewpoint that reduces nature through impoverished artificial landscapes that are not sustainable. (Makhzoumi and Pungetti 1999)

In the context of a sustainable landscape, one interpretation of this statement is that the public finally tired of the preponderance of generic, artificial-looking landscapes packed with sheared shrubs and large expanses of bark mulch (Figure 5-1). They wanted something different—something that looked more natural, reflected the local native landscape, and did not require a lot of weekly maintenance. Because of this demand for a different type of landscape, designers began to modify how they approached the design process.

The result of this critical review of existing landscape design and development practices over the past two decades is an improved approach to landscaping. Many in the landscape design professions now take a comprehensive systems approach. In terms of problem solving and design, a systems approach takes into account how one change will influence every other part of the design (or system). The designer

Figure 5-1 This landscape requires significant maintenance inputs to keep the hedge sheared, trees limbed up, and herbaceous plants lined up in rows without touching each other.

hopes to predict an outcome of the entire design, having considered the impact that each component will have on the end result. Landscape designers using this approach will possess an increased awareness of what impact the design will have on the environment as the plantings develop and mature into a functional ecosystem.

HOW LANDSCAPES FUNCTION AS ECOSYSTEMS

Landscapes should be multifunctional, fulfilling utilitarian, recreational, and aesthetic needs as well as contributing to ecological cycles and environmental enhancements (Dunnett and Clayden 2000). An ecological approach to design and management will help the landscape become a multifaceted ecosystem.

John Tillman Lyle's work (1985) has been particularly important in shaping this new approach to design and to viewing landscapes as ecosystems. There are two aspects of his work with direct relevance to designing and managing landscapes as ecosystems:

- There needs to be a critical investigation of the landscape design process in the context of an ecosystem—its function, structure, and ecology—rather than just economic rationality.
- Management issues need to be addressed as an integral part of ecosystem design because ecosystems have a variable future and it is difficult to predict what changes will take place over time.

The general implication of his work is that design is an ongoing process; it should not be the objective. His work was forward thinking because it acknowledged the need for management strategies to develop over time while accounting for how the landscape has matured. In some cases, the management strategy may include redesigning a portion of the landscape to make it more functional.

Along with Lyle's approach to design is an understanding of the impact plant selection can have on how the landscape functions as an ecosystem. Proper plant selection can influence the designed landscape in two ways: an increase in habitat and biodiversity and an increase in the genus loci (local distinctiveness or sense of place) of the landscape. Plantings with a local distinctiveness help maintain the ecological diversity of an area and make aesthetic sense (Color Plate 5-1). These types of plantings are usually based on local native plant communities and can also reflect local cultural uses of plants in gardens and the wider landscape (Kendle, Rose, and Oikawa 2000).

As stated earlier, biodiversity is essential to a sustainable ecosystem. Traditional landscape plantings more closely represent a monoculture with a smattering of trees and shrubs and a few annuals thrown in for color (Figure 5-2). This is partly a result of limited plant availability, an unimaginative design approach, and the planned management of the site aimed at preserving a desired species mix and size (Dunnett and Clayden 2000). Combining a mix of species with varied mature sizes, branching habits, and growth rates with a dynamic and adaptive management strategy can result in a functional and

Figure 5-2 Yews (*Taxus* spp.) are a staple in many commercial landscapes because of their low maintenance and general adaptability. This landscape includes a limited number of species and no annual color.

aesthetic planting that also increases habitat value. This planting approach can be an important part of naturalistic areas in a landscape as well as more managed spaces.

Historically, many landscape design concepts focused on the short-term goals of a project. Yet the overall design of the landscape will have both short- and long-term impacts on how it functions. Similar to Lyle, Wann (1996) introduced a different approach to design. He highlighted the need for a more enduring view of the landscape. Much of his work addressed the importance of designing sustainable landscapes that allow the integrity of the original landscape design to be maintained indefinitely.

Designing for a sustainable landscape necessitates a holistic and integrative outlook that is based on ecological understanding and awareness of the potentialities and limitations of a given landscape. Such understanding ensures that in accommodating future uses their impact on existing ecosystems and essential ecological processes and biological and landscape diversity is anticipated. This will allow for healthy ecosystems and long-term ecological stability (Wann 1996).

Lyle (1985) and Wann (1996) both acknowledged the role of humans in the design, installation, and management of landscape ecosystems. In their work, they successfully incorporate the human species in ecological theory rather than suggest that humans are separate from nature and that our impact on an ecosystem is always negative. Both suggested that landscape professionals can initiate positive environmental changes within a landscape ecosystem. One example of the positive role humans can have on developing and managing an ecosystem can be seen in many gardens and parks. Numerous ecology studies, including Gaublomme et al. (2008) and Loram et al. (2008), demonstrate that gardens and parks typically have greater biodiversity than natural systems because they include a select number of non-native species. In comparison, landscapes devoted wholly to native plant species have a much more limited level of diversity.

Building on the work of Lyle (1985) and Wann (1996), today's landscape designers, installers, and managers have an operational framework on which to base their effort. Using this paradigm, the landscape ecosystem can be viewed as a set of complex relationships among the growing environment (soil, moisture, light patterns, and temperature), plants (trees, shrubs, annuals and perennials, ground covers, and turfgrass), animals (wildlife, birds, and insects), and people. These multiple relationships and the interactions among them result in a landscape ecosystem.

CONSIDERATIONS IN DESIGNING A NEW LANDSCAPE ECOSYSTEM

Careful design and plant selection can produce beautiful and functional plant communities that are ecologically sophisticated. This section will address both the designer's intent and the plant materials in regard to creating a landscape ecosystem. Chapters 2 and 3 describe plant materials—existing vegetation and selecting new species—in the broad context of sustainable design. This chapter will focus on plant materials in the context of creating landscape ecosystems.

Designer's Intent in Creating a Landscape Ecosystem

Chapter 2 outlined the concept of design intent as part of the landscape design process. This concept is also relevant when creating a landscape ecosystem. In addition to focusing on the aesthetic and functional goals of the landscape, however, the designer must also address ecosystem services. The design focus may be on creating new ecosystem services or on enhancing existing services such as erosion and sediment control or habitat function. Whatever the intent, in order for the goals to be achieved, the designer, landscape contractor, and maintenance professionals must communicate throughout the project.

Much of current conventional landscape planting design is characterized by the use of a limited number of species and cultivars with relatively simple compositions (Figure 5-3). These compositions include shrub masses with or without ground covers, street trees with or without turf below, and mown amenity turf (Thoday, Kendle, and Hitchmough 1995). A result of this design approach is that most of these plantings fill aesthetic and functional roles but provide limited ecosystem services. Often the plantings are maintained to produce a static effect. To achieve this effect, considerable resource inputs in site preparation, plant establishment, and long-term maintenance are required (Benson and Roe 2000).

Amenity turf is turf used for aesthetic purposes.

Figure 5-3 Upright evergreens are combined with deciduous flowering shrubs to create a simple composition that provides year-round aesthetic appeal.

In broad terms, the designer's intent for a landscape ecosystem should meet these minimum criteria:

- Require limited inputs, albeit more during the plant establishment phase and less during the long-term management phase.
- Reflect local character.
- Include native or site-adapted species.
- Contribute to the local biodiversity.
- Have a dynamic growth and development progression that allows for self-regeneration and nutrient cycling.

A final consideration is the social implications of the design. In order for a landscape ecosystem to be truly sustainable, it must also be publicly acceptable and aesthetically pleasing. In some cases to gain larger acceptability, it may be necessary to include landscape elements, such as annual plantings for color, that do not meet the objectives listed previously. One approach is to have a multidimensional design with showy and highly manicured areas near building entrances. As you move away from this public space, the landscape becomes more natural and less maintained. This approach helps a designer satisfy

Considerations in Designing a New Landscape Ecosystem

Figure 5-4 In this housing development, a large portion of the site was developed to re-create the native habitat and function as a wetland ecosystem.

multiple objectives. Provided the overall move is toward sustainability, sometimes both pragmatic and flexible approaches are necessary when meeting social or cultural needs (Dunnett and Hitchmough 1996).

When all of the objectives that constitute the designer's intent are achieved, a sustainable landscape ecosystem is created (Figure 5-4). This ecosystem will meet the aesthetic needs of the project, serve in a functional capacity, and provide multiple ecosystem services.

Plant Materials for Creating a Landscape Ecosystem

A logical first step in landscape ecosystem development is to start with existing materials on the site. This includes the existing vegetation, soil conditions, drainage patterns, and light exposure. Retaining existing vegetation of value provides both a cost savings and an initial framework for additional species selection and design. It also influences whether all or just part of the site must be designed and planted. Preserving and integrating existing vegetation where possible has aesthetic, functional, and ecological value (Dunnett and Clayden 2000).

Natural Regeneration of Site-Adapted Species to Create a Landscape Ecosystem

An alternative to retaining existing vegetation or incorporating new plant species is to encourage natural regeneration of vegetation on the site. Natural regeneration requires little management input and allows species already adapted to the growing environment to colonize the area. The natural competition that develops as a result of the colonization will result in a diverse mix of species, each well suited to the unique microclimates on the site. However, this type of natural regeneration is also unpredictable. There is no guarantee that the preferred species will regenerate and that the desired plant community will develop (Dunnett and Clayden 2000). The natural progression may result in a landscape ecosystem that lacks biodiversity and is not aesthetically acceptable during early successional phases. Often plant species introduced by birds and animals can have a major influence on the plant community that develops (see Table 10-1). In these instances, some form of landscape management, including the removal of unwanted species and the addition of desirable species, may be required to achieve a fully functional landscape ecosystem.

Sometimes soil management may be necessary to ensure the desired species mix establishes on the site. A minimal amount of soil modification, such as adding organic matter to improve drainage and nutrient content, may be necessary to allow these desirable, though less well adapted, species to thrive. When possible, soil modifications should be done early in the site regeneration process to minimize damage to roots.

Selecting New Species to Create a Landscape Ecosystem

When natural regeneration does not result in the desired landscape ecosystem, or when little to no

---

Successional phase refers to the succession, or change, in the vegetation found in a plant community over time.

existing vegetation has been left on a landscape site, it will be necessary to select species to create the landscape ecosystem. Although many plant species grow best in a narrow range of environmental conditions, most can still grow adequately across a broader range. This is important in a landscape ecosystem because of the desire for a diverse species mix, which is often linked to the need for diverse growing requirements. Further, as successional growth in the landscape occurs, some of the environmental conditions on the site will change, and plants must adapt to these changes in order to survive.

Selecting regionally adapted species or those from similar native habitats gives the landscape the best chance of survival and increases the likelihood it will reach its full potential and the designer's intent. One example of using regionally adapted species is incorporating species native to the Mediterranean area in plantings located in the western United States. Mediterranean species are adapted to growing in mild climates with extended dry periods. Because of this, many of these species (Table 5-2) are well suited to growing in western Washington and Oregon and parts of California, where the climate, including seasonal precipitation patterns, is similar (Figure 5-5).

The ultimate goal of a functional landscape ecosystem is twofold. First, it should serve the needs of those who use the landscape, mainly humans and animals. Second, the resulting plant community should require minimal inputs (water, fertilizer, pesticides, maintenance labor) as it matures and reaches a level of natural equilibrium. Incorporating existing vegetation, allowing natural regeneration to occur, and adding site-adapted plant species all contribute to successfully creating a functional landscape ecosystem.

ESTABLISHMENT STRATEGIES FOR A NEW LANDSCAPE ECOSYSTEM

The twin forces of succession and disturbance are constantly at work in a newly planted landscape. The

TABLE 5-2 Abbreviated List of Mediterranean Native Species Well Adapted to the Growing Climates of Western Oregon and Washington

Common Name	Scientific Name
Herbaceous Perennials	
Artemisias	*Artemisia* spp.
Bear's breeches	*Acanthus mollis*
Cupid's dart	*Catananche caerulea*
Mulleins	*Verbascum* spp.
Rockrose	*Cistus* spp.
Spurge	*Euphorbia* spp.
Ground Covers	
Candytuft	*Iberis sempervirens*
Saint-John's-wort	*Hypericum calycinum*
Thyme	*Thymus* spp.
Vinca, common periwinkle	*Vinca minor; Vinca* spp.
Evergreen Shrubs	
Heath	*Erica* spp.
Laurustinus	*Viburnum tinus*
Lavender	*Lavandula* spp.
Rosemary	*Rosmarinus officinalis*
Trees	
Atlas cedar	*Cedrus atlantica*
Italian cypress	*Cupressus sempervirens*
Portugal laurel	*Prunus lusitanica* (can be invasive)
Savin juniper	*Juniperus sabina*
Strawberry tree	*Arbutus unedo*

Source: Table compiled from Bell, VanDerZanden, and McMahan (2001); Mesogeo Gardens and Greenhouse (http://mesogeogarden.com/wpblog/); and the Mediterranean Garden Society (http://www.mediterraneangardensociety.org/).

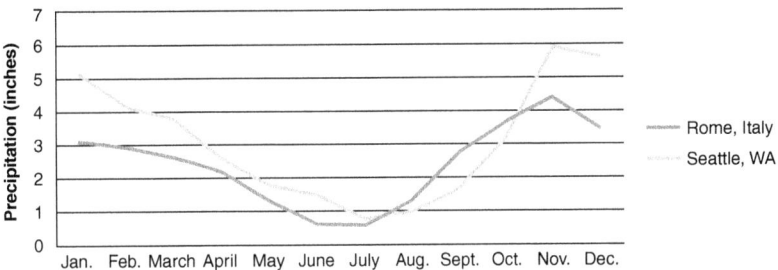

Figure 5-5 Seasonal rainfall distribution for Seattle, Washington, and Rome, Italy, both of which have a Mediterranean growing climate.

disturbance created by installing a new landscape creates the opportunity for seeds existing on the site to germinate and sets in motion the forces of succession. The new plant community that has been installed will change over time and, without some form of human intervention (landscape management), will develop into an ecosystem that may or may not meet the designer's intent. (Refer to Chapter 8 for specific strategies on the planting and establishment of landscape plants.)

As the serial progression of a landscape ecosystem occurs and the planting moves from the establishment phase into the growth and maturation phase, there will be a change in management needs (Figure 5-6). The establishment phase requires intensive management, including limiting competition from weeds for water and nutrients and mulching to conserve soil moisture and limit weed germination. This input-intensive phase enables the planting to become well established and grow rapidly into a functional ecosystem. The level of inputs should decrease as the landscape progresses toward a climax phase. During this phase, plantings will still require some level of management if they are to develop into a functional landscape ecosystem. Allowing a planting to revert to its natural pattern and processes, with no management input, is seldom a desirable approach to short- and long-term management of the site.

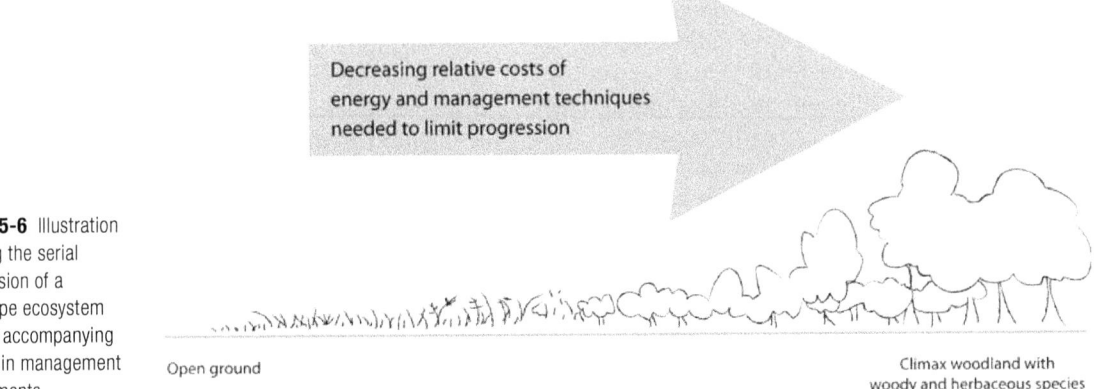

Figure 5-6 Illustration showing the serial progression of a landscape ecosystem and the accompanying change in management requirements.

MANAGEMENT STRATEGIES FOR A LANDSCAPE ECOSYSTEM

Postplanting Succession, Plant Attrition due to Changing Microclimates, and Encroachment of Nonplanted Species

A landscape manager's involvement with a site normally encompasses a much longer time frame than that of the designer or installation contractor. Because of this long-term interaction with the site, landscape managers should be involved in discussions and decisions about the project from the very beginning. To help landscape managers approach landscape maintenance in a sustainable way, the Sustainable Sites Initiative (2009a) has developed a comprehensive guide to developing and implementing a landscape maintenance plan (Table 5-3). The guide can be used by the integrated team (designer, installation contractor, and landscape manager) to develop a landscape maintenance plan that identifies the long-term desired outcomes for the site and the short-term plans to achieve these goals. This tool provides an excellent framework for communication between all parties involved in the project.

Management of a landscape ecosystem requires an understanding of natural plant cycles and a flexible and dynamic approach to plant care. Purposeful management throughout the life span of the planting is necessary. When possible, the focus of this type of management should be on the natural evolutionary change of the landscape over time. Research has shown that ecosystems near their climax successional state, or natural equilibrium, need less management than landscapes that are in an early successional state (Brooker and Corder 1986; Handley and Bulmer 1987). However, the ecosystem that results from a designed and managed landscape is far from natural and will always require some management.

In fact, these ecosystems are often in a slowly progressing state of flux over the lifetime of the planting. Sometimes this fluctuation is small, progressive, and easy to integrate. An example of this type of change is the attrition of full-sun species due to the increasing shade density from maturing tree canopies (Figure 5-7). In other cases, larger, more extreme influences will impact the ecosystem's growth and development. An example of this type of change is the loss of overstory trees as a result of extreme weather events such as flooding or ice storm damage (Figure 5-8). In these extreme cases, significant management intervention will be necessary to preserve the overall functionality of the landscape.

A major component of long-term landscape ecosystem management is postplanting succession. The species mix of the planting often changes over time due to microclimate changes and plant attrition. Occurring parallel with this serial progression is the encroachment of nondesirable species into the landscape ecosystem. Although these species may not be desirable, not all of these new arrivals are invasive. Invasive species, on the other hand, do need to be managed intensively to preserve the ecosystem and to limit their impact on surrounding natural and artificial landscapes.

Postplanting Succession

Plant succession accounts for the change in species mix of a plant community over time. Landscape succession can be seen on many scales. Examples of large-scale succession include the thousands of acres (hectares) burned in Yellowstone National Park in the United States in 1988, the extreme flooding that remade the landscape in Northern Italy in 2000, and the decimation of the native pine population in the first decade of this century in the Rocky Mountains of the United States due to the mountain pine beetle (*Dendroctonus ponderosae*). Small-scale succession may occur when a new building site is cleared or a gap in the existing tree canopy is created when a mature shade tree is removed in an urban landscape. The multiple types of succession are often due in part to changes in microclimates within the plant community. The serial progression, or succession, of a new landscape ecosystem is unavoidable, and landscape managers are responsible for directing succession in a desirable way (Figure 5-9).

TABLE 5-3 Sustainable Sites Initiative Sample Landscape Maintenance Plan Matrix

\	\	\	\	\	\	\
WORKSHEET: SITE MANAGEMENT PLAN						
Maintenance plan topics to be addressed by the integrated design team (including the maintenance contractor or manager)	Required or optional?	10-year desired outcome from maintenance practice	Required actions to achieve 10-year desired outcome (include specific details below)			
			Specific activities	Skill level required	Timeline/ schedule	Other details
Plant Stewardship						
Plant maintenance: Describe the process for maintaining vegetation according to long-term plans for the site and adhering to recognized standards for professional horticultural practice.	Required for all sites					
Plant health: Describe the process for monitoring plant health to prevent problems. Identify the proper techniques for addressing dead, diseased, or pest-infested vegetation.	Required for all sites					
Site safety: Describe the process for maintaining vegetation to ensure site safety and meet the needs of the intended users of the site.	Required for all sites					
Plant replacement: Provide a list (include the common and scientific names) of potential appropriate, noninvasive plants that can be used for replacing plants. When replacing plants, consider maintenance needs of plants and design approach.	Required for all sites					
Pest management: Control pests, diseases, and any unwanted species of plants and animals using integrated pest management (IPM) techniques.	Required for all sites					
Invasive Species Management						
Provide a list (include common and scientific names) of plant species identified in the area that are currently on any of the following lists as invasive: regional lists, state noxious weed laws, or federal noxious weed laws.	Required for all sites					

Figure 5-7 The sun-loving perennials originally planted in this landscape have died out over time as the tree canopies above have matured. Those that remain are weak and should be replaced with shade-tolerant species.

Figure 5-8 These mature trees are being pruned significantly or removed entirely as a result of a major ice storm. The resulting landscape will look much different as new plants are installed based on the changed site conditions.

Plant Attrition Due to Changing Microclimates

Landscapes transform over time as a result of environmental changes (including changes in site microclimates), variations in plant growth rates, and plant death (attrition). A body of research describes the important role population dynamics play in plant attrition in an ecosystem (Breshears et al. 2008; Stilma, Keesman, and Van der Werf 2009). The continual and dynamic biological and environmental processes that impact a landscape

DOES MAINTENANCE OF NATURALISTIC LANDSCAPES ALWAYS REQUIRE FEWER INPUTS?

A common assumption is that maintenance of naturalistic landscapes requires fewer inputs compared to other types of landscapes (Dunnett and Clayden 2000). This type of blanket statement doesn't always hold true. One example is the maintenance of amenity turf. A naturalistic approach might include fewer mowings over the course of the growing season so the turf has a taller, more natural appearance. Clearly, this would require fewer inputs (i.e., labor and fuel) than mowing the turf more frequently to maintain it at a shorter mowing height. However, it isn't quite that simple. Although the taller turf requires fewer mowings, each mowing requires more time and energy compared to more frequent mowings that remove less leaf tissue each time. Another issue with this maintenance approach is that the taller grass will generate significant green waste with each mowing, which must be disposed of off-site. This results in an additional cost compared to mowing more frequently with a mulching mower and leaving the clippings on-site, because less leaf tissue is being removed. A better approach is to analyze the desired outcome of the maintenance practice and then balance the maintenance inputs with outputs.

DISCUSSION POINTS

At this 10-acre (4 ha) commercial landscape site, the landscape manager has recently noticed a significant increase in the number of broadleaf weeds in the planting beds and turf area. What are some probable causes for this change to the landscape? Describe potential management strategies for this scenario.

ecosystem result in an ever-changing mix of species. As some species lose their ability to grow in the new environment, they are replaced by better-adapted species.

Examples of species changes due to microclimate changes include the following:

- Full-sun species being replaced by those that can handle an increasing shade level due to maturing tree canopies (Color Plate 5-2)
- Loss of some herbaceous species because they are unable to compete for the reduced soil moisture as trees and shrubs mature and require more water
- Loss of some species because of an increase in foliar diseases due to decreased air circulation caused by increased foliage density from the maturing plants

Figure 5-9 This commercial landscape is carefully managed to maintain the native species that were planted and to create the appropriate genus loci.

Courtesy Rick Martinson, WinterCreek Restoration, Bend, Oregon.

NATURAL SUCCESSION

The natural process of succession generally includes a sequential series of events. Included here is a succession scenario for an eastern deciduous forest in the United States described by the Brooklyn Botanic Garden (2009). It describes vegetation change, acknowledging some regional differences, on abandoned farmland left undisturbed for many years.

> Millions of seeds that lay dormant in the exposed soil germinate, causing an explosion of physiologically tough, aggressive annuals like horseweed (*Conyza canadensis*) and common ragweed (*Ambrosia artemisiifolia*). These plants, called pioneer species, dominate the first season. In a few years, biennials like mullein (*Verbascum* spp.) and Queen Anne's lace (*Daucus carota*) become common, along with a few perennial wildflowers like asters (*Aster* spp.) and goldenrods (*Solidago* spp.). After five years or so, grasses and wildflowers turn the area into a meadow. Within a few years young maples (*Acer* spp.), ashes (*Fraxinus* spp.), dogwoods (*Cornus* spp.), cherries (*Prunus* spp.), pines (*Pinus* spp.), and cedars (*Cedrus* spp.), many present as seedlings in the earliest stages, rapidly transform the meadow into "old field." This habitat is an extremely rich, floriferous blend of pioneer trees, shrubs, and herbaceous species particularly favored by wildlife. Given enough time without major disturbance, perhaps several centuries, a mature or old-growth forest will once again be found on the site.

As this natural attrition takes place, it is often necessary for a landscape manager to add new species to ensure the ecosystem continues to have adequate biodiversity. One strategy landscape managers can use to limit the amount of replacement species needed is to incorporate plants that grow in a range of light conditions (Table 5-4). These species can adapt over time to the changing light levels and still perform their ecosystem function. Landscape managers must monitor these progressive changes and make the necessary adjustments to direct the changing species mix in order to preserve the aesthetic, functional, and ecosystem services of the landscape.

TABLE 5-4 Ornamental Trees, Shrubs, Perennials, and Ground Covers That Are Adaptable to Growing in a Range of Light Conditions from Full Sun to Full Shade

Scientific Name	Common Name
Evergreen Trees	
Picea glauca	White spruce
Picea glauca var. *densata*	Black Hills spruce
Pinus cembra	Swiss stone pine
Pinus flexilis	Limber pine
Pinus mugo	Mugo pine
Pinus strobus	White pine
Taxus cuspidata 'Capitata'	Japanese yew
Thuja occidentalis 'Techny'	Techny arborvitae
Deciduous Trees	
Acer saccharinum	Silver maple
Nyssa sylvatica	Black gum
Sassafras albidum	Common sassafras
Evergreen Shrubs	
Large (5–10 feet) (1.5 to 3 meters)	
Juniperus chinensis 'Maney'	Chinese juniper
Picea glauca 'Conica'	Dwarf Alberta spruce
Rhododendron ×	Numerous hybrids, including 'Helsinki University', 'Mikkeli', 'Northern Starburst', 'Olga Mezitt'
Taxus × *media*	Anglojap yew
Tsuga canadensis 'Lewis'	Lewis hemlock

Scientific Name	Common Name
Small (under 5 feet) (under 1.5 meters)	
Buxus microphylla var. *koreana* 'Wintergreen'	Wintergreen boxwood
Euonymus fortunei 'Emerald 'n' Gold'	Emerald 'n' Gold wintercreeper
Euonymus fortunei 'Moonshadow'	Moonshadow wintercreeper
Juniperus horizontalis 'Mother Lode'	Mother Lode creeping juniper
Juniperus horizontalis 'Wiltonii'	Blue rug creeping juniper
Juniperus sabina 'Blue Forest'	Blue Forest savin juniper
Picea abies 'Nidiformis'	Bird's nest spruce
Picea pungens 'Montgomery'	Montgomery Colorado blue spruce
Rhododendron ×	Numerous hybrids, including: 'Pink Beauty' and 'Snowbird'
Deciduous Shrubs	
Large (8–12 feet) (2.5 to 3.5 meters)	
Exochorda racemosa	Common pearlbush
Exochorda serratifolia 'Northern Pearls'	Northern Pearls pearlbush
Hamamelis vernalis 'Autumn Embers'	Autumn Embers vernal witch hazel
Philadelphus coronarius	Sweet mock orange
Rhamnus frangula 'Columnaris'	Columnar glossy buckthorn
Viburnum × *burkwoodii*	Burkwood viburnum
Viburnum dentatum 'Morton'	Northern Burgundy viburnum
Viburnum dentatum 'Ralph Senior'	Autumn Jazz viburnum
Viburnum dentatum 'Synnestvedt'	Chicago Lustre viburnum
Viburnum farreri	Fragrant viburnum
Viburnum lantana	Wayfaringtree viburnum
Viburnum × *rhytidophylloides*	Lantanaphyllum viburnum
Viburnum × *rhytidophylloides* 'Alleghany'	Alleghany lantanaphyllum viburnum
Medium (4–8 feet) (1 to 2.5 meters)	
Aronia arbutifolia	Red chokeberry
Calycanthus floridus	Common sweetshrub
Clethra alnifolia	Summersweet clethra

(*Continued*)

TABLE 5-4 (Continued)

Scientific Name	Common Name
Clethra alnifolia 'Ruby Spice'	Ruby Spice clethra
Exochorda serratifolia	Korean pearlbush
Fothergilla major	Large fothergilla
Hydrangea arborescens 'Annabelle'	Annabelle hydrangea
Ilex glabra	Inkberry
Kerria japonica	Japanese kerria
Myrica pensylvanica	Northern bayberry
Rhodotypos scandens	Black jetbead
Spiraea × vanhouttei	Vanhoutte spirea
Symphoricarpos albus	White snowberry
Small (under 4 feet) (under 1.5 meters)	
Daphne × burkwoodii	Burkwood daphne
Daphne × burkwoodii 'Carol Mackie'	Carol Mackie daphne
Daphne × burkwoodii 'Somerset'	Somerset burkwood daphne
*Forsythia × * 'Arnold Dwarf'	Arnold Dwarf forsythia
Itea virginica	Virginia sweetspire
Itea virginica 'Henry's Garnet'	Henry's Garnet sweetspire
Itea virginica 'Sprich'	Little Henry sweetspire
Rhus aromatica 'Gro-Low'	Gro-Low sumac
Salix purpurea 'Nana'	Dwarf purple oiser willow
Stephanandra incisa 'Crispa'	Cutleaf stephanandra
Symphoricarpos × chenaultii 'Hancock'	Chenault coralberry
Ground Covers	
Ajuga reptans	Bugleweed
Euonymus fortunei	Wintercreeper euonymus
Euonymus fortunei 'Coloratus'	Purple wintercreeper
Vinca minor	Common periwinkle

Scientific Name	Common Name
Perennials	
Achillea spp.	Yarrow
Aquilegia hybrids	Columbine
Campanula carpatica	Carpathian bellflower
Centaurea montana	Mountain bluet
Chelone lyonii	Turtlehead
Heuchera hybrids	Coralbells

Encroachment of Nonplanted Species

Part of the constantly changing landscape ecosystem is the encroachment of nonplanted species on the site. Many forces lead to this distribution, including humans, animals, and environmental factors such as wind and water. Recently, some landscape ecology research has evaluated how and what changes to both natural and managed landscapes may be attributed to climate change (Breshears et al. 2008; Kelly and Goulden 2008; Kendle, Rose, and Oikawa 2000). In particular, they are focusing on what impact climate change has on plant distribution and encroachment into landscape ecosystems.

Even a subtle change in plant distribution can have a significant impact on the landscape. It is important for landscape managers to be able to distinguish between the arrival of species that will have a clear and undesirable impact on ecosystem function (invasive species) from those that simply represent ecosystem flux due to serial progression. The arrival of invasive species in natural and managed landscapes leads to a number of problems, including displacement of native species, which must be addressed through sound landscape management strategies (California State Parks 2009) (Figure 5-10). In contrast, the species representing flux can be essential to maintaining a level of ecosystem stability. These new species are able to grow where previously established species have become less viable (Williams 1997) and can ensure the landscape will still fill its aesthetic, functional, and ecosystem service roles.

Identifying Invasive Species

In contrast to native species that are indigenous to a particular area or region, invasive species are plants that are not native to a given ecosystem and that cause, or are likely to cause, economic, ecological, or environmental harm (Wikipedia 2010b). It is often because of this economic and environmental impact that some of the "introduced," "exotic," or "alien" species used in landscapes today get a bad name. Clearly, not all introduced species are invasive. In many cases, they are well-behaved, functional, and aesthetic parts of a landscape.

In general, invasive species are more often associated with a species of plant rather than a plant cultivar. Because the majority of cultivars are reproduced through budding or grafting, which requires human intervention, there is little likelihood they will spread extensively unless planted by humans. Further, many

---

Population dynamics is the branch of life sciences that studies short- and long-term changes in the size and age composition of populations, and the biological and environmental processes influencing those changes (Wikipedia 2010a).

Figure 5-10 (a) Butterfly bush (*Buddleia* spp.) has invaded the edge of this stream and has choked out native vegetation. (b) English ivy (*Hedera helix*), seen here climbing up tree trunks, has become a significant problem in some parts of the United States.
Images courtesy of Linda R. McMahan and Brad Withrow-Robinson, Oregon State University Extension Service.

of the newer tree cultivars readily available through the nursery industry do not produce viable seed via pollination so seed dispersal and subsequent spread of the plant does not occur (Ramstad and Orlando 2009).

However, there are exceptions. Recent data suggests that cultivars of two common urban trees, Norway maple (*Acer platanoides*) and Bradford pear (*Pyrus calleryana*), have exhibited invasive tendencies in native woodland areas (Ramstad and Orlando 2009). There is similar evidence that some native species, western juniper (*Juniperus occidentalis*) for example, are spreading beyond their native habitats and significantly changing otherwise intact ecosystems. Table 5-5 lists a number of native species that have become invasive in certain parts of the world. While native plants are an important part of a sustainable landscape, the species in the overall context of the design and growing environment must be considered when determining if it is the best choice. Although a particular species is native, in some instances it may become a landscape liability. It is important to check local resources to determine if these species are a problem in your area.

COMMON INVASIVE SPECIES TRAITS INCLUDE THE FOLLOWING:

- Ability to reproduce both asexually and sexually
- Fast growth rate
- Rapid reproduction
- High dispersal ability
- Phenotypic plasticity (the ability of a plant to alter its growth form to suit current environmental conditions)
- Tolerance of a wide range of environmental conditions
- History or evidence of successful invasions

Source: Wikipedia (2001b).

TABLE 5-5 Plant Species Native to the United States That Have Been Classified as Invasive

Scientific Name	Common Name
Shrubs and Subshrubs	
Bocconia frutescens	Plume poppy
Caragana arborescens	Siberian peashrub
Citharexylum caudatum	Juniper berry
Clidemia hirta	Soapbush
Hypericum canariense	Canary Island Saint-John's-wort
Lantana camara	Large-leaf lantana
Maclura pomifera	Osage orange
Mahonia nervosa	Oregon grape
Rubus argutus	Highbush blackberry
Trees	
Calocedrus decurrens	Incense cedar
Catalpa bignonioides	Southern catalpa
Catalpa speciosa	Northern catalpa
Juniperus virginiana	Eastern red cedar
Pinus ponderosa	Ponderosa pine
Pinus strobus	Eastern white pine
Populus balsamifera	Balsam poplar
Pseudotsuga menziesii	Douglas fir
Robinia pseudoacacia	Black locust
Thuja occidentalis	Eastern arborvitae

Source: Adapted from the Invasive Plant Atlas of the United States (http://www.invasiveplantatlas.org/index.html).

SUMMARY

Landscape ecosystems are multifunctional and fulfill aesthetic and functional needs while providing ecosystem services. Ecosystem services contribute to ecological cycles and environmental enhancements. Ongoing collaboration among the landscape designer, installation contractor, and landscape manager is essential to creating landscape ecosystems that function in both the short term and the long term. A well-designed and well-managed landscape ecosystem will require more inputs (labor, resources such as water, fertilizer, pesticides) during the early phases of succession but will ultimately require fewer inputs as the entire system evolves into a functional ecosystem at a semi–steady state of equilibrium. To accomplish this, the landscape management plan must account for planting succession due to plant attrition and the encroachment of nonplanted species.

STUDY QUESTIONS

1. Describe the climax stage of an ecosystem.
2. Define "ecosystem services." List 10 examples.
3. Describe the concept of "ecological design" from the 1960s through the late 1980s. How has this influenced current landscape design approaches?
4. Define "amenity turf."
5. Describe what is meant by design intent with regard to creating landscape ecosystems.
6. Define "succession phase."
7. Describe natural regeneration in a landscape context. Give an example in a natural landscape and in a built landscape.
8. What is postplanting succession? What can landscape managers do to address this situation?
9. Describe the relationship between plant attrition and microclimates.
10. List five factors that contribute to plant attrition.
11. Define an "invasive species." What happens when they invade a landscape? Why should they be managed?
12. If a species is invasive in one part of the world, is it necessarily invasive in another part of the world? Explain.
13. Should only plants native to an area be used to create a landscape ecosystem? Explain.

Building a Sustainable Future

CHANGE OCCURRED RAPIDLY in the twentieth century—more so than at any other time period in the history of humanity. Arguably, the most significant change has been the number of people living on earth and depending on its resources for survival. Within a hundred-year time span, the global population grew from 1.6 to 6 billion, and for the first time in history over 50 percent of the population—80 percent in the United States and Europe—is concentrated in urban areas. Cities are hastily expanding to accommodate the rapid influx. In the United States alone, 1.5 million acres (0.6 million hectares) of farmland, forest, or other rural land is being converted to urban development each year (American Farmland Trust 2009). In the coming decades, the rapid population increase is expected to continue, with projections of 7 billion in 2011, 8 billion in 2024, and 9 billion by 2045.

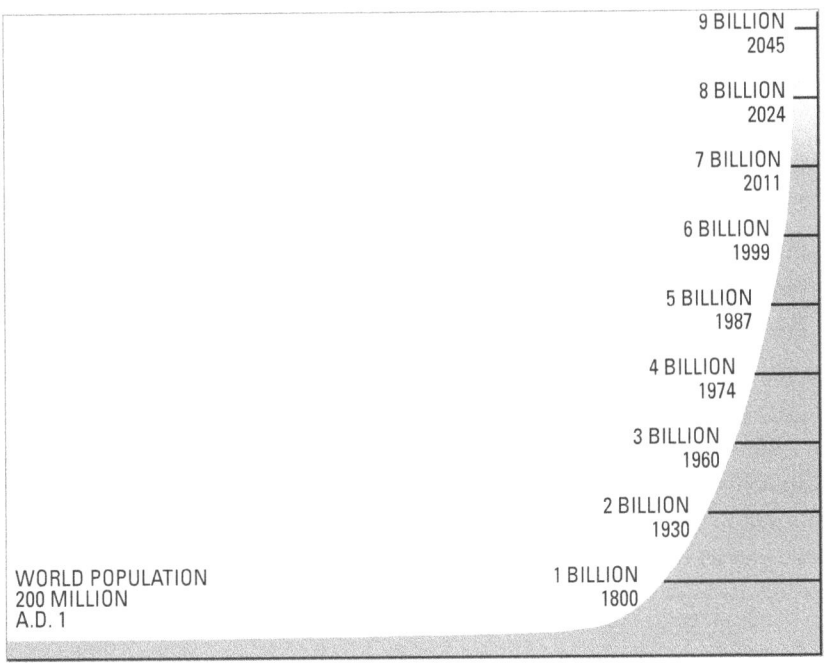

FIGURE 1.2
Global population growth.

CHAPTER 1: Building a Sustainable Future

As human populations increase, so do the demands on the earth's resources. Unprecedented pressure is being placed on the planet's soils, waters, forests, and other natural capital (Brundtland 1987). It is projected that at current rates, humanity will soon need the capacity of two earths to absorb CO_2 waste and keep up with natural resource consumption (World Wildlife Fund 2010).

To maintain their physical and mental health, every individual needs and *deserves* clean air, clean water, healthy productive soils, opportunities for physical activity and mental respite, and other benefits or "ecosystem services" provided by the natural environment. Historically, we have not required urban sites to function as sustainable and productive ecosystems but instead have relied on wildlands or rural areas to provide the services that sustain human life. Sadly, two-thirds of ecosystem services are now in decline worldwide (UN Foundation 2005).

Urban sites and other developed landscapes can help reverse this trend. A sustainable future for the growing population is not out of reach, but achieving it will require dramatically changing the ways in which sites are developed and maintained. To adequately provide for the next generation, the protection and restoration of ecosystem services must become standard practice for all sites—both urban and rural.

■ ECOSYSTEM SERVICES: A KEY ATTRIBUTE OF A SUSTAINABLE SITE

Ecosystems provide a multitude of resources and processes that sustain and fulfill human life. These benefits, collectively known as ecosystem services, are essential to our well-being and are a key attribute of a sustainable site. Examples of ecosystem services include:

- Regulate temperature and precipitation.
- Sequester greenhouse gases.
- Cleanse the air and water.
- Provide habitat.
- Maintain soil health and fertility.
- Retain and store fresh water.
- Control erosion.
- Provide recreation.
- Recycle nutrients.
- Produce food and other raw materials such as timber, medicine, and fuel.
- Mitigate natural hazards such as flooding, wildfire, and drought.
- Provide inspiration, intellectual stimulation, and cultural enhancement.
- Enhance opportunities for mental respite.

Many of the goods and services provided by nature are often taken for granted, in large part because they are supplied for "free" and are not part of our traditional accounting systems. To underscore their importance and inform land-use decisions, scientists have begun estimating the wealth of ecosystem services and have found the monetary value to be an average of $33 trillion per year, or nearly twice the global gross national product (Costanza et al. 1997).

Issues that plague urban environments, such as flooding, urban heat islands, and water pollution, are often caused or exacerbated by the disturbance or removal of natural systems and the benefits they provide. Sustainable sites seek to improve the quality of life of site users and the surrounding communities by creating regenerative systems that protect and restore ecosystem services.

Regenerative Systems

The building industry has been an early adopter of the sustainability movement and has documented success in reducing energy, water use, greenhouse gas emissions, and solid waste. Although reducing environmental impacts is definitely a step in the right direction, it is not enough to provide a sustainable future for the burgeoning human population. In addition to doing less damage, we must also reverse the degradation of the earth's natural resources by creating regenerative and resilient systems that sustain and increase the provision of ecosystem services. Landscape practitioners can lead the green building movement to a higher level of sustainable design by helping project teams realize this goal and integrate living systems into all aspects of the site.

Previously developed sites that have limited ecological or cultural value present the greatest opportunity for the type of regenerative change we need. The redevelopment of environmentally degraded sites, such as greyfields or brownfields, provides a mechanism not only for protecting native ecosystems and agricultural lands (via diversion of development pressure) but also for restoring natural systems and the ecosystem services they provide. Encouraging development within existing communities and developed places also conserves the natural and financial resources required to construct and maintain infrastructure. This stands in contrast to the development of greenfield sites, which has a much greater potential of reducing or destroying healthy, functioning ecosystems and the goods and services they provide. Greenfield development that diminishes ecosystem services ultimately contributes to the global decline of natural capital and the overall benefits humanity receives from nature.

FIGURE 1.3
High Line Park, Twenty-sixth Street viewing spur. The elevated public park constructed on an abandoned railway in Manhattan repurposes existing structures and provides a ribbon of green space that restores a variety of ecosystem services in a dense urban environment.

What Is Site Sustainability?

Sustainable development is commonly defined as "development that meets the needs of the present without compromising the ability of future generations to meet their own needs" (Brundtland 1987). It recognizes the interdependency between the environment, human health, and the economy and considers all three when measuring success.

The three pillars of sustainability and their relationship to site development are outlined below:

- **PLANET:** Environmental or ecological sustainability stems from the realization that human life (and the life of other creatures as well) is dependent upon the natural environment and its provision of ecosystem services. It recognizes that there are limits to the bounty ecosystems can provide and to the harvest and degradation they can withstand. To ensure the longevity and viability of the earth's resources, sites must protect and restore ecosystem services and humans must act as stewards of the environment. Sustainable sites help society build an environmental ethic by providing everyday opportunities for people to connect with nature.

- **PROFIT:** Traditionally, the success of development has primarily been evaluated by economic measures. Placing such a strong focus on financial gains alone has led to significant environmental and human health costs. For any endeavor to work long term, it must certainly be profitable; however, other factors must also be considered. Sustainable sites base decisions not only on their economic merits but also on their environmental and social costs and benefits. Including the impacts on people and the planet in the project accounting brings to light the full cost of doing business and encourages more social and environmental responsibility.

- **PEOPLE:** Social equity and human health is an aspect of sustainability that is commonly overlooked and can be the most difficult to address. It extends the opportunity to aspire to a better quality of life to all individuals. Social equity addresses basic provisions such as clean air and water, the right to education, access to safe and healthy green space, and other factors that impact our quality of life. Sustainable sites play an important role in supporting human health and create opportunities for all site users to improve their physical, mental, and social well-being.

TABLE 1.1
Example Characteristics of Conventional and Sustainable Sites

	CONVENTIONAL SITE	SUSTAINABLE SITE
TEAM CULTURE OR PHILOSOPHY	Perceives nature and development as being in opposition. May incorporate sustainable practices into the design if it does not increase time or immediate costs.	Values nature and the ecosystem services it provides. Accepts the responsibility of sustainability and providing a meaningful quality of life to future generations. Strives to reverse the degradation of the earth's natural resources by creating regenerative and resilient systems.
MEASURES OF SUCCESS	Primarily evaluated by the economic success of the project.	Success is measured by not only the economic outcomes but also the environmental and human health impacts of the project.
DESIGN PROCESS	Site design is compartmentalized, and the landscape and buildings are viewed as separate entities. Landscape design often begins after the building design or construction is complete. Consultants work independently on their area of the project and communicate information as needed.	Building and landscape practitioners, engineers, construction and maintenance professionals, and other consultants are collectively involved in the design process and work together to optimize the performance of the site toward common goals.

	CONVENTIONAL SITE	SUSTAINABLE SITE
AESTHETICS	Somewhat homogenous, replicating standard templates similar to sites from other regions or parts of the world.	Design solutions grow from the place and are representative of the local soils, vegetation, materials, and culture.
ENERGY	Relies heavily on nonrenewable resources that harm the environment and human health.	Minimizes energy consumption and the use of fossil fuels. Whenever feasible, energy is derived from the sun and wind, biomass, or other renewable resources.
	The building and landscape do not work together to reduce energy consumption.	The landscape creates favorable microclimates that reduce the energy consumption of buildings and increase the comfort of site users.
SOILS	Construction and maintenance practices commonly damage soils.	The disturbance of healthy soils is minimized. Degraded soils are restored prior to replanting.
	Require regular applications of fertilizers to promote healthy plant growth.	Soil biota and organic matter from on-site vegetation promote healthy plant growth.
VEGETATION	Preserves large trees.	Maximizes the integration of all existing native and ecologically appropriate vegetation into the site design.
	Plant selection is primarily based on site conditions and aesthetic considerations.	Plant selection considers a broad range of factors, including growing conditions, beauty, resiliency, ecological function, native range and habitat, invasiveness, and maintenance requirements.
WATER	Quickly conveys stormwater runoff and other wastewater resources off-site.	Captures rain and wastewater for reuse on-site or on adjacent properties.
	Strongly relies upon potable water for irrigation.	Landscape primarily relies upon precipitation or wastewater resources such as air-conditioner condensate, greywater, or reclaimed water.
MATERIALS	Removes and disposes of much of the existing building and landscape materials.	Maximizes the reuse of existing structures, landscape, and building materials.
	The reuse of site structures or materials at the end of the project life is not considered in the design process.	Sites are designed to minimize the disposal of materials. Site structures and features can be adapted and reused in place or easily deconstructed and reclaimed or recycled.
MAINTENANCE	The individuals responsible for maintenance are not aware of the goals of the project or how maintenance practices impact the site's ecological and cultural function.	The individuals responsible for maintenance understand and support the goals of the project. Education and training is provided to ensure that maintenance optimizes the site's ecological and cultural performance.
	Maintenance occurs on a regular schedule and is not informed by the performance of the site. Land-care practices focus on keeping the site somewhat static and limiting change.	Postoccupancy evaluations and monitoring guide land-care practices. The site evolves and adapts in a way that continually improves its ecological function and the visitor's experience.
CONTINUED LEARNING	No postoccupancy evaluations or monitoring is conducted to improve future projects.	Monitoring is built into the design and information gathered is used to improve future projects and the success of the sustainable design industry.

The Importance of Education and Stewardship

Design alone cannot ensure a sustainable site; what is created on paper must be translated into a tangible project constructed and cared for in a way that perpetuates its success. Landscape practitioners often guide the design and construction process but are commonly separated from the long-term management of the site. Many project teams that have worked so diligently to minimize resource consumption, cleanse water, restore ecological processes, and address other aspects of sustainability discover after some time that their sustainable site does not function as intended or live up to its accolades. This is often due to a lack of performance monitoring and misguided or omitted operations and maintenance procedures. These important practices are frequently overlooked or cut from the project for one or all of following reasons:

- Budget restraints
- A belief that landscapes are natural systems and as such can care for themselves
- A lack of individuals who take ownership of the site and see themselves as stewards of the land
- A general ignorance or apathy toward the concept of sustainability and how the site must function in order to support it

Regardless of the reason, the fact stands true: constructed landscapes and many natural systems do require monitoring and strategic management and *stewardship* in order to continue to function properly and optimize their provision of ecosystem services. Accepting this, we must ask ourselves, how do we get people to embrace sustainability and care about the ecological health of our landscapes? How do we instill a sense of stewardship for our built and natural ecosystems? The answer is twofold: (1) illustrate both the short- and long-term economic and human health benefits, and (2) provide educational and meaningful experiences that connect people to nature. In addition to project teams working with the client, maintenance staff, or volunteers to help them understand why monitoring and stewardship are central to long-term success; project teams can also create landscapes that help humanity build an environmental ethic.

Aldo Leopold, in his writings on the subject, recognized the need for a land ethic—a moral principle or value—that "simply enlarges the boundaries of our community to include soils, waters, plants, and animals, or collectively: the land." Leopold notes, "An ethic to supplement and guide the economic relation of land presupposes the existence of some mental image of land as a biotic mechanism. We can be ethical only in relation to something we can see, feel, understand, love, or otherwise have faith in" (Leopold 1949).

FIGURE 1.4
Infiltration planters filled with trees, grasses, and perennial wildflowers manage stormwater and connect the surrounding community to the natural environment at the Taylor 28 streetscape.

In other words, nature must become relevant to our everyday lives. Proving opportunities for society to see and experience nature in this way should be the charge of landscape practitioners and one of the primary purposes of a sustainable site. In this respect, a successfully designed site functions as a living teaching tool.

There are many different ways to learn, and the best teachers make a topic relevant to their students. In a landscape setting this can be accomplished through both active education or outreach and experiential learning. In addition to commonly used conventional teaching methods such as interpretation, guided tours, or volunteer activities, landscapes can also teach by being a source of inspiration, evoking emotion and providing a physical connection to the environment. Constructed landscapes can reveal the ecological processes, rhythms, and cycles of nature and provide restorative settings that allow us to reflect upon our place in the world and to notice the environment around us (Meyer 2008). Hands-on interaction and exploration of diverse and healthy ecosystems can build a broader understanding of the natural world and provide the motivational basis for more formal learning (Wells and Lekies 2006). Positive and spontaneous interaction with nature in our homes, schools, and places of work can build a familiarity with and love for the natural environment that translates into a sense of stewardship. Landscapes that improve our understanding of nature and make it relevant to our lives can ultimately have a sphere of influence that extends well beyond the boundaries of the site. Though the number of people who visit the site may be relatively small in comparison to the global population, their environmental ethic can be very influential and a catalyst for change, impacting the government officials they elect, their vote on key issues, the purchase of products, and decisions on where to live and how to commute (Meyer 2008).

CASE STUDY

UNDERWOOD FAMILY SONORAN LANDSCAPE LABORATORY

PROJECT TYPE: Public institution

LOCATION: Tucson, Arizona

SIZE: 1 acre (0.4 hectare)

HIGHLIGHTED SUSTAINABLE PRACTICES:

- Redevelopment of a greyfield site
- Use of harvested wastewater
- Increased vegetative biomass
- Habitat for endangered species
- Landscape irrigation requirements balanced with the available wastewater supply
- Comfortable outdoor microclimate that encourages interaction with nature
- On-site monitoring and documentation of sustainable practices to evaluate performance over time

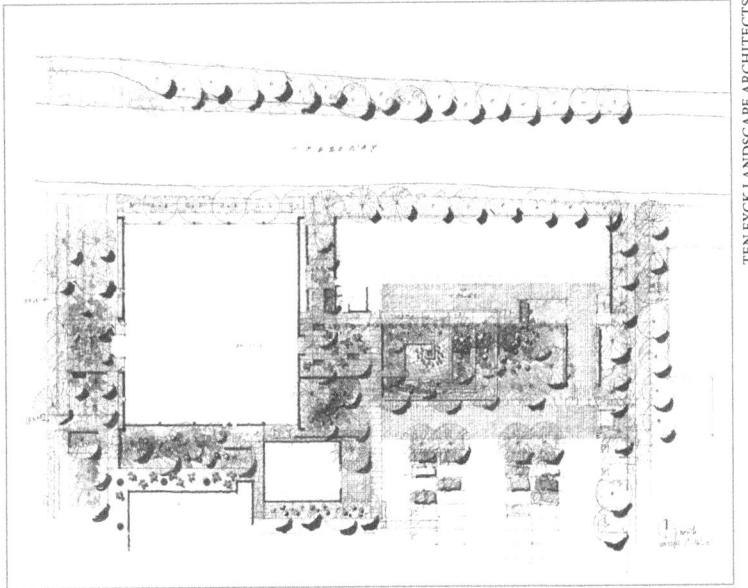

■ FIGURE 1.5 Site plan.

THE SITE: Asphalt campus parking lot located adjacent to the School of Architecture and Landscape Architecture at the University of Arizona. The Tucson climate is hot during the summer and cool in winter. Average annual precipitation is 12 inches.

continues

UNDERWOOD FAMILY SONORAN LANDSCAPE LABORATORY *(CONTINUED)*

Design Overview

In 2006, the University of Arizona built a new expansion facility that brings students from architecture, planning, and landscape architecture under one roof to provide an integrated learning environment. The asphalt parking lot adjacent to the school was transformed into the Underwood Family Sonoran Landscape Laboratory, which functions as both an outdoor classroom and entry plaza. The research-oriented garden serves as a demonstration facility that focuses on water-conscious design solutions and functions as a cleansing biosponge for stormwater runoff and building wastewater (see Figure 1.5).

Five distinct ecological communities of the Sonoran Desert are represented in the desert laboratory. The 5,000-gallon (18,900 L) pond provides habitat for endangered fish and is listed by the U.S. Fish and Wildlife Service as a "safe harbor" urban site (see Figure 1.6). The diverse garden is vegetated with native drought-resistant plants appropriate for each biome. A vertical scrim extends along the south side of the building and is vegetated with vines that have climbed 50 feet (15.24 m) high, which help to reduce the building's energy consumption.

■ FIGURE 1.6
Wetland pond and shaded lower court. The 5,000-gallon (18,900 L) pond provides habitat for endangered fish and is listed by the U.S. Fish and Wildlife Service as a "safe harbor" urban site.

UNDERWOOD FAMILY SONORAN LANDSCAPE LABORATORY *(CONTINUED)*

Extensive collaboration between the project architect, landscape architect, engineers, and irrigation consultant resulted in an impressive water harvesting system that collects rainwater from the roof, air-conditioning condensate, and greywater from the building's drinking fountains. The water is stored in an 11,600-gallon (43,911 L) cistern and over the course of a year, 244,000 gallons (922,320 L) are harvested. The recycled water is comprised of approximately 40 percent condensate, 33 percent rainwater runoff, 18 percent well water blowoff and 9 percent greywater. The well's operation requires daily flushing, which was sending 200 gallons (757 L) per day to the city storm drain system. The fresh water from the blowoff is now diverted into the desert riparian pond and helps to maintain water levels and the appropriate conditions for the desert fish species. After the initial establishment period, the site's water use will be balanced; potable water will likely no longer be required, and the garden will rely solely on reclaimed water sources (see Figure 1.7).

FIGURE 1.7
Native plants adapted to the site conditions are planted throughout the site. Once the vegetation is established, potable water will likely no longer be required, and the garden will rely solely on reclaimed water sources.

continues

UNDERWOOD FAMILY SONORAN LANDSCAPE LABORATORY *(CONTINUED)*

PROJECT TEAM

- **LANDSCAPE ARCHITECTS**
  Christine E. Ten Eyck, FASLA
  Todd Briggs, ASLA, project manager
  www.teneyckla.com

- **ARCHITECT**
  Jones Studio
  www.jonesstudioinc.com

- **CIVIL ENGINEER**
  Evans Kuhn
  www.evanskuhn.com

- **MECHANICAL ENGINEER**
  Kunka Engineering
  www.kunka.com

- **IRRIGATION DESIGN**
  Carl Kominsky

- **WETLAND CONSULTANT**
  Wass Gerke & Associates
  www.azwetlands.com

- **GENERAL CONTRACTOR**
  Lloyd Construction Company, Inc.
  www.lloydconstruction.com

- **LANDSCAPE CONTRACTOR**
  AAA Landscape
  www.aaalandscape.com

Creating a Love for Nature in Our Children

Children who feel connected to the natural environment and the ecological processes that sustain humanity are better equipped to face the challenge of building a sustainable society. Unfortunately, today's children are spending less and less time outdoors and as a result, their knowledge and appreciation of the natural world is dwindling (Louv 2005). The increasing disconnect with nature can be attributed, in part, to residential and schoolyard landscapes that children often find boring and uninspiring and to the layout of our neighborhoods and communities, which often limits safe access to natural settings (Moore and Marcus 2008).

Children are fascinated by nature and have an innate desire to splash in water, chase butterflies, get muddy, and explore their surroundings (see Figure 1.8). If their curiosity is not given an opportunity to flourish, an aversion to nature—or biophobia—may develop, which can result in a general discomfort, fear, or disregard for the natural environment (Kellert and Wilson 1993).

FIGURE 1.8 Children playing with rocks and water that are part of a cleansing biotope at Tanner Springs Park.

HENRY KUNOWSKI / A ATELIER DREISEITL

In order to cultivate a love for nature within children, they must first have fun playing outdoors and immersing themselves in healthy ecosystems and all of their components. Providing these opportunities where children spend their days—at home or school, or in a local park—enables spontaneous interaction with nature to become part of everyday life and relieves parents of the need to program time in the natural world into children's lives (Moore and Marcus 2008). Unstructured, child-directed play in "wild" settings—as opposed to structured or programmed activities such as planting a tree or caring for a plant—has been found to be more effective at encouraging developmental impacts that support an environmental ethic in adults (Wells and Lekies 2006). Sites can serve a special and valuable purpose when they encourage children to play outdoors and explore the natural environment (see Figure 1.9).

FIGURE 1.9
Fifty-foot-long hillside slide integrated into the Adventure Garden at the San Francisco School. The terraced garden is built from recycled concrete taken from a demolished basketball court located on-site. The schoolyard integrates concepts of sustainability, recycling, and reuse into the physical form of the landscape.

Continual Improvement: Monitoring and Adaptive Management

The living systems that make up a sustainable site do not exist in a fixed state. Similar to natural ecosystems, they grow, senesce, and evolve over time. The same is true for the culture of a site and how people choose to use and experience the landscape. Acknowledging that change is an unavoidable and essential component of a site is key to the long-term success of the project.

Postoccupancy evaluations and the monitoring of sustainable design practices are necessary for continued improvement and informed site stewardship. Adaptive management uses the information gathered to continually adjust maintenance practices and improve the overall function of the site.

Planning for information gathering and adaptive management begins in the design phase. Project teams can incorporate tracking mechanisms into the site design for water and energy use, waste disposal, and other performance targets. And the design of the site can ease the gathering of information and encourage monitoring.

To understand which components of a site to monitor, the goals and performance targets of the project must first be agreed upon. How monitoring will be used to improve site performance should be clear to all those involved. Projects are more likely to be successful when the individuals collecting and using the data are included in the design process.

Project teams may need to educate clients about the public perception and monetary benefits of monitoring and adaptive management, which include:

    Avoiding trial and error maintenance practices

    Reducing replacement costs

    Preventing extreme overhauls of failing systems

In addition to the on-site benefits, postoccupancy evaluations and monitoring also provide invaluable opportunities for continued learning that can improve the body of knowledge and success of the sustainable design industry.

TABLE 1.2 Guiding principles are commonly held values or fundamental beliefs that steer an organization, team, or individual's decision making. They are the foundation of the design process and help articulate expectations and evaluate success.

GUIDING PRINCIPLES OF A SUSTAINABLE SITE

DO NO HARM.
Avoid making changes to the site that will degrade the surrounding environment. Promote projects on sites where previous disturbance or development presents an opportunity to regenerate ecosystem services through sustainable design.

OBSERVE THE PRECAUTIONARY PRINCIPLE.
Be cautious in making decisions that could create risk to human and environmental health. Some actions can cause irreversible damage. Examine a full range of alternatives—including no action—and be open to contributions from all affected parties.

DESIGN WITH NATURE AND CULTURE.
Create and implement designs that are responsive to economic, environmental, and cultural conditions.

PROVIDE REGENERATIVE SYSTEMS AS INTERGENERATIONAL EQUITY.
Provide future generations with a sustainable environment supported by regenerative systems and endowed with regenerative resources.

SUPPORT A LIVING PROCESS.
Continuously reevaluate assumptions and values and adapt to demographic and environmental change.

USE A SYSTEMS-THINKING APPROACH.
Understand and value the relationships in an ecosystem and use an approach that reflects and sustains ecosystem services; reestablish the integral and essential relationship between natural processes and human activity.

USE A COLLABORATIVE AND ETHICAL APPROACH.
Encourage direct and open communication among colleagues, clients, manufacturers, and users to link long-term sustainability with ethical responsibility.

CONTINUALLY IMPROVE SITE PRACTICES.
Conduct postoccupancy evaluations and ecological monitoring to inform the maintenance of the site and provide opportunities for continued learning that improves the field of sustainable design.

FOSTER ENVIRONMENTAL STEWARDSHIP.
In all aspects of land development and management, foster an ethic of environmental stewardship—an understanding that responsible management of healthy ecosystems improves the quality of life for present and future generations.

CONNECT PEOPLE TO NATURE.
Create environments where all people can receive and enjoy the benefits of nature in their everyday lives.

SOURCE: THE SUSTAINABLE SITES INITIATIVE GUIDELINES AND PERFORMANCE BENCHMARKS, 2009

CASE STUDY

PACIFIC CANNERY LOFTS

PROJECT TYPE: Mixed-use, multifamily development

LOCATION: Oakland, California

SIZE: 2.7 acres (1.1 hectares)

COMPLETION DATE: 2008

CLIENT: Holliday Development

HIGHLIGHTED SUSTAINABLE PRACTICES:

- Redevelopment of a brownfield site
- Within walking distance to mass public transportation
- Reuse of existing on-site materials
- Reduces impervious cover
- Increases vegetative biomass
- Gardens include edible plants
- Mitigates the urban heat island
- Utilizes reclaimed water in a drip irrigation system

THE SITE: Industrial brownfield site located in West Oakland. The historic neighborhood was characterized by abandoned warehouses, a crumbling train station, and a maze of raised freeways, frontage roads, and rail lines.

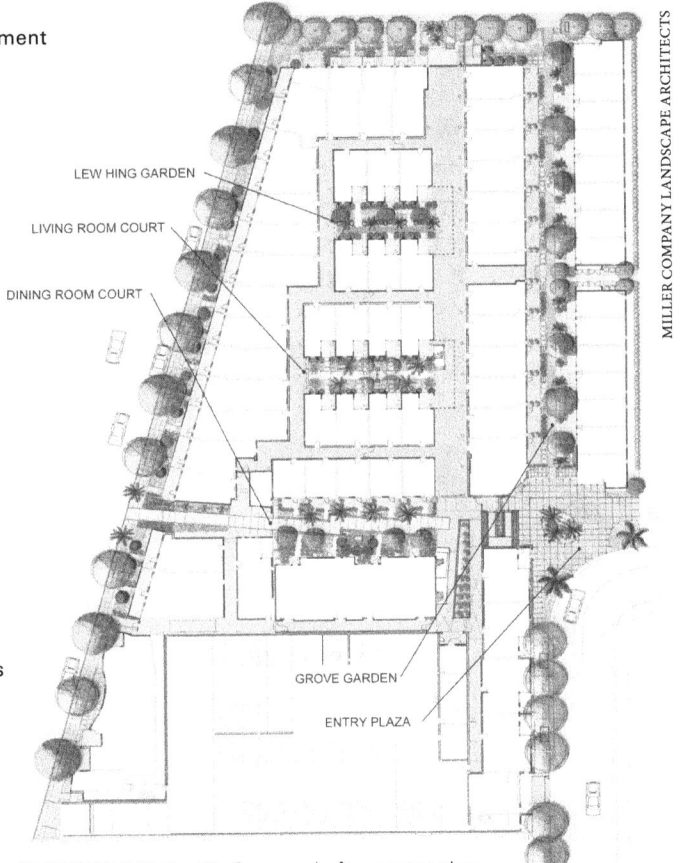

FIGURE 1.10 Pacific Cannery Lofts master plan.

Design Overview

Pacific Cannery Lofts is an adaptive reuse project that has transformed a historic vegetable cannery into 163 contemporary loft and town house units (see Figure 1.11). The site is part of a vision to redevelop nearly 30 acres of brownfield into a new Central Station neighborhood that brings together a number of developers to build parks with improved streets, commercial spaces, an urban farm, and over 1,000 new housing units around the renovated train station.

    The site design features three internal garden courtyards that are linked by a 350-foot-long (107 m) double-height corridor known as the Gallery, which serves as the internal "main street" of the project. A sense of retreat and privacy for residents was created through a thoughtful organization of space, rich detail in the lushly planted courtyards, and a linear grove court featuring fruit trees and edible plants. Central walkways focus circulation to the middle of the spaces, leaving room adjacent to the buildings for individual entry garden zones and privacy plantings designed to screen private unit patio areas (see Figure 1.11). Incorporating edible plants and highlighting natural wind and stormwater events in the gardens tempers the heavily built atmosphere of the site.

continues

PACIFIC CANNERY LOFTS *(CONTINUED)*

The main entry courtyard is designed as a rain garden. Flagstone paths lead to individual unit entries furnished with a dual-purpose bench and aqueduct. Water cascades from the pebble-filled aqueduct into linear "rivers" adjacent to the main walkway that hold and cleanse the water before it infiltrates into the local aquifer. Recycled tumbled glass installed at the surface of the channels is underlit with LED strands marking the path and giving the courtyard a warm glow at night (see Figure 1.12). Reclaimed gears and valve heads embedded in the walkway provide rhythm and indicate locations of drain inlets set immediately below the recycled tumbled glass. The drain inlets relieve the courtyard when extreme downpours deluge the infiltration system, thereby protecting the building from flooding.

Abandoned cannery relics are reused throughout the Pacific Cannery Lofts project as industrial sculpture. Ten-foot diameter cast-iron wheels, originally part of the cannery's ice-making equipment, mark the west entry, along with engines, mounts, and other related machine parts. The cannery's original scale marks the east entry, and slate-plated switching stations are set in the building's new gallery arcade.

■ **FIGURE 1.11**
Central walkways in the dining room courtyard focus circulation to the middle of the space, leaving room adjacent to the buildings for individual entry garden zones and privacy plantings designed to screen private unit patio areas.

■ **FIGURE 1.12**
Flagstone paths lead to individual unit entries furnished with a dual-purpose bench and aqueduct. Water cascades from the pebble-filled aqueduct into linear "rivers" adjacent to the main walkway that hold and cleanse the water before it infiltrates into the local aquifer. Recycled tumbled glass installed at the surface of the channels is underlit with LED strands marking the path and giving the courtyard a warm glow at night.

PACIFIC CANNERY LOFTS (CONTINUED)

PROJECT TEAM

LANDSCAPE ARCHITECTS
Miller Company Landscape Architects
www.millercomp.com
Jeffrey Miller, Principal Landscape Architect
Leah Hickey, project assistant

ARCHITECTS
David Baker + Partners Architects
www.dbarchitect.com

GENERAL CONTRACTOR
Cannon Constructors
www.cannongroup.com

LANDSCAPE CONTRACTOR
Miller Company Landscape Contractors
William Rogers, project manager
www.millercomp.com

■ FIGURE 1.13
Brightly hued custom concrete banquettes and low tables flank the central walkway in the living room courtyard. The tandem U-shaped seating design invites conversation and provides respite. Large leaf and flower plantings create a tropical effect, while the low-water-use understory provides texture and fragrance.

REFERENCES

American Farmland Trust. 2009. Farming on the edge report. http://www.farmland.org/resources/fote/default.asp; accessed 10/11/11.

Brundtland, G. H. 1987. *Our common future: Report of the World Commission on Environment and Development.* Oxford University Press.

Costanza, R., et al. 1997. The value of the world's ecosystem services and natural capital. *Nature* 387 (May 15): 253–60.

Kellert, S., and E. O. Wilson. (1993). *The biophilia hypothesis.* Washington, DC: Island Press.

Leopold, A. 1949. *A Sand County almanac: And sketches here and there.* Oxford University Press.

Meyer, E. K. 2008. Sustaining beauty: The performance of appearance. *Journal of Landscape Architecture* (Spring).

Moore, R.C., and C. C. Marcus. (2008). Healthy planet, healthy children: designing nature into the daily spaces of childhood. In *Biophilic design*, by S. Kellert, J. Heerwagen, and M. Mador. Hoboken, NJ: John Wiley & Sons, pp. 153–204.

Wells, N. M., and S. K. Lekies. 2006. Nature and life course pathways to environmentalism. *Children, Youth and Environments* 16:1–24.

World Wildlife Fund. 2010. Living planet report 2010: Biodiversity, biocapacity and development.

THE SUSTAINABLE SITES INITIATIVE

THE CASE FOR SUSTAINABLE LANDSCAPES

American Society of Landscape Architects

Lady Bird Johnson Wildflower Center
at The University of Texas at Austin

United States Botanic Garden

The Sustainable Sites Initiative is a partnership of the American Society of Landscape Architects, the Lady Bird Johnson Wildflower Center, and the United States Botanic Garden in conjunction with a diverse group of stakeholder organizations to establish and encourage sustainable practices in landscape design, construction, operations, and maintenance.

The Sustainable Sites Initiative 2009

EXECUTIVE SUMMARY

This document, The Case for Sustainable Landscapes, *is a companion volume to the much larger report titled* The Sustainable Sites Initiative: Guidelines and Performance Benchmarks 2009. *It provides background on the Sustainable Sites Initiative™; a set of arguments—economic, environmental, and social—for the adoption of sustainable land practices; additional background on the science behind the performance criteria in the* Guidelines and Performance Benchmarks 2009; *and a sampling of some of the case studies the Initiative has been following. For more information, or to download copies of either volume, please see www.sustainablesites.org.*

By aligning land development and management practices with the functions of healthy ecosystems, the Sustainable Sites Initiative believes that developers, property owners, site managers, and others can restore or enhance the ecosystem services provided by their built landscapes. Moreover, adopting such sustainable practices not only helps the environment but also enhances human health and well-being and is economically cost-effective. For the Initiative's purposes, "sustainability" is defined as design, construction, operations, and maintenance practices that meet the needs of the present without compromising the ability of future generations to meet their own needs. This definition embraces the definition of sustainable development first put forward by the United Nations World Commission on Environment and Development in 1987.

The Sustainable Sites Initiative, an interdisciplinary partnership of the American Society of Landscape Architects, the Lady Bird Johnson Wildflower Center, and the United States Botanic Garden, has spent several years developing guidelines for sustainable land practices that are grounded in rigorous science and can be applied on a site-by-site basis nationwide. These guidelines—*The Sustainable Sites Initiative: Guidelines and Performance Benchmarks 2009*—acknowledge that different regions of the country will have different requirements and therefore include performance levels appropriate to each region as needed.

The impetus for creating the guidelines came from the recognition that although buildings have national standards for "green" construction, little existed for the space beyond the building skin. Modeled after the LEED® (Leadership in Energy and Environmental Design) Green Building Rating System™ of the U.S. Green Building Council, the Initiative's rating system gives credits for the sustainable use of water, the conservation of soils, wise choices of vegetation and materials, and design that supports human health and well-being.

Executive Summary

The term "ecosystem services" describes the goods and services provided by healthy ecosystems—the pollination of crops by bees, bats, or birds, for example, or the flood protection provided by wetlands, or the filtration of air and water by vegetation and soils. Ecosystem services provide benefits to humankind and other organisms but are not generally reflected in our current economic accounting. Nature doesn't submit an invoice for them, so humans often underestimate or ignore their value when making land-use decisions. However, efforts to determine the monetary value of ecosystem services have placed that figure at an estimated global average of $33 trillion annually (in 1997 dollars).

Increased understanding of the value of these services has led to acknowledgment of the way current land practices can imperil such essential benefits as air purification, water retention, climate regulation, and erosion control. As many communities have found, it is difficult, expensive, and sometimes impossible to duplicate these natural services once they are destroyed.

The good news is that we can model the creation of our landscapes after healthy systems and thereby increase the ecosystem services they provide after development—whether that development is a backyard garden, a housing development, or a state park. Water on the site can be managed to imitate natural water cycling, vegetation can be used strategically to cool the area and filter water, and soils can be restored to support healthy vegetation and filter pollutants.

The Initiative's development of site-specific performance benchmarks is grounded in an understanding of healthy systems and natural processes. Achieving these benchmarks will help to maintain or support those natural processes and the services that they provide to humans. This volume, *The Case for Sustainable Landscapes*, is intended to provide readers with more background on the science underlying the guidelines for sustainable practices—to explain the connection, for example, between excessive use of nitrogen fertilizers and the increase in "dead zones" in coastal waters downstream, or between an increase in impervious cover and reduced base flow to creeks, streams, and rivers.

The Case for Sustainable Landscapes also offers evidence for the economic benefits that can accrue from adopting sustainable practices. For example, as a number of developers have found, bioswales, raingardens and other low-impact development strategies to reduce runoff not only help recharge groundwater but also can save developers anywhere from 15 to 80 percent in total capital costs. And as New York City has found, a long-term investment in protecting its watershed can save billions in avoided costs for a new water treatment plant—a cost saving passed on to rate payers.

The science demonstrates that humans are an integral part of the environment. As people acknowledge this link, they recognize that human decisions and behavior are in fact components of a global feedback loop: what people do affects the health and well-being of the rest of the natural world, which in turn affects human health and well-being—physical, mental, economic, and social.

Swan River Foreshore, Point Fraser Development, Perth, Western Australia

1 PURPOSE AND PRINCIPLES OF THE SUSTAINABLE SITES INITIATIVE

A little more than two decades ago, the United Nations World Commission on Environment and Development, headed by Gro Harlem Brundtland, then-Prime Minister of Norway, presented its report to the UN General Assembly. Titled *Our Common Future* but better known as the Brundtland Report, it made an eloquent argument for sustainable development, which it defined as "development that meets the needs of the present without compromising the ability of future generations to meet their own needs."[1]

> We came to see that a new development path was required, one that sustained human progress not just in a few places for a few years, but for the entire planet into the distant future.
>
> GRO HARLEM BRUNDTLAND, 1987

Over the intervening years, the Brundtland Report's prescription for sustainability has gained wide acceptance. In corporate boardrooms and grade-school classrooms, at neighborhood gatherings and in councils of government, growing numbers of citizens are embracing the opportunity to live sustainably. As people acknowledge that humans are an integral part of the environment, they recognize that human decisions and behavior are in fact components of a global feedback loop: what people do affects the health and well-being of the natural world, which in turn affects human health and well-being—physical, mental, economic, and social.

1 Purpose and Principles of the Sustainable Sites Initiative

The Sustainable Sites Initiative, founded in 2005, embraced the Brundtland Report's forward-looking definition of sustainability.[2] In the Initiative's words, "sustainability is defined as design, construction, operations, and maintenance practices that meet the needs of the present without compromising the ability of future generations to meet their own needs."

This definition guides the formulation of the Initiative's voluntary guidelines and performance benchmarks for sustainable land development and management. Presented in the document *The Sustainable Sites Initiative: Guidelines and Performance Benchmarks 2009*, these benchmarks are designed to preserve or restore a site's sustainability within the context of ecosystem services—the idea that healthy ecosystems provide goods and services of benefit to humans and other organisms.[3] As Dr. Brundtland put it, "the 'environment' is where we all live; and 'development' is what we all do in attempting to improve our lot within that abode. The two are inseparable."[4]

The benchmarks are meant to guide, measure, and recognize sustainable landscape practices on a site-by-site basis. They may also inform larger scale projects or planning efforts although they are not intended to be a tool for regional planning. Similarly, although the guidelines and benchmarks encourage edible landscapes and small-scale food production as components of a site, they do not address sustainable agricultural products or large-scale agricultural or farming practices; other organizations, such as the Leonardo Academy and the Rainforest Alliance, are developing or have already developed systems to do so. The U.S. Green Building Council anticipates incorporating the Sustainable Sites benchmarks into future versions of its LEED® (Leadership in Energy and Environmental Design) rating system.

Roots of Sustainability

The word "sustainability" may be relatively new, but its underlying ethic has deep roots on the North American continent. Native Americans have historically held to the "seven generations" rule, meaning that all decisions should take into account the impact on seven generations into the future. Well aware that people have the power to manipulate the world around them, Native Americans use their ceremonies and traditions to help them to maintain respect for life and to remind them that, as one Native American proverb puts it, "We do not inherit the earth from our ancestors, we borrow it from our children."[5]

Another strand of sustainable resource use can be traced back more than a hundred years to Gifford Pinchot, the first head of the U.S. Forest Service. Pinchot coined the term "conservation ethic," and his philosophy "to provide the greatest amount of good for the greatest amount of people in the long run" infused the fledgling agency. Today, the stated mission of the Forest Service is to "sustain the health, diversity, and productivity of the nation's forests and grasslands to meet the needs of present and future generations."[6]

GUIDING PRINCIPLES

Throughout the life cycle of each site—from design and construction through operations and maintenance—sustainable performance benchmarks will enable built landscapes to support natural ecological functions by protecting existing ecosystems and regenerating ecological capacity where it has been lost. To that end, the Initiative's guiding principles (see page 9) not only inform its own work but should also inform all aspects of sustainable site development.

1   Purpose and Principles of the Sustainable Sites Initiative

GROWING AWARENESS

The Millennium Ecosystem Assessment, a United Nations study completed in 2005, highlighted the need for all development to address considerations in three key arenas: social, environmental, and economic.[7] Unless all three aspects are equally vibrant, true sustainability is not possible.

As with sustainable development in general, a sustainable site also needs to take into account the challenges on all three fronts. An environmentally sustainable site that does not engage its users on multiple levels—physical, aesthetic, cultural, spiritual—will lose crucial human stewardship. By the same token, creation and maintenance of the site must be economically feasible for the site to exist at all.

Guiding Principles of a Sustainable Site

Do no harm
Make no changes to the site that will degrade the surrounding environment. Promote projects on sites where previous disturbance or development presents an opportunity to regenerate ecosystem services through sustainable design.

Precautionary principle
Be cautious in making decisions that could create risk to human and environmental health. Some actions can cause irreversible damage. Examine a full range of alternatives—including no action—and be open to contributions from all affected parties.

Design with nature and culture
Create and implement designs that are responsive to economic, environmental, and cultural conditions with respect to the local, regional, and global context.

Use a decision-making hierarchy of preservation, conservation, and regeneration
Maximize and mimic the benefits of ecosystem services by preserving existing environmental features, conserving resources in a sustainable manner, and regenerating lost or damaged ecosystem services.

Provide regenerative systems as intergenerational equity
Provide future generations with a sustainable environment supported by regenerative systems and endowed with regenerative resources.

Support a living process
Continuously re-evaluate assumptions and values and adapt to demographic and environmental change.

Use a systems thinking approach
Understand and value the relationships in an ecosystem and use an approach that reflects and sustains ecosystem services; re-establish the integral and essential relationship between natural processes and human activity.

Use a collaborative and ethical approach
Encourage direct and open communication among colleagues, clients, manufacturers, and users to link long-term sustainability with ethical responsibility.

Maintain integrity in leadership and research
Implement transparent and participatory leadership, develop research with technical rigor, and communicate new findings in a clear, consistent, and timely manner.

Foster environmental stewardship
In all aspects of land development and management, foster an ethic of environmental stewardship—an understanding that responsible management of healthy ecosystems improves the quality of life for present and future generations.

1 Purpose and Principles of the Sustainable Sites Initiative

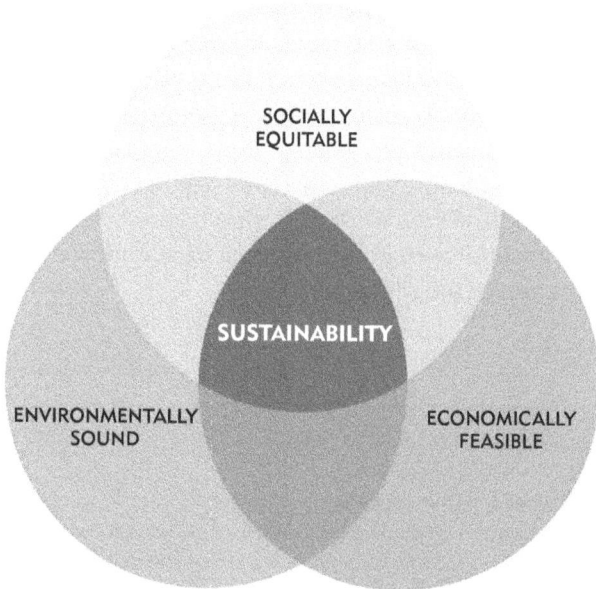

Fig. 1.1 SUSTAINABLE DEVELOPMENT. Of the three components of sustainability, the primary focus for the Sustainable Sites Initiative is the environment, including those aspects of economic feasibility and social equity that intersect with the environment.

In view of the pressing need for an economy less reliant on fossil fuels and more attuned to potential climate change, the Sustainable Sites Initiative hopes to encourage land design, development, and management professionals to engage in a re-evaluation of conventional practices—and a new valuation of ecosystem services—so that built landscapes will support natural ecological functions throughout the life cycle of each site. Encouragingly, growing numbers of projects are adopting the philosophy of low-impact development (see Chapter 2) and many local and regional efforts now provide guidelines for improved land development and management practices. The Initiative is interested in information sharing and partnering with all interested parties. At the same time, the Initiative hopes that its products will be able to serve as stand-alone guidelines for anyone who wishes to embrace landscape sustainability.

Beginning in April 2010, a number of pilot projects will help test and refine the *Guidelines and Performance Benchmarks 2009* and its rating system over the course of two years. The Initiative expects to incorporate knowledge gained from working with the pilot projects into development of *The Sustainable Sites Initiative Reference Guide*.

Meanwhile, the Initiative has been following a number of case studies—projects that have incorporated sustainable practices in a wide variety of situations. A selection of those studies is presented in Chapter 4. The case studies pre-date the development of the *Guidelines and Performance Benchmarks 2009* and are separate from the Initiative's pilot program. For more information on the pilot program, please visit *http://www.sustainablesites.org/pilot/*.

1 Purpose and Principles of the Sustainable Sites Initiative

1. UN General Assembly, *Our Common Future: Report of the World Commission on Environment and Development*, 1987, chap. 2, "Towards Sustainable Development," http://www.worldinbalance.net/agreements/1987-brundtland.html (accessed October 11, 2009).

2. For a history of the Initiative, see http://sustainablesites.org/history.html.

3. G Daily, ed., *Nature's Services: Societal Dependence on Natural Ecosystems* (Washington, DC: Island Press, 1997).

4. *Our Common Future*, Foreword, http://www.worldinbalance.net/agreements/1987-brundtland.html (accessed October 11, 2009).

5. "In our every deliberation we must consider the impact of our decisions on the next seven generations." from the Great Law of the Iroquois Confederacy. For more information on the Great Law: http://www.indigenouspeople.net/iroqcon.htm (accessed September 26, 2009); "Native American communities are some of the most sustainable on earth because they live in balance with their environment. They follow the seven-generation rule: How will what we do today impact seven generations from now?" L Miller, "A Native American Teacher Talks About Biotechnology," Aldo Leopold Center, Iowa State University, http://www.leopold.iastate.edu/pubs/nwl/2001/2001-2-leoletter/michael.htm (accessed September 26, 2009); proverb from http://www.quotegarden.com/environment.html.

6. USDA Forest Service, "Sustainable Operations," http://www.fs.fed.us/sustainableoperations/ (accessed September 26, 2009).

7. Millennium Ecosystem Assessment, *Ecosystems and Human Well-being: Message from the Board* (Washington, DC: Island Press, 2003), p.3.

SECTION II: SOIL HEALTH & MANAGEMENT

IN THIS SECTION	PAGE
Sustainable Soils for Landscapes *Source: Chapter 7 of Sustainable Landscape Management: Design, Construction, and Maintenance*	135
Building Soils: A Summary of "Building Soil Best Management Practices for Western Washington *Source: Building Soils, www.BuildingSoils.org*	149
When to Amend: Construction Sequencing for Soil Protection & Restoration *Source: Building Soils, www.BuildingSoils.org*	151
Erosion Control With Compost: Using Compost To Meet TESC & Soil Quality Requirements on Building Sites *Source: Building Soils, www.BuildingSoils.org*	153
Estimating Soil Textures *Source: Washington State University*	154

chapter 7
Sustainable Soils for Landscapes

INTRODUCTION

Healthy soil is central to the development of sustainable landscapes. Healthy soils are biologically active and texturally and structurally suited to healthy root growth of trees, shrubs, and lawns. In the context of landscapes, soils serve many functions, including that of plant growth medium, substrate/habitat for soil fauna/flora, nutrient recycling, sink for pollutants, and source of pollutants (Bullock and Gregory 1991). Unfortunately, soils are often damaged during building and landscape construction, resulting in an altered growing environment that may suffer from compaction, poor drainage, and altered soil fertility.

This chapter will discuss the following:

- Healthy soils
- Sustainable options in developing soils for landscapes
- Managing soils sustainably

HEALTHY SOILS

An excerpt from the National Cooperative Soil Survey describes soil as "natural bodies, made up of mineral and organic materials that cover much of the earth's surface, contain living matter and can support vegetation outdoors, and have in places been changed by human activity.... Soil consists of the horizons near the earth's surface which, in contrast to the underlying rock material, have been altered by the interactions, over time, between climate, relief, parent materials, and living organisms" (Fenton and Collins 2000).

The principal components of the mineral fraction of soils are sand, silt, and clay. Under natural conditions, these minerals plus organic matter develop over long periods of time into defined layers called "soil horizons." The conditions under which soils develop determine their properties and morphology. In the U.S. system, there are 12 orders that characterize soil (Table 7-1). Each order of soil can be further subdivided into as many as six additional taxonomic categories, with the lowest level called a "soil series." A soil series is a group of soils that have horizons similar in arrangement and characteristics (Fenton and Collins 2000). This hierarchical system demonstrates that in nature soils are highly ordered with predictable properties.

Urban soils don't fit well into the categories used to describe natural soils. Urban soils may consist of material having a nonagricultural, artificial surface layer more than 20 inches (50 cm) thick that has been produced by mixing, by filling, or

TABLE 7-1 Natural Soil Orders Based on the U.S. System of Classification

Order	Percentage of World's Ice-Free Land Surface	Characteristics
Alfisols	10	Soils with clay minerals leached out of the surface layer and into the subsoil layer. Form under forest or mixed vegetation and are productive crop soils. Located in semiarid to moist areas.
Andisols	1	Minerals lack orderly crystalline structure, and soil has high nutrient- and water-holding capacity. Highly productive crop soils. Common in cool areas with high precipitation.
Aridisols	12	Minimally weathered soils that often accumulate gypsum, salt, and calcium carbonate. Common desert soils.
Entisols	16	Occur in areas with recently deposited parent materials. Found in many environments, including floodplains, dunes, and steep slopes.
Gelisols	9	Soils with permafrost near the soil surface. May be affected by frost churning and ice segregation. Found at higher latitudes and higher elevations.
Histosols	1	Soils with high organic matter and no permafrost. Can be saturated or free-draining. Commonly called bogs, moors, peats, or mucks.
Inceptisols	17	Moderately weathered soils common to semiarid and humid environments. These soils have a wide range of characteristics and are found in many different climates.
Mollisols	7	Soils with a dark surface horizon relatively high in organic matter. Tend to be quite fertile. These form under grass in climates with pronounced seasonal dry periods.
Oxisols	7	Highly weathered soils common in tropical and subtropical regions. Found on land surfaces that have been stable for a long time. Tend to be infertile and have low cation exchange capacity.
Spodosols	4	Weathered soils with organic matter and aluminum deposited in the subsoil. Common where soils are formed from coarse-textured deposits. Common in coniferous forest regions and tend to be acidic and infertile.
Ultisols	8	Humid-area soils formed from intense weathering and leaching. Typically acidic with nutrients concentrated near the surface.
Vertisols	2	Soils containing high levels of expanding clay minerals. Expand when wet and shrink when dry. Fertile soils but retain water when wet.

Source: Adapted from http://soils.usda.gov/technical/soil_orders/.

by contamination of the land surface (Maechling, Cooke, and Bockheim 1974). Taxonomists struggle to categorize urban soils because of their extreme diversity (Evans, Fanning, and Short 2000).

In spite of the taxonomic difficulties, healthy urban soils are achievable. Healthy soils are characterized by the composite of their physical, chemical, and biological properties. Physical properties such as structure and water-holding capacity; chemical properties such as pH, nutrient-supplying ability, and salt content; and biological properties such as mineralization capacity and microbial associations are specific examples of factors affecting soil health (Pankhurst, Doube, and Gupta 1997).

Soil health has been defined by Doran and Safley (1997) as "the continued capacity of soil to function as a vital living system, within ecosystem and land use boundaries, to sustain biological productivity, promote the quality of air and water environments, and maintain plant, animal and human health." While soil quality focuses primarily on the physical and chemical properties of a soil, soil health factors soil biota into the equation. Soil biota include living roots, microflora (e.g., bacteria and fungi), microfauna (e.g., nematodes, protozoa, and rotifers), mesofauna (e.g., mites, collembolans, and enchytraeids), and macrofauna (e.g., spiders, larger insects, earthworms, ants, and termites) (Coleman and Wall 2007). The living biological components of soil make up less than 10 percent of the total organic matter in the soil but are involved in a wide range of soil processes, including nutrient cycling, organic matter decomposition, soil structure development, and the fate of agrochemicals and soil pollutants. Of the soil organisms, microflora (e.g., fungi and bacteria) make up 75 to 90 percent of the total while microfauna and macrofauna (nematodes, earthworms, microarthropods, and protozoa) make up 5 to 10 percent (Coleman and Wall 2007).

Soil health indicators collectively tell whether the soil is functioning normally (Pankhurst, Doube, and Gupta 1997). Physical indicators of soil health include bulk densities low enough to allow normal root development, water-holding capacity high enough to support plant growth between irrigation or precipitation events, and adequate pore space to maintain aerobic conditions suitable for root growth. Chemical indicators include pH in the range of 5 to 7.5, low to moderate electrical conductivity, cation exchange capacity adequate to retain nutrients, organic matter levels high enough to support high microbial activity, presence of major nutrient elements, and absence of heavy metals. The physical and chemical indicators are fairly constant and do not change much over time unless humans intervene.

Biological Factors

Biological indicators of soil health are harder to interpret (Pankhurst 1994). Scientists are still learning how soil micro-, meso-, and macroorganisms interact to produce healthy soils. Some of the attributes that have been considered include microbial biomass, abundance of microorganisms, soil respiration rates, microbial biodiversity, and soil microfauna and macrofauna biodiversity. Soil enzymes mediate and catalyze most soil processes and have the potential to provide an assessment of soil health (Dick 1997). At present, we lack simple meaningful measures of biological activity as indicators of soil health.

Soil Ecological Food Web

In contrast to simple measures, studies of soil ecological food webs prove useful in characterizing communities of micro- and macroorganisms normally associated with different plant communities. For example, ecologists have used nematode population and community structure to determine the characteristics of the detritus food web (the community of organisms that decompose organic material). Because nematodes feed on bacteria and fungi, the assemblage of microbial populations will be reflected in the makeup of the nematode population (Ferris and Matute 2003). Lawn soil food webs are categorized as highly enriched (high fertility) but poorly to moderately structured (less microbial diversity) compared to undisturbed natural grasslands that are usually highly structured (high microbial diversity) but poorly enriched (low soil fertility) (Cheng et al. 2008). Fertilizer inputs increased the enrichment index in this study, but had no impact on the nematode community. Disturbance such as tillage or application of organic materials with high nitrogen content (low carbon-to-nitrogen ratio) increased the enrichment-opportunistic nematodes due to stimulation of bacterial growth by the organic source material (Ferris and Matute 2003).

WHAT IS THE SIGNIFICANCE OF THE CARBON-TO-NITROGEN RATIO?

The C/N ratio refers to the relative amount of carbon in organic material compared to the amount of nitrogen. Organic material that is high in carbon but low in nitrogen is slow to decompose, because microorganisms cannot get enough nitrogen to grow and assimilate the carbon in the organic matter. To initiate decomposition, the microbes scavenge for soil nitrogen, which depletes the amount available for plants to use. When organic debris is composted properly by adding nitrogen fertilizer or green waste that is high in nitrogen, microbes rapidly break down the organic matter and produce the finished compost, which has a much lower C/N ratio. The relatively higher amount of nitrogen in the finished compost is released from dead microbes and is available to plants as a fertilizer.

Mycorrhizae

Mycorrhizal fungi are essential components of native plant communities, including forests and grasslands. Mycorrhizae form symbiotic associations with the vast majority of vascular plants. Plant benefits include increased uptake of water and phosphorus and protection against root pathogens (Bardgett 2005). Because mycorrhizae benefit some plants more than others, they can affect the structure of plant communities by preferentially increasing the competitiveness of certain plants (Grime et al. 1987). Soils with strong mycorrhizal associations are generally healthy soils, but many plants can perform well without mycorrhizae. Management inputs of fertilizers or fungicides may or may not decrease mycorrhizal activity.

Earthworms

Earthworms are important contributors to healthy soils in constructed landscapes. They facilitate aggregate and crumb formation in soil and increase pore formation. They also facilitate the breakdown of organic matter via fragmentation, burial, and mixing of residues (Coleman and Wall 2007) (Figure 7-1). Earthworms are generally abundant in natural forests and grasslands in temperate and tropical climates. In constructed landscapes, earthworms may be present or absent, depending on the source of soil. Soils can be improved by introducing earthworms. Several insecticides and fungicides are toxic to earthworms and can reduce or eliminate populations when used regularly. Lawn thatch levels increase when earthworms are killed by pesticides because the fragmentation and mixing function is gone (Potter, Powell, and Smith 1990).

The dominant earthworms in many constructed landscapes in cool temperate climates include *Lumbricus terrestris* L., *L. rubellus* Hoff., *Apporectodea longa* Ude., and *A. trapezoides* Duges. High soil organic matter, periodic fertilizer applications, and soils kept moist via regular irrigation foster higher species diversity and density.

Figure 7-1 Healthy earthworm population in a lawn as indicated by worm casts.

The picture emerging from the limited research on lawn community ecosystems indicates a system with a range of flora and fauna, grazing and detritus food webs that are well developed but skewed toward high enrichment (high fertility) and low structure (less microbial diversity), and a key role for earthworms in system development. Tree and shrub plantings in landscapes have been less well researched than lawns so it is difficult to describe the structure of soil food webs associated with them. In healthy plantings, strong mycorrhizal associations may or may not be present, detritus food webs in typical acidic soils will be dominated by fungi rather than by bacteria (Cheng et al. 2008), and strong earthworm populations are likely. These factors will result in good soil structure and healthy vigorous plants.

Figure 7-2 Layering quality topsoil over compacted subsoil and gravel is a poor way to produce a good growing medium.

SUSTAINABLE OPTIONS IN DEVELOPING SOILS FOR LANDSCAPES

A landscape soil conservation plan should be developed before building construction occurs. This plan designates protected areas, creates soil stockpiling areas, and orchestrates the entry and exit areas for machinery. The goal is to do no harm to on-site soils when possible and to maintain the integrity of existing topsoil. Unfortunately, given the nature of building construction, soil planning is often neglected early in the process and may only involve bringing in topsoil to assist in achieving final grades. The following sections introduce options for addressing soil issues. For soil specifications and engineering standards, see Craul (1999) and Urban (2008).

Fill Soils

Fill soils may include sand and gravel, subsoil construction spoils, or construction debris such as concrete rubble and asphalt chunks. In a given fill area, there is rarely continuity so physical characteristics may vary significantly from one section to another. Fill material is often heavily compacted after placement to avoid settling prior to landscape installation. Soil scientists refer to fill material as "having great spatial variability."

Fill soils are generally not intended for use as planting soils but, in effect, become the subsoil to whatever topsoil is placed over them. Because of the poor water movement properties of compacted fill soils, drainage system installation has to be considered prior to or after adding topsoil. If drainage is not accounted for, the finished landscape will suffer from poor drainage, because water moving through the topsoil cannot move into and through the fill material below (Figure 7-2).

On-Site Soils

Because much urban and suburban development occurs in areas of former farmland, it is possible that on-site soils are of good quality and generally suitable for a wide range of landscape plantings. The strategy in these situations is to remove the topsoil from the building footprint area and parking lot areas and place it in stockpiles for later use. Areas that will be undisturbed during building construction should be fenced and otherwise protected to prevent unplanned heavy-equipment traffic, dumping, and contamination during construction. Once elevations have been established, the stockpiled soil can be incorporated with existing topsoil to achieve final grades.

The advantages of using on-site soils include:

Soil uniformity across the site

Unimpeded natural drainage through the profile

Minimal need for amendments

Known fertility status

Minimal need to import soil

The disadvantages of using on-site soils include:

Soil type may not be suitable for planting.

Quantity may not be adequate to meet grades.

Soil seed bank may contain noxious weeds.

The 2009 version of the Sustainable Sites Initiative offers soil restoration criteria, including a root zone depth of 12 inches (30 cm), maximum dry bulk density or cone penetrometer readings appropriate for a range of soil textures from sand to clay, appropriate soil organic matter levels, and restoration of soil organism activity and diversity based on on-site reference soils. For details, see: http://www.sustainablesites.org/report/.

Amending On-Site Soils

Even when on-site soils are generally suitable, they may have been compacted during construction or require pH adjustment prior to use. Soils slated for flower or shrub beds may be too fine textured (excess clay) and require amendments to decrease the bulk density and raise the porosity to acceptable levels.

Amending on-site bed soils is commonly done by adding composted organic matter at rates ranging from 10 to 50 percent by volume (Figure 7-3). Adding 33 percent food waste compost by volume to a sandy loam soil reduced the bulk density from 1.5 g/cm^3 to 1.2 g/cm^3 in uncompacted soil and from 1.8 g/cm^3 to 1.5 g/cm^3 in compacted soil. In

Figure 7-3 Adding and then tilling compost into surface soils can improve fertility, aeration, and water retention.

both cases, the bulk density of the amended soil was below the threshold for potential root restriction (Rivenshield and Bassuk 2007). Root restriction in sands occurs at bulk densities above 1.6 g/cm^3 (Aubertin and Kardos 1965). When compost was added to clay loam soils, the bulk density actually increased at the 33 percent volume and didn't decrease until the compost volume increased to 50 percent (Rivenshield and Bassuk 2007). This may be an anomaly because this particular compost contained sand, but it appears that using compost to reduce the bulk density of clay soils may require too much amendment to be practical.

Because commercial composts are only partially composted, decomposition continues once they are incorporated into soil. The ultimate volume reduction of the incorporated compost due to decomposition may run 50 to 75 percent (Urban 2008). When large amounts of compost are mixed with soil, significant settling will occur. Incorporating compost into the top 8 inches (20 cm) of soil will alleviate compaction to that depth, will decrease the bulk density initially by physical dilution, and may provide long-term structure enhancement as the compost decomposes. Settling and decomposition loss of added

Figure 7-4 Prior to planting, the soil on the right side of this photo was amended with 6 inches (15 cm) of compost, while the soil on the left received nothing. Note the increased growth in the amended soil.

organic matter of an 80 percent/20 percent compost mix may reduce final soil volume by 10 to 15 percent to the depth of incorporation (Urban 2008).

Compost may also affect numerous soil characteristics. These include pH and nutrient status, and if the original soil is sandy, compost will increase the water-holding capacity. Composts vary in their state of decomposition, pH, and nutrient status, and, without testing, there is no way of knowing what impact individual materials might have. Except in annual flower beds, compost can only be incorporated into soil once. In planting beds with herbaceous perennials and woody plants, additional applications can only be made from the surface. The impact of a one-time compost incorporation in a silty clay soil on the growth of rhododendrons (*Rhododendron* spp.) is illustrated in Figure 7-4.

There are several potential problems with adding compost, including:

- Uniform on-site mixing is difficult to achieve.
- Amended soil volume may settle significantly as compost decomposes.
- Excessive tilling during mixing may destroy the original soil structure.
- Effective incorporation depth is limited so there is no impact on soil deeper than the tillage depth.
- Soil may become loaded with phosphorus from compost.
- Compost may be cost prohibitive on large areas.

From a practical point of view, bed areas are often amended with organic matter, whereas lawn areas are not. Where existing soils are used for lawns, general preparation requires only enough tillage to facilitate grading.

Adding sand to heavy-textured on-site soils to improve porosity and drainage is a risky endeavor. Research has shown that small quantities of sand, even when mixed uniformly, decrease the porosity (micropores and macropores) of amended soils (Spomer 1983). As sand proportions increase, the porosity decreases until the quantity of sand is large enough that remaining soil particles cannot fill all the voids between sand grains. Practically speaking, sand must make up in excess of 80 percent of the final amended soil by volume before it increases macropore space. This in itself makes adding and tilling sand into on-site soils impractical.

Importing, Manufacturing, or Augmenting Landscape Soils

Often existing soils have not been protected, and construction activities have ruined the soil via compaction, layering, gravel incorporation, or contamination with paint or other chemicals. In such situations, a common practical option is to remove the existing surface soil to a depth of 10 to 18 inches (25 to 45 cm) and replace it with imported soil. Though effective, this is the least sustainable approach for improving soil because the original soil is now suited only for fill and the imported soil has to be mined from another location. This is probably the most common strategy in use currently, and it will be a difficult practice to abandon for most contractors.

Figure 7-5 In this case, a loamy sand soil was placed over the original silty clay loam soil, resulting in nutritional and drainage issues.

It was once possible to obtain true topsoil harvested from farmlands or stripped from other construction sites. Today, it is more common to get whatever soil is being harvested as gravel operations open up new pits. These soils are variable, often ranging from sandy loams to loamy sands. By nature, they are easy to work, relatively free-draining, nutrient poor, and may contain undesirable weeds such as horsetail (*Equisetum* spp.) or nutsedge (*Cyperus* spp.). Sometimes imported soils are not topsoil but instead are clean fill soil harvested from deep pits (Figure 7-5).

Imported soils are often placed over subsoils to fill up the excavated area. Where excavation has exposed subsoils and created a pit surrounded by foundations and sidewalks, drainage problems may result. Because the imported soils are often porous, the subsoils are impervious, and the pit is surrounded on all sides, water tends to accumulate, leading to perpetually wet soils. To avoid this, drainage needs to be installed at the interface between subsoil and topsoil. Details on drainage design can be found in Craul (1999).

When soil is imported to augment existing soil and establish final grades, it is most often layered over the original soil. When possible, use soil that is similar in texture to the original soil and till on-site soil lightly before placement to break up the interface between the original soil and the imported soil. If sandy soil is placed as a shallow layer over an existing finer-textured soil, it should be uniformly incorporated to eliminate layering.

Manufactured soils are typically mixtures of soil, sand, and organic matter or just sandy soil plus organic matter. These are mixed off-site and delivered as a homogeneous product. Premixed soils may be proprietary and may be inoculated with mycorrhizae or other microorganisms. Where project value is high enough, custom mixes may be specified by landscape architects or consulting engineers.

Sustainable soils are manufactured soils that use sustainable components such as sand from river dredging, composted garden waste, mine tailings, or other waste materials suitable for use in manufactured soil mixes (Craul 1999). The goal is to assemble a mix that will support plant growth, drain well but hold adequate water, and retain nutrients. Organic sources such as peat moss are not considered sustainable because of current fears that peat bogs are being destroyed by overharvesting. Thorough testing of prospective mixes is necessary to determine their suitability for use (Craul 1999).

Structural soils have been developed to improve the survival potential of urban street trees planted in paved areas (Grabosky, Bassuk, and Trowbridge 2002). The planting mix consists of a stone matrix mixed with a small portion of clay loam soil. The stone provides a stable medium to support the trees, and the soil provides nutrient-holding capacity and enhances water retention. Roots grow in the voids between rocks. The system is compatible with engineering compaction needs and allows root growth to develop in an aerated environment that is not prone to plugging or further compaction (Grabosky, Bassuk, and Trowbridge 2002).

This approach has shown promise in difficult planting situations during establishment and early development, but because it is new, the long-term function of the system is unknown. In North Carolina, tree growth in structural soil was equal to growth of the same trees in compacted soil and produced greater total root length than other treatments. Tree growth in uncompacted soil was notably better than that in structural soil (Smiley et al. 2006). This reinforces the notion of using structural soils only in situations where uncompacted soils are not feasible to maintain.

MANAGING SOILS SUSTAINABLY

Once bed soils are in place, regardless of how they were selected or amended, the goals become the same. In order for soil to function over time, it needs to support healthy soil fauna and flora communities, absorb and move water, maintain soil oxygen levels high enough to sustain healthy root growth, and replenish organic matter to fuel growth of soil organisms. The natural process in tree and shrub bed soils is for added organic matter to decompose down to an end point organic matter percentage. The structure resulting from decomposition by-products is transient without continued inputs of organic matter. As a result, infiltration and percolation rates decline along with soil aeration. Without continued inputs, bed soils become harder, less receptive to water, and less hospitable for root growth.

Lawns, by nature, tend to build soil organic matter, and the fibrous nature of the root systems builds structure (Figure 7-6). Returning clippings to the lawn encourages general vigor and can stimulate earthworm activity, which incorporates clipping debris, reduces thatch accumulation, enhances aeration, and may increase infiltration rates (Potter, Powell, and Smith 1990). The main threat to this process is compaction resulting from foot and machinery traffic. If compaction is severe, the natural system breaks down, and soil becomes denser, more impermeable, and less suitable for root growth.

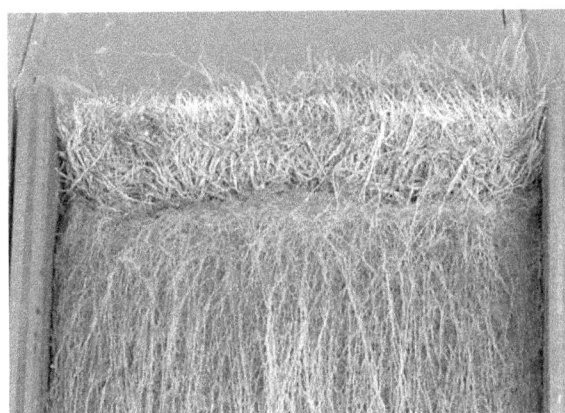

Figure 7-6 The fibrous nature of grass roots helps to improve soil structure.

Mulch

In bed areas, mulching is an important means for maintaining surface permeability, enhancing soil biological activity, conserving water, and preventing a general decline in soil health. Mulches may also help with weed suppression, as discussed in Chapter 10. The impact of organic mulch depends somewhat on its composition.

Mulches with high carbon-to-nitrogen (C/N) ratios include the following:

- Most bark materials (large and small nuggets, fine grades, hardwood, and softwood; most have high lignin content)
- Wood chips (cellulose)
- Sawdust (cellulose)
- Pine needles (lignin, cellulose)
- Coconut husks (lignin, cellulose)
- Ground recycled pallets (cellulose)
- Arborist mulch (mix of wood chips, bark, and leaves)

Materials with high C/N ratios are slow to decompose. It is not clear what impact these mulches might have on soil properties, and there is only a limited amount of research from which to draw. In a study comparing ground recycled pallets with composted garden refuse and unmulched bare soil, Tiquia et al. (2002) measured several soil and microbial properties over a three-year period. The ground wood pallets had a C/N ratio of 114:1 at the time of application. After three years, this mulch had no effect on soil nutrient status, pH, or soil microbial biomass compared to the unmulched bare soil area.

Low C/N mulches include:

Composts

Hemlock bark

Mulches that have been thoroughly hot composted have low C/N ratios. In theory, they should provide nutrients, improve soil structure, and enhance soil microbial activity. In the trial by Tiquia et al. (2002) discussed earlier, composted garden refuse with a C/N ratio of 17:1 increased soil organic matter, soil potassium, soil pH, soil respiration, extractable nitrogen, and microbial biomass compared to bare soil. Compared to ground recycled pallets, it increased soil organic matter, weak Bray extractable soil phosphorus, soil potassium, total extractable soil nitrogen, and dissolved organic nitrogen. In this case, compost really did have significant impacts on the soil. Other research has demonstrated that low C/N composted garden refuse not only stimulates soil microorganism growth but also increases the available soil nitrogen and stimulates both growth and flowering of rhododendron (*Rhododendron* spp.) and growth of river birch (*Betula nigra*) (Lloyd et al. 2002).

There are many reasons for applying mulch to planting beds, but if the goal is to enhance physical, chemical, and biological soil properties, the best choice is compost. For weed control, mulches with high C/N ratios are the ideal choice. Bark products are among the slowest mulches to decompose so they last longer than other organic materials. After many years' use of high C/N mulches, it is probable that impact on soil properties will be similar to compost effects measured in short-term trials.

One of the problems associated with conventional landscape management is that virtually all plant debris is removed from the landscape. In a natural setting, plant debris falls to the ground and becomes part of the detritus food web. In typical constructed landscapes, natural debris is collected and hauled to recycling facilities and then returned to the landscape as compost. Finding ways to keep plant debris in beds will not only reduce waste but will also contribute to the development of healthy soils in a sustainable way.

WHAT IS HOT COMPOSTING?

Hot composting describes aerobic decomposition of organic material in which a series of microorganisms attack the organic matter using carbon in the organic material as an energy source. As mesophilic organisms (which tolerate moderate temperatures) attack raw organic matter, respiration rates increase and heat is produced. At about 110°F (45°C), thermophilic microorganisms (which are heat tolerant) take over and raise temperatures as high as 150°F (65°C) as they consume the remaining organic matter. At these high temperatures, pathogenic organisms and most weed seeds are killed, and decomposition proceeds rapidly, causing a reduction in the volume of organic material. Turning the pile maintains aerobic conditions, and decomposition occurs rapidly before temperatures drop, mesophilic organisms recolonize, and the compost cures. Hot composting is a controlled process that yields a predictable product with a low C/N ratio that is stable and rich in nutrients.

Moisture, Compaction, and Aeration

Soil moisture, compaction, and aeration are all interrelated. Compaction reduces macropores in soil and hampers aeration. Infiltration and percolation rates

Figure 7-7 In compacted soils, trees often develop very shallow root systems with many surface roots.

Figure 7-8 Mulch is useful for retaining soil moisture, but when coupled with regular irrigation or lots of rain, soils under mulch can become saturated and anaerobic. This image shows saturated soil with excess water at the mulch-soil interface.

of water decline under compacted conditions. Compaction also reduces root depth and may result in surface rooting (Figure 7-7). Compacted soils are difficult to wet when dry and, once wet, are slow to dry out. Wet soils are more prone to further compaction and further reductions in soil aeration. The goal in managing soils is to minimize compaction and optimize aeration. It is then possible to manage moisture with careful irrigation.

Moist aerated soil with a ready source of organic matter stimulates strong soil fauna and flora communities. Mulching combined with periodic irrigation during extended dry periods helps maintain soil moisture at optimal levels. This combination will maintain vigorous microflora, microfauna, and macrofauna growth throughout the growing season. Excessive irrigation, common in many mulch beds, may result in wet surface soils and can cause anaerobic conditions to develop (Figure 7-8). Anaerobic soils will kill aerobic microorganisms. Sustainable irrigation strategies for beds are discussed in Chapter 8.

Mechanical options for compaction relief and aeration for lawns include coring machines and solid-tine aerators. Unfortunately, these machines are not suited for use in landscape beds, and there are limited practical options available for improving aeration in landscape beds. Traditional methods include soil augering with or without backfills, vertical slotted pipes placed in auger holes with or without gravel, and water jets used to bore into soils around plants. Using these techniques, researchers found no differences in tree growth over a two-year period (Pittenger and Stamen 1990). They also concluded that where soil moisture is consistently maintained in the readily available range, tree growth in compacted sandy loam soils does not appear to be affected.

Other approaches have been developed to relieve soil compaction in tree root zones. The Grow Gun and Terralift both use high-pressure air discharge to blow holes in the soil and then fill the holes with some type of porous material. In sandy clay and clay loam soils, neither machine decreased the bulk density. Oxygen diffusion was increased at soil fracture layers but not beyond, and the long-term impact was not measured (Smiley et al. 1990). Other research has demonstrated decreased bulk density, increased macroporosity, and increased saturated hydraulic conductivity when the Terralift was used in sandy loam soil but not in a loam soil (Rolf 1992). Soil injection with high-pressure nitrogen gas using the Terrravent machine was not effective in decreasing the soil bulk density or improving tree growth in compacted soils (Hascher and Wells 2007; Smiley 2001).

A detailed review of compaction and amelioration treatments failed to find any postplanting treatments that could be recommended with confidence (Day and Bassuk 1994). The authors commented that multiple site-specific variables make it difficult to predict results. The difficulties in relieving compaction in planted landscape beds attest to the importance of proper bed preparation prior to planting and the need to maintain mulch cover after planting to minimize compaction.

SUMMARY

Long-term sustainability of landscapes is dependent on a healthy growing environment for plants. Healthy growing conditions start with quality soil that is biologically healthy. Sustainable site preparation uses on-site soils when possible. Soils high in sand tend to be well aerated but prone to drought, whereas soils high in clay tend to be fertile but prone to compaction and poor water movement. Both extremes of soil types can be amended with organic matter prior to planting to enhance performance after planting and meet sustainability goals. In situations where on-site soil is not suitable for use, manufactured soils are a viable option. Once soils are in place and plants are growing, ongoing efforts are needed to minimize the negative impacts of compaction on soil aeration and soil moisture status. Mulch plays a major role in maintaining soil health and preventing compaction after landscape installation while relatively few options are available for alleviating compaction in existing landscapes.

STUDY QUESTIONS

1. Define "soil." What are soil orders? Where do urban soils fit into the traditional soil classification system?
2. Define "soil health." How does soil health differ from soil quality?
3. What are the important types of soil biota? What makes them so important in determining soil health?
4. What are the key physical and chemical components contributing to soil health?
5. How do soil ecological food webs relate to soil health? What are examples of soil food webs?
6. What does it mean to say that lawn soil food webs are highly enriched but poorly structured? Is that a value judgment or just a way of categorizing lawn soils? Explain.
7. What is the difference between mycorrhizae and endophytic fungi (see Chapter 10)? What functions does each serve?
8. Do earthworms serve any beneficial purpose in landscape soils? Explain.
9. Compare the properties of fill soils, undisturbed on-site topsoils, and imported soils.
10. Why is it desirable to save on-site soils? Are there any notable problems with keeping on-site soils?
11. What are the goals of amending on-site topsoils? What is bulk density and why is it important? How do amendments affect bulk density?
12. What soil properties are affected by added compost? Is there a difference in soil response to compost and noncomposted amendments?
13. How effective is sand in improving soil physical properties? How much sand is needed to improve soil porosity?
14. Importing soils to landscape sites is almost standard practice. From a sustainable perspective, what is wrong with imported soils? Are imported soils generally more or less fertile than undisturbed on-site soils?
15. What kind of weed problems are associated with imported soils? Is there any way to avoid these problems?

16. What is the difference between manufactured soils and sustainable soils?
17. What are structural soils and where in the landscape are they best used? Are they intended to replace topsoils in all bed and lawn areas?
18. What happens to compost after it is incorporated into on-site soils? Once in place, is there any way to further enhance soil organic matter content?
19. Explain the concept of the carbon-to-nitrogen ratio in organic mulches. Why is the carbon-to-nitrogen ratio important? What is the optimum carbon-to-nitrogen ratio to enhance soil properties? What if the mulch is intended for weed control?
20. What happens to soil aeration, drainage, and rooting when soils become compacted? What choices do you have to effectively decrease compaction in bed soils?

What's in the Building Soil Manual?

Summary of "Building Soil: Guidelines and Resources for Implementing Soil Quality and Depth BMP T5.13 in WDOE Stormwater Management Manual for Western Washington"

View or print the full manual at www.BuildingSoil.org

What happens when the rain can't soak in?

The Role of Soil Quality in Stormwater Management

Native forest soils in western Washington soak rainfall quickly down into the groundwater, so that little runs off. But during development soils are often stripped and compacted, resulting in rapid runoff that damages streams and downstream properties. The Department of Ecology has decided to require a minimum post-construction soil standard on all building sites around western Washington, to protect water quality, streams, Puget Sound, and downstream property owners.

BMP T5.13 "Post Construction Soil Quality and Depth"

This new "best management practice" (BMP), which local governments around western Washington are now adding to their stormwater codes, requires:

- **Soil retention** – preserving existing site vegetation and soil, uncompacted by equipment, <u>or</u>
- **Soil restoration** – correcting compaction to a 12-inch depth, and amending soils with compost or bringing in/reusing an amended topsoil to an 8-inch depth, <u>plus</u>
- **Soil protection** – protecting restored soils from re-compaction, and mulching after planting to prevent erosion and support healthy plant growth.

Summary of Steps for Implementing BMP T5.13

The Ecology BMP requires a 12-inch finished uncompacted soil depth, including 8 inches of topsoil amended to meet a minimum "soil organic matter" (SOM – by loss-on-combustion test) of 10% for planting beds or 5% for turf areas.

Building and landscape professionals worked with soil scientists and planners to create this "Building Soil" manual and website, to help builders, landscapers, and designers implement BMP T5.13 in a practical and cost-effective way.

Amendment Options

The Department of Ecology's BMP T5.13 lays out **four options** for soil management in different areas of each site:

1) **Leave native vegetation and soil undisturbed**, and protect from compaction during construction. This is the least expensive option, because undisturbed soils don't have to be restored.

2) **Amend existing site topsoil or subsoil with compost** to meet the "soil organic matter" requirements. (Pre-approved rates are 3 inches of compost tilled in to an 8-inch depth for planting beds, or 1.75 inches of compost tilled in 8 inches for turf areas.)

3) **Stockpile existing topsoil during grading**. Amend as needed to meet the organic matter requirement, and replace 8 inches of topsoil before planting, again scarifying to break up compaction to a 12-inch depth.

4) **Import a topsoil mix that meets the organic content and depth requirements**. Topsoil mixes around 40% compost by volume meet the 10% SOM requirement for planting beds. Mixes around 25% by volume compost meet the 5% SOM required for turf areas. Scarifying to a 12 inch depth, or tilling in the first layer of topsoil, will allow water and roots to penetrate the subsoil. It's important not to have too many fine particles (silt or clay, which can plug up drainage) in the mix. Compost quality is also important, so the manual lists Washington permitted compost facilities, as well as soil labs that can do testing for custom soil mixes if desired.

Building Soil — Foundation for Success

Learn more at **www.BuildingSoil.org**

Developing a Soil Management Plan

The *Building Soil* manual walks through the steps to develop a "Soil Management Plan":

1) **Review site landscape plans and grading plans.** Identify areas where existing soil and vegetation can be left undisturbed and protected from compaction. For areas that will be graded, decide whether to stockpile and reuse site topsoil, amend soils on-site with compost, or bring in an amended topsoil mix that meets requirements.

2) **Visit site to determine soil conditions.** Identify trees and other vegetation to be preserved. Check existing soil conditions and compacted areas. Flag and fence protected areas, and make sure they fit with grading plans.

3) **Select amendment options for each area of the site.**

4) **Identify compost, topsoils, and other organic materials for amendment and mulch.**

5) **Calculate amendment, topsoil, and mulch volumes required for this site**, and record them on a soil management plan form. That form becomes part of permit and landscaping specifications.

Field Guide for Verifying Soil Quality and Depth

The manual describes simple field tests:

1) Verify that compost, topsoil mixes, and mulch have been delivered to the site as specified in the soil management plan.

2) Dig a few test holes to see that soils have been amended to an 8-inch depth. Push a metal rod into the soil to verify that soils are un-compacted to the required 12-inch depth.

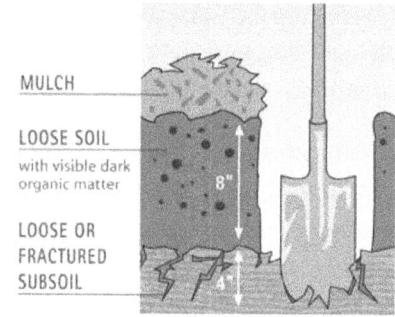
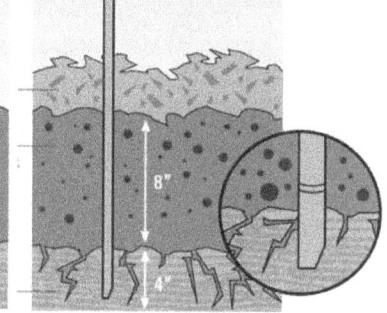

Why build healthy soil?

- More marketable buildings and landscapes
- Better site erosion control
- Reduced need for water and chemicals
- Less stormwater runoff, better water quality, lower costs to comply with new regulations
- Healthy landscapes, for satisfied customers

Resources

The *Building Soil* manual also contains a number of useful resources for builders and designers:

- **Calculating Custom Amendment Rates** – formula & spreadsheet
  The website also has an online Excel spreadsheet calculator,
  click here → www.BuildingSoil.org/tools/Compost_Calculator.xls

- **Permitted Composting Facilities in Western Washington** – contact information for suppliers

- **Soil and Compost Analysis Labs** serving the Northwest

- **Model Soil Amendment Specifications** in APWA and CSI formats

- **Additional Resources** on compost quality and use, and the role of soil quality in stormwater management and successful landscaping

View or download the complete manual at
click here → www.BuildingSoil.org/tools/Soil_BMP_Manual.pdf

Learn more at **www.BuildingSoil.org**

When to Amend?
Construction Sequencing for Soil Protection and Restoration

The goal: healthy soil under every landscape
Washington State DOE's stormwater BMP T5.13 "Post Construction Soil Quality and Depth" requires that every construction site be left with at least 12 inches of un-compacted soil, and that the upper 8 inches have sufficient organic content to support a healthy landscape and soak up most rainfall. The State BMP (available with a how-to manual at www.BuildingSoil.org) lays out four options for soil management on different areas of sites. Soil best practices fit into construction projects from start to finish.

Design phase: plan to preserve or restore soil
Disturbed soils must be restored (see options at right), so it's better to preserve and protect existing soil and vegetation where possible.

- Identify trees and other vegetation to be preserved.
- Flag and fence off soil areas that will be protected from compaction and not graded. Pay attention to tree root zones (typically twice the width of the tree's canopy or "drip line").
- Once grading plans are complete, make a "Soil Management Plan" that identifies soil areas to be preserved, and compost or amended topsoil and mulch that will be needed to restore the soil areas that are disturbed during grading or compacted by equipment. (See the *Building Soil* manual for a blank Soil Management Plan form, and easy calculator for soil materials.)
- Dig a few holes around site to examine soil quality. Soil tests can determine how much amendment is needed. Or just plan to use "pre-approved" rates.

Four Options for Soil Management
1) **Leave native vegetation and soil undisturbed**, and protect from compaction during construction. This is the least expensive option, because undisturbed soils don't have to be restored.
2) **Amend existing site topsoil or subsoil with compost** to meet the "soil organic matter" requirements. (Pre-approved rates are 3 inches of compost tilled in to an 8-inch depth for planting beds, or 1.75 inches of compost tilled in 8 inches for turf areas. Alternatively, custom rates may be calculated from soil tests.) Scarify the subsoil, to provide 12 inches of un-compacted soil depth.
3) **Stockpile existing topsoil during grading**, and replace 8 inches of topsoil before planting. Amend if needed to meet the organic matter requirement, and scarify subsoil to break up compaction to a 12-inch depth.
4) **Import a topsoil mix that meets the organic content and depth requirements.** Topsoil mixes around 40% compost by volume meet the 10% organic matter requirement for planting beds. Mixes around 25% by volume compost meet the 5% organic matter required for turf areas. Scarifying to a 12 inch depth, or tilling in some of the topsoil, will help water and roots to penetrate the subsoil.

Land clearing and grading: reuse soil and organic materials
- Land clearing debris can often be chipped on-site and used immediately as erosion-control cover, or stockpiled for re-use as landscape mulch at the end of the project. (Don't mix un-composted debris into the soil – it's better used as mulch.)
- Root zones of trees should be fenced, and protected from compaction by equipment traffic wherever possible. Where traffic is unavoidable, a 6 inch layer of coarse wood chips (hog fuel) or quarry rock will reduce root damage.
- Topsoil removed during grading can be stockpiled and covered with wood chips, plastic, or breathable fabric.
- If amended topsoils will be placed at the end of the project, grade 8-12 inches below finish grade to allow for placing them.

At Redmond Ridge, Quadrant Homes fences and protects areas of existing forest, as an amenity and stormwater filter. They chip land clearing debris. Then they grade to 12 inches below finish grade, stockpiling topsoil for reuse. Next step is to place rock pads for roads and driveways.

Site prep and construction traffic: the cheapest messes are the ones we don't make
- Lay out the roads and driveways, and get the rock bases down for them as soon as possible. Then keep as much construction traffic as possible on the road base, and off open soils. Besides reducing soil compaction, this helps with erosion compliance, and with site safety by keeping rolling equipment on a firm base.
- Maintain barriers to keep construction traffic off soil, vegetation, and tree root zones that are being preserved.

Building Soil
Foundation for Success

Learn more at **www.BuildingSoil.org**

ecoPRO Handbook

Erosion control <u>and</u> soil quality – a two-for-one with compost

- Required temporary erosion and sediment control (TESC) can be accomplished by spreading a "blanket" of 1-3 inches of coarse compost to protect open soils during construction. At the end of the project, the compost can just be tilled in to create a healthy planting soil, or planted through on slopes too steep to till, saving the expense of removing erosion covers.
- Compost berms or socks often work better as perimeter sediment controls than silt fence, straw bales, etc. Again, the compost can just be knocked down or tilled in and left on site. See *Erosion Control with Compost* at www.BuildingSoil.org .

Reducing compaction: just rip it

- At the end of the project an inspector should be able to push a 3/8" metal bar 12 inches into the soil just with body weight. Compaction could be from an existing hardpan layer in the subsoil (found during the design phase), or caused by unavoidable construction traffic over an area.
- De-compaction can be done with a cat-mounted ripper, tractor-mounted disc, or tiller, before or after placing topsoil or compost. Scarifying through the first lift of applied soil or compost will mix it into subsoil, so that roots and water will penetrate deeper.

Placing and protecting amended topsoils

- Topsoils (from stockpiles or off-site) should be amended with compost as needed to meet the minimum organic matter requirements in the WA State "Post Construction Soil Quality and Depth" BMP T5.13 (see the *Building Soil* manual). The default pre-approved rates are 3 inches of compost blended into the upper 8 inches of soil for planting beds, and 1.75 inches of compost blended into 8-inch depth for turf areas. Custom rates based on soil tests may be lower, and save money on larger sites (see *Building Soil* manual).
- Amended topsoils can be placed as soon as building exterior work is complete, if contractors understand that vehicles must stay on road and driveway pads to prevent soil compaction. Compost/soil blends provide good erosion protection.

Amending soils with compost on-site

- Rather than purchasing "topsoil" of unknown quality (weed seeds or too much clay are common problems), it's often more cost effective to amend existing site top or sub-soils with compost to restore final soil quality. Because Washington composting facilities must follow strict State quality regulations, compost quality is more dependable than purchased soil.
- If compost blankets, berms, and socks have been used for site erosion and sediment control during construction, just till the compost at least 8 inches into the soil before planting. Avoid tilling through tree roots.
- When planting turf (by seed or sod), a pass with a rock rake may be needed to create a smooth seedbed. Roll to firm soil before seeding.

"When to amend?" – it depends

Soil protection starts with initial site planning and continues through to final sale. Compost or wood chip blankets can be great for erosion control during construction. But final soil quality and depth restoration, whether by placing imported or reused topsoil or by amending site soils with compost, should wait at least until building exteriors are finished and trade crews have moved indoors. Before sodding or seeding turf, tilled soils need to be rolled or allowed to settle with rainfall – but trees and shrubs can go in right away. Beds should be mulched right after planting with wood chips or coarse bark, to prevent weeds and erosion, conserve water, and improve plant survival and growth.

Talk to your landscape architect, site prep, grading, and landscape contractors about when and how soil BMPs fit best into <u>your</u> team's construction schedule.

Building Soil — Foundation for Success

Learn more at **www.BuildingSoil.org**

Erosion Control with Compost

Using compost to meet TESC <u>and</u> Soil Quality requirements on building sites

Washington Department of Transportation specifies compost blankets, for cost-effective erosion control and excellent long-term plant establishment.

EPA-approved Erosion Control BMP's

Compost blankets, berms, and socks are US EPA-approved for temporary erosion and sediment control (TESC) on construction sites. Unlike other erosion BMPs that can be expensive to remove and dispose of, compost can be left on-site to permanently enhance plant growth. Compost can be tilled into the soil before planting to meet the Washington Department of Ecology's "BMP T5.13 – Post Construction Soil Quality and Depth". On sites too steep or sensitive for tilling, seed can be blown in with the compost, or plants can be planted through the compost blanket. This provides much better plant survival, long-term growth, and erosion prevention, even on difficult sites.

"Two for one" – construction erosion control <u>and</u> soil quality BMPs are met with compost at Issaquah Highlands.

Compost Blankets

Compost blankets are usually 1 to 3 inches thick (2 inches is common in Washington). They can be installed by blowing compost onto slopes up to 2:1 (up to 1:1 with additional stabilization), or on shallower slopes by spreading compost with conventional equipment. In general, the compost used for all these erosion control methods has larger particle sizes (usually a 1 inch-minus screened compost, as compared to ½ inch-minus screen for garden compost) to allow more rainfall to be absorbed and filtered rapidly. The compost makes excellent surface contact, prevent rilling underneath.

Compost Berms

Compost berms are a perimeter sediment control, increasingly used instead of silt fence. Berm width is twice its height – 3ft. x 18 inches high or 2 ft.. x 12 inches high are common. They can be blown in place (see photo) or just placed with a front-end loader. Again, the compost is coarser (3/4 or 1 inch-minus screened) to filter a lot of turbid water quickly. Besides sediment removal, compost excels at removing oil and grease, metals, and buffering pH (such as from fresh concrete wash off).

Compost Socks

Compost socks are fast replacing silt fence and straw bales as a cost-effective control for sediment and other pollutants, because they excel at filtration and dependable ground contact. Sock material may be biodegradable, for protection up to six months that can be planted and left in place. If non-biodegradable socks are used, only the light fabric must be removed while the compost is left on-site – still much cheaper than silt fence removal. Socks can be filled in place by compost suppliers, or delivered filled on pallets. Unlike many wattle BMPs, they don't have to be trenched in – just walk down them to ensure good soil contact, and stake through the sock on slopes.

Standard Specifications and Suppliers

- **US EPA's standard specifications for compost blankets, berms, and socks:**
  click here → www.BuildingSoil.org/tools/EPA-erosion-control-specs.pdf

- Contact your local compost supplier or see "Composting Facilities" on page 20 of the Building Soil manual, at www.BuildingSoil.org

Building Soil — Foundation for Success

Learn more at **www.BuildingSoil.org**

Estimating Soil Texture

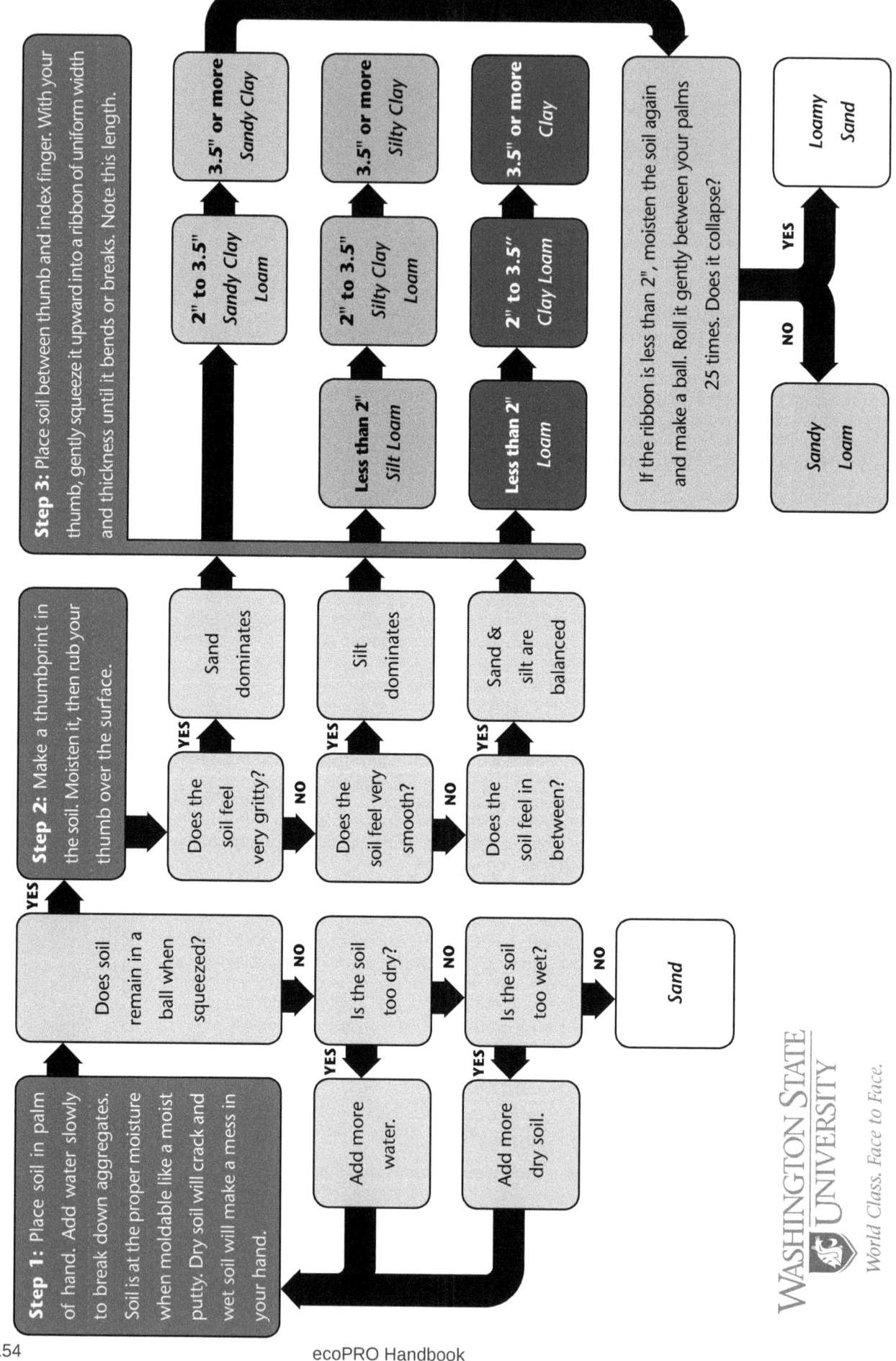

Estimando la Textura del Suelo

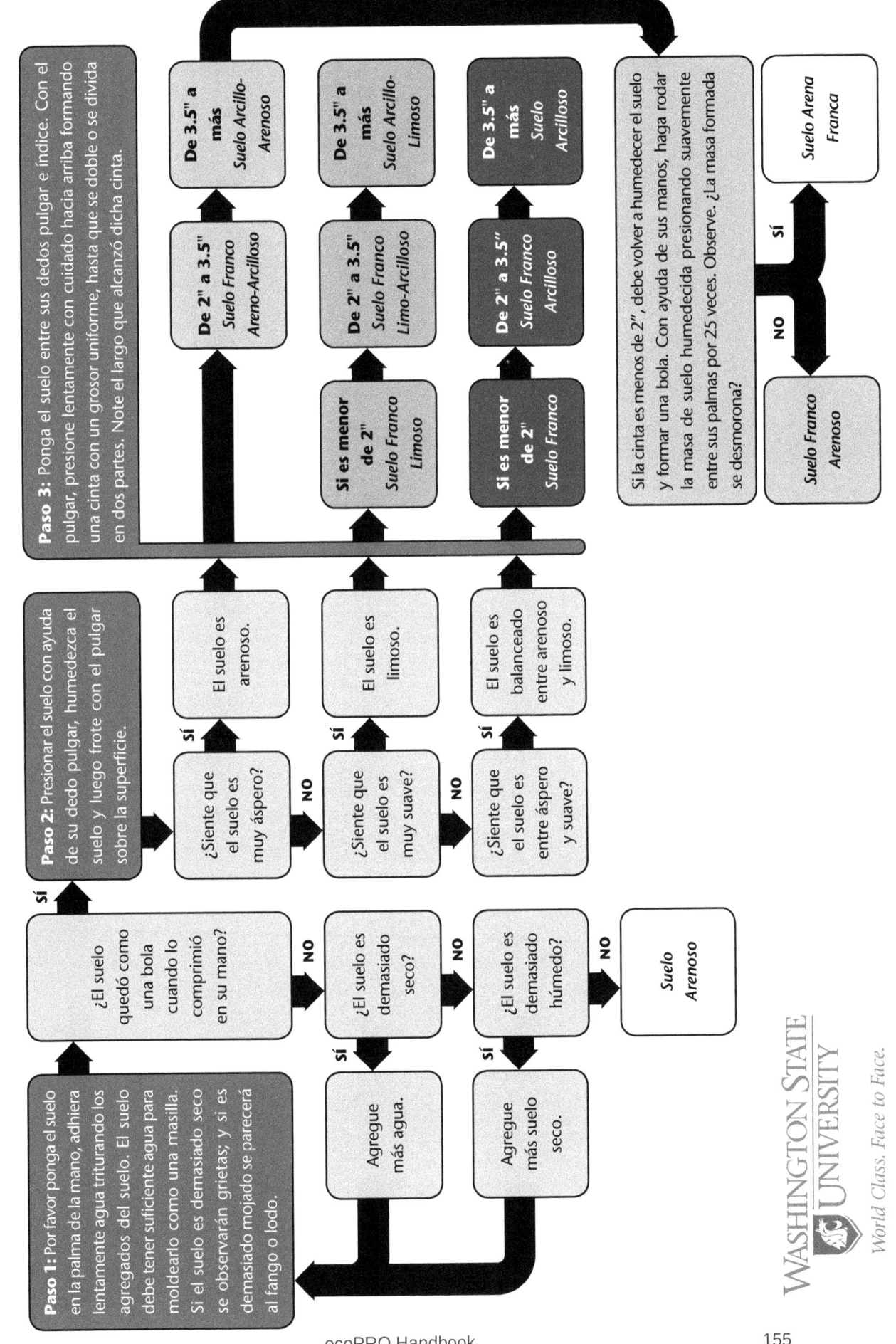

SECTION III: PLANT HEALTH CARE

IN THIS SECTION	PAGE
Managing Trees, Shrubs & Beds Sustainably *Source: Chapter 8 of Sustainable Landscape Management: Design, Construction, and Maintenance*	157
Sustainable Lawn Care, Installation & Maintenace *Source: Seattle Public Utilities*	185
ProIPM: Integrated Pest Management Solutions for the Landscape Professional *Source: Seattle Public Utilities*	193
Integrated Pest Management Flowchart *Source: Local Hazardous Waste Management Program*	195
Gardening without Pesticides *Source: Grow Smart; Grow Safe Program*	196

chapter 8
Managing Trees, Shrubs, and Beds Sustainably

INTRODUCTION

Sustainable management of trees and shrubs requires proper planting, thoughtful care during establishment, and regular follow-up. Maintenance contractors often spend a great deal of time rescuing plants that suffer from poor planting, lack of follow-up fertilization, misguided pruning, and inadequate irrigation. Attentive pruning, intelligent irrigation, and periodic tasks such as edging, mulching, and weed control will develop sound trees, shrubs, and ground covers.

This chapter will discuss sustainable strategies for:

- Planting
- Fertilization
- Irrigation
- Pruning
- Managing the waste stream

PLANTING

This section will discuss preparation of the planting hole and the planting process. Opportunities for handling and placing soils during construction were discussed in Chapter 7.

One of the basic goals in planting is to place plant roots in contact with the soil in which they will be growing. While this seems simple and intuitive, failure to achieve good root-to-soil contact is one of the most common reasons for planting failures. Techniques used to grow plants in nurseries may contribute to planting problems due to extreme root loss or root system distortion. Characteristics of the most common production systems are discussed next.

Field-Grown Bare-Root Stock

Field-grown bare-root stock is a technique for producing deciduous trees and some deciduous shrubs. It involves growing plants in soil until they reach market size and then harvesting them with mechanical diggers that undercut the plants and sever the roots. Plants are harvested in late fall or early winter once the plants are fully dormant. After digging, plants are graded and stored in sawdust or other mulch prior to shipping to nurseries where they are sold locally in early spring prior to leaf-out. Bare-root plants are typically small with stems around 0.75 to 1.5 inches (2 to 4 cm) in diameter, and they have up to 95 percent of their roots removed during digging (Figure 8-1). Planting can only be done for a short time in spring while they are still dormant so the window of opportunity for bare-root stock is small.

133

Figure 8-1 Most of the roots on this bare-root tree have been removed during digging.

Bare-root plants are easily planted because they are free of soil and roots are immediately placed in contact with soil, thus avoiding interface problems common to other plant production systems. Because the planting season for bare-root stock is short, leftover plants are often transferred to pots filled with organic planting media. If held in the nursery for most of the season, they essentially become container-grown plants and face the same challenges associated with that method of plant production.

Balled-and-Burlapped and Spade-Dug Stock

Field-grown stock not suited to bare-root transplanting was historically hand dug with the intact and undisturbed root-ball placed in burlap, which was then bound with twine (Figure 8-2). With the

(a)

(b)

Figure 8-2 (a) This balled-and-burlapped Oregon grape (*Mahonia aquifolium*) (plant on right) has about 5 percent of the root system remaining after digging. Root-balls should be handled carefully to avoid breaking up the soil mass. (b) This much larger spade-dug tree is placed in burlap lining the wire basket. The basket ensures the root-ball will not fall apart during handling.

development of mechanical spades, trees today are commonly dug and placed in wire baskets lined with burlap. The burlap and basket are then secured with twine. This system is widely used for conifers, larger deciduous trees, and many shrubs. Even though as much as 95 percent of the root system is removed during digging, the remaining roots are undisturbed and the fine roots are intact, resulting in generally high transplant survival rates. In many cases, stock can be stored and then planted at any time during the growing season. Balled-and-burlapped and spade-dug plants are heavy and must be handled with care to avoid fracturing the root-ball. Plants placed in pots after digging often develop distorted root systems with proliferation of roots at the surface, which increases the potential for girdling roots once the plants are planted out. Postplanting irrigation problems arise when the soil in the ball differs significantly from the backfill soil. Problems also result from failure to remove the twine from around the plant stem at the time of planting. This is particularly important if nonbiodegradable twine is used to secure the root-ball.

Tree spades are frequently used to transplant large trees with trunk diameters 2 to 10 inches (5 to 25 cm) or larger. In these situations, trees are generally dug and placed in wire baskets or boxes for transport (Figure 8-2b). In cases where trees are already growing on-site, tree spades can be used to move them directly to their new location. This involves digging the planting hole with the spade, discarding the soil on-site, and then digging the tree and placing it in the new planting hole. Large spade-dug trees have generally high survival rates but often grow slowly after planting for several years until the root system regenerates.

Container-Grown Stock

Container-grown nursery plants are the most common plants available today. The system employed by most growers uses lightweight organic growing media designed to drain rapidly once placed in plastic containers. Media may be entirely composed of ground bark or a mixture of bark with small portions of sand, soil, or other material. Container-grown plants are easily transported and can be planted at any time of the year. Root systems tend to be vigorous and often become distorted as roots quickly fill the container and either circle around the base of the container or grow upward to the surface (Figure 8-3a). Roots may develop on the surface of the container and develop into girdling roots as they enlarge over time (Figure 8-3b). Container stock planted in spring establishes well in most cases. Stock held over through the growing season, however, often becomes pot bound and is more likely to struggle after planting. Container plants tend to have high transplant survival rates but often grow poorly once planted in the landscape. Because most landscaping is done during the main growing season and into the fall, containers are the system of choice for planting shrubs.

The Planting Hole

People have been planting plants for a long time, so it is not surprising that there are many different recommendations on how to plant properly. Many time-honored practices work just fine but often involve more effort than is necessary. As research has caught up to folklore, planting guidelines have changed significantly. Current recommendations stress the following.

Planting holes should be wider than they are deep. Typical recommendations call for the planting hole to be two to three times the diameter of the root-ball. Therefore, a plant with a 12-inch (30-cm) root-ball should be placed in a hole 24 to 36 inches (60 to 90 cm) across. The outer edges of the hole can be tapered down from the edge of the hole to the bottom, creating a bowl-like cross section (Figure 8-4). This recommendation is based on studies demonstrating that roots tend to develop laterally from the ends of cut roots or from within the center of the root-ball and that relatively few roots initially develop downward (Watson and Himelick 1997).

136 Managing Trees, Shrubs, and Beds Sustainably

(a)

(b)

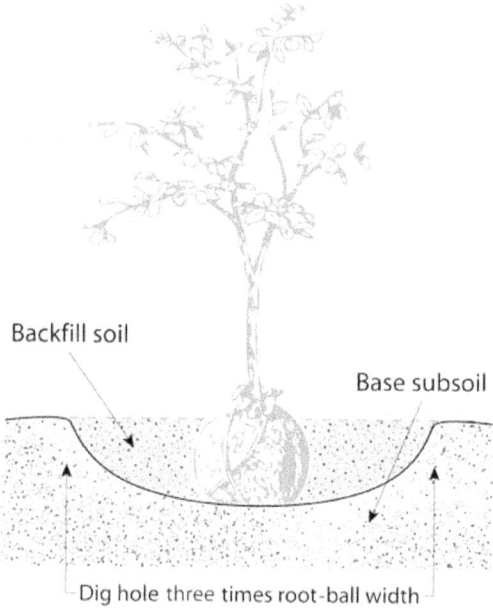

Figure 8-4 Planting holes that are wide and tapered from the edges to the center provide optimum conditions for rapid establishment and root system recovery.

Planting holes should be just deep enough to accommodate the plant. Digging a giant pit is a lot of work that accomplishes very little and may cause plants to sink below grade when settling occurs. This is particularly true when planting balled-and-burlapped or spade-dug trees. The holes should be just deep enough so that when the root mass is placed on the compacted bottom of the hole, the root-stem juncture is at or slightly above grade level (Watson and Himelick 1997).

Figure 8-3 (a) Plants that grow too long in containers often have distorted root systems. (b) This maple was held too long in a small container and then moved to the field, with its distorted root system intact. Now several potential girdling roots are apparent.

In normal soils with average structure, there is no need to amend the soil prior to backfilling (Gilman 2004; Smalley and Wood 1995; Whitcomb 1975, 1987). Because amending soils with organic matter is one of the time-honored practices in horticulture, this may seem counterintuitive. Most research shows that plant growth in sites with amended soils is about the same as plant growth in unamended soils. Under normal conditions, amending the backfill soil in a planting hole does not affect the rate of transplant survival.

In highly compacted soils (or disturbed soils with poor structure), soil replacement or large-scale amendment of the entire area may be needed (see Chapter 7). Amending the soil in the planting hole may provide a better environment for initial establishment but only if drainage is included to prevent accumulation of water in the amended planting hole. For detailed information on working with these soils, consult Craul (1999) or Urban (2008).

Plants grown in containers are prone to becoming root bound, and the root system structure is often tangled and circular. Breaking up this container mass immediately before planting will improve root contact with the soil. When plants are removed from containers and planted with this compacted root mass intact, an interface is created between the soil and the porous, free-draining container medium. In these instances, water entering the container plant root zone tends to drain freely into the surrounding soil. Because water is held more tightly in the soil than in the container medium, it does not move back into the container plant root zone and drought stress occurs (Costello and Paul 1975; Spomer 1980). Further, because plant roots often stay in the container medium, which does not retain nutrients, deficiencies often occur. The result is a plant that is under drought and nutritional stress and therefore slow to establish roots into the surrounding soil (Figure 8-5).

There are two common options available to avoid the container interface problem. In young container plants that are not yet root bound, shake out some of the medium or bare-root the plant com-

Figure 8-5 This container plant was planted undisturbed in gray clay. After five years, the plant had not grown and showed several nutrient deficiencies. After it was dug up, it was apparent that the roots had never grown into the surrounding soil.

pletely (Color Plate 8-1). Feather out the roots and spread them into the surrounding soil prior to backfilling. If planting in the spring or fall under moist conditions, some root pruning can be done to reduce tangling roots and to improve the lateral spread of the root system. A faster and simpler strategy involves laying the plant on its side and using a spade to slice through the root mass from the base toward the root-stem interface. This technique, commonly

Figure 8-6 One year after planting in soil, note the greater root development in the butterflied plant on the right versus the undisturbed container plant on the left.

called "butterflying," opens up the root system, thus facilitating better root-to-soil contact without severely damaging the root system (Figure 8-6).

Firmly pack the soil into the hole after plant placement but do not compact. The goal is to pack the soil returned to the hole enough to securely hold the plant in place and prevent tipping. Additional packing causes loss of soil structure and increases compaction. It is okay for the soil to have clods and small air pockets when planting is completed.

Other Amendments

There are many proponents of adding microbial preparations such as mycorrhizae, compost tea, and biostimulants such as cytokinins and humic substances to the backfill soil or after planting as surface applications. These materials are successfully marketed because they promise a healthy soil teeming with microbes and the ability to withstand the rigors of environmental stress (Lowenfels and Lewis 2006). Anecdotal testimonies often predict dramatic effects and claim these additives are the most important part of the planting process.

There is limited research to support claims about compost tea, cytokinins, and humic substances, and it remains to be seen whether research bears out the initial claims. Results from extensive research conducted over decades supports the general role mycorrhizae play in plant growth and survival in natural habitats such as forests. In natural environments, mycorrhizal effects on increased phosphorus uptake are well documented (as are increased survival rates in stressful environments particularly where drought is severe) (Steinfeld, Amaranthus, and Cazares 2003). Growth responses in landscape environments where plants have been inoculated with commercial preparations of mycorrhizae have been difficult to demonstrate (Appleton et al. 2003; Gilman 2001). Following is a summary of plant responses to mycorrhizal associations under natural and landscape conditions:

- A high level of mycorrhizal infection of roots is normal in any soil formerly supporting forests (Iyer, Corey, and Wilde 1980). In constructed landscapes planted with nursery-grown plants, the mycorrhizal infection rate is variable and ranges from no infection to levels typically found in natural settings.
- The principal impact of mycorrhizae is increased absorption of nutrients by host plants. This is particularly valuable in nutrient-poor soils. Phosphorus is the best-documented nutrient.
- Mycorrhizal associations often decrease when plants are grown in fertile, irrigated soil.
- Fertilization and irrigation in landscapes can largely substitute for mycorrhizal functions in many cases.

Because of the trend toward more sustainable landscapes that receive fewer inputs such as fertilizer and irrigation, it is likely mycorrhizae will become increasingly important for healthy plant growth. Since most landscape plants have some level of natural mycorrhizal infection, it is important to determine the degree of natural infection to avoid needlessly applying commercial mycorrhizal products (Iyer, Corey, and Wilde 1980).

Postplanting Care

The goal of postplanting care is to encourage rapid establishment of roots and to enhance plant vigor. In commercial settings, postplanting care for trees may include minimizing competition by removing grass or ground covers around the base, staking, mulching, fertilizing, and irrigating. Pruning at the time of planting may also occur.

Minimizing Competition

Creating a free space around the base of newly planted trees reduces the chances that trees will get struck by mowers and reduces competition between grass roots and developing tree roots for nitrogen and moisture. Numerous studies have demonstrated that grass roots can significantly reduce tree root growth, root extension rates, and shoot extension (Messenger 1976; Green and Watson 1989; Harris, Clark, and Matheny 2003). A circular free space 4 to 5 feet (1 to 1.5 m) in diameter will generally minimize competition during the establishment period and reduce the chance that trees will be damaged by landscape maintenance equipment.

Staking

Researchers generally conclude that, in most cases, staking is not necessary and may even delay establishment by reducing root development and slowing trunk diameter growth (Harris, Leiser, and Davis 1978). The value of staking is holding trees straight and protecting them from damage. Problems with staking often result from staking rigidly, which prevents normal root and trunk development, and from using wire or plastic ties that girdle trunks as the tree diameter increases over time (Figure 8-7).

Staking should meet the following criteria:

- Avoid staking when trees are able to stand straight without assistance and there is no need for protection from wind or machinery.
- Place stakes away from the trunk and below the lowest branches. When planting balled-and-

Figure 8-7 Staking causes damage in the landscape when stakes and ties are left on too long. Wire ties eventually will cut into and girdle stems if not removed in a timely fashion.

burlapped or spade-dug trees, avoid driving stakes into the intact root-ball.
- Attach ties to the trunk loosely and as low as possible. The idea is to support the tree while allowing some movement of the trunk. Movement is what stimulates both increased root growth and trunk diameter growth.
- Remove stakes and ties as soon as possible. In many cases, the stakes can be removed by the end of the first growing season after planting (Figure 8-8).

(a)

(b)

Mulching after Planting

Mulching after planting gives the installation a finished look and provides sustainable benefits by reducing weed encroachment and preventing the soil surface from rapidly drying (thereby assisting in quicker establishment and increased shoot growth) (Ferrini et al. 2008; Montague et al. 2007).

In general, mulches derived from composted organic debris with a carbon-to-nitrogen ratio (C/N) of 20:1 or lower positively affect establishment in new plantings as compared with noncomposted wood waste with a C/N ratio above 50:1, which tends to tie up soil nitrogen during subsequent decomposition. Due to the volume of compost mulches applied around the base of newly planted trees or shrubs, much of the increased growth observed may be due to nitrogen release by the mulch. Mulch should be 2 to 4 inches (5 to 10 cm) deep and applied so as not to cover the base of the tree trunk.

FERTILIZATION

Fertilization of landscape plants is a surprisingly controversial topic among researchers and landscape professionals (Siewart et al. 2000). In its simplest form, fertilization involves determining optimum rates of fertilizer, application timing, and the combination of nutrients needed to produce vigorous healthy landscape plants in much the same manner as for other crop plants. While in many cases it is that simple, some experts question the very idea of fertilizing because trees and shrubs growing in the wild seem to do just fine without fertilizer (Miller 2000). Others argue that conditions at landscape sites are vastly different from natural environments; soils are more likely to be impoverished, and fertilizer is absolutely necessary. Research trials often add

Figure 8-8 This example of staking shows (a) the optimum placement of stakes originally and (b) how removing stakes one year after planting avoided damage to the trunk.

to the confusion: some demonstrate strong growth responses to fertilizer while others show no response at all.

Goals in developing a fertilization program include the following:

- Enhancing establishment and early growth after transplanting
- Stimulating growth to more rapidly achieve functional landscape size
- Maintaining plant health over time
- Overcoming known nutrient deficiencies that affect plant health

There are other situations where fertilization is likely to be necessary, including trees growing in confined root zones caused by construction activities or plants growing in containers. This section will address fertilizing new transplants, stimulating growth in young trees, and maintaining plant health over time.

Fertilizing Transplants during Establishment

Young trees in new landscapes may take several years before they become big enough to impact the landscape. During the establishment period, which can last from one to four years, trees may grow weakly or not at all (Color Plate 8-2). Several studies have demonstrated significant growth from annual applications of nitrogen fertilizer to trees, particularly those with continuous (indeterminate) growth habits such as tulip poplar (*Liriodendron tulipifera*) (Figure 8-9), sweet gum (*Liquidambar styraciflua*), and elm (*Ulmus* spp.). Typical response patterns show modest increases in growth and color in the first year, followed by increased growth in height, caliper, and canopy spread in succeeding years (van de Werken 1981). Trees in temperate climates receiving annual fertilizer applications generally develop denser branching and retain leaves longer during fall as noted in Color Plate 8-3.

Other research has found that some newly transplanted trees do not respond to added fertilizer for the first one to three years after planting (Day and Harris 2007). This may be due to local environmental conditions or because determinate species were used that are less responsive to nitrogen fertilizer than the indeterminate species discussed earlier. Determinate trees generally don't show much response in year 1 other than darker foliage color in nitrogen-deficient soils as shown in Color Plate 8-4.

Maintaining Long-Term Plant Health

In generally healthy growing environments with mature trees or shrubs, it is hard to recommend continuous annual fertilization. Mature trees growing in lawns typically have extensive root development extending out into the lawn area (Figure 8-10). Because tree and lawn roots largely occupy the same area, trees compete freely for fertilizer applied to the lawn area. Likewise, trees near or in planting beds will compete for nutrients with shrubs. Maintaining an aerated root zone, which encourages strong microbial activity, and alleviating compaction in tree root zones are probably more important than regular fertilization in mature landscapes.

Alleviating Nutrient Deficiencies

Iron deficiency occurs in soils with a pH above 7.5, because iron tends to form insoluble compounds at high pH and is unavailable for plant root absorption. Research has shown that soil injections of iron solutions can alleviate symptoms for one or more years. Iron trunk implants can have a similar effect. A better solution is to avoid planting trees like pin oak (*Quercus palustris*) and maples (*Acer* spp.), which are prone to iron deficiency, in areas with high-pH soils. Sustainable practice dictates that the best approach is to avoid these types of landscape problems rather than to create problems and then search for solutions.

Figure 8-9 Trees like tulip poplar (*Liriodendron tulipifera*) with indeterminate growth are very responsive to nitrogen fertilizers even when young. (a) In this trial, unfertilized trees were tall and spindly with small canopies. (b) Fertilized trees were taller with nearly double the trunk diameter and much larger canopies.

DETERMINATE VERSUS INDETERMINATE GROWTH

In temperate climates, all trees start growth in spring by elongation of preformed shoots contained in terminal buds. With determinate trees, the preformed leaves and shoots elongate and may produce a few more leaves before setting a new bud. Under normal conditions, once the bud is set, growth is finished for the rest of the year. The actual period of shoot elongation may last only a few weeks. With indeterminate trees, growth starts out by elongation of the preformed leaves and stems, but the apical meristem (growing point) continues to produce new leaves as long as conditions are conducive to growth. Indeterminate trees may continue to grow throughout the entire growing season sometimes for as long as 150 days.

HOW IS TREE RESPONSE TO FERTILIZER MEASURED?

There are a number of different parameters that can be used to evaluate the effect of fertilizer on plant growth. These include increase in vertical height, increase in lateral shoot extension, increase in canopy area, and increase in trunk caliper at a specified height above the ground. Because it is easy to measure increases in trunk caliper, this measure is often the choice of researchers.

COMMON TREE RESPONSES TO SPECIFIC NUTRIENTS AND APPLICATION METHODS

- Nitrogen is the most important nutrient and is most likely to stimulate growth.
- All types of nitrogen fertilizers are effective in stimulating color and growth.
- Growth responses to phosphorus are likely only when a deficiency is demonstrated.
- Potassium does not appear to affect growth in a measurable way.
- Tree responses are similar for all methods of application.
- Broadcasted tree fertilizer tends to stimulate weed growth in mulch beds and overstimulate lawn grasses.
- Tree responses to nitrogen applied by the broadcast method have been reported at rates ranging from 1 to 6 pounds N/1000 square feet (5 to 30 g N/m^2).
- Maximum plant growth occurs from early-spring applications, followed closely by fall and summer applications.
- Fertilizer growth responses continue to show for one or more years after applications are stopped.
- Fertilizer responses are less apparent in mature trees with larger root spreads.

Figure 8-10 Tree roots generally spread a long way from the base of the trunk as shown in this photo of elm tree roots uncovered over 50 feet (15 m) from the tree.

Assessing Fertilizer Needs

Accurate techniques for assessing landscape fertilizer needs could help landscapers use fertilizers more efficiently. Soil testing and plant tissue analysis are the most common methods used to estimate fertilizer needs, but both have limitations. For example, there are no simple and effective soil tests to help guide nitrogen applications (Scharenbroch and Lloyd 2004). In general, more research is needed to develop the potential of soil and plant analyses for guiding landscape fertilizer applications.

IRRIGATION

Irrigation is an important practice for landscapes in many different climate zones. While criticism of landscape water use is often directed at lawns, it is fair to say that a significant amount of total water use occurs in bed areas. Because landscape watering is so visible and water is such a precious commodity, it is important that it be used efficiently. The following sections will address options for improving irrigation efficiency and reducing water use in general.

Irrigating New Plantings

In many climates, irrigation is critical for successful establishment of transplanted plants (Anella, Hennessey, and Lorenzi 2008). Bare-root, balled-and-burlapped, and spade-dug trees all suffer in excess of 95 percent root loss during digging. Container plants retain their root systems, but due to excessive drainage from porous container media, they often suffer from rapid drought stress (Costello and Paul 1975). As a result, all types of plants benefit from regular irrigation for at least the first year after transplanting. Research has demonstrated that regular irrigation during the establishment year benefits root system development as much as five years later, even if no additional irrigation occurs after the first year (Gilman et al. 2003; Gilman 2004). In situations in which automated irrigation is not feasible for street trees, soaker bags provide an effective way to maintain consistent moisture during establishment (Figure 8-11).

Irrigating Mature Plantings

Pop-up sprays are the most common heads for beds. With precipitation rates of 1.5 to 2 inches/ h (4 to 5 cm/h), water application rates far exceed the infiltration rates of even the most porous soils. A general strategy has evolved toward daily irrigation or every-other-day irrigation, often in conjunction with lawn irrigation systems. This is the case in spite of

Figure 8-11 Tree survival in areas without irrigation systems has been improved by using soaker bags like the one shown here.

a general consensus that shrubs and trees are more tolerant of drought than lawns and require less irrigation. Until recently, irrigators have had limited methods to reduce irrigation in bed areas other than using judgment based on personal experience. New head technology such as stream rotor nozzles for pop-up spray head bodies offers a chance to reduce precipitation rates significantly and help reduce runoff potential in shrub bed areas.

With the advent of weather-based controllers, it is now possible to irrigate based on evapotranspiration (ET). Evapotranspiration is the water lost from surface evaporation added to that lost from transpiration from plants. Using weather station data, computers calculate the daily ET and adjust the run times of controllers to match the total ET since the last irrigation event. Properly analyzed, ET is a fairly accurate measure of water use by plants. (For more information on ET measurements, see Chapter 9.) The use of calculated ET values to guide irrigation is an improvement, but there are still many obstacles that make efficient irrigation difficult. Some of these difficulties include excessive precipitation rates, poor system uniformity or unknown system uniformity, and unknown water requirements for most commonly used landscape plants.

Researchers have determined regionally accurate ET values for lawn grasses, but it has been difficult to measure water needs for landscape plants, although some research in this area has been conducted. Costello et al. (2000) used two methods to estimate water requirements for landscape plants in California.

One approach involves landscape coefficients and potential ET measurements, which are useful for estimating actual irrigation needs in landscapes. The other approach is Water Use Classification of Landscape Species (WUCOLS), which relies heavily on expert opinions based on field observations to categorize plant water requirements for 1900 plant species. Water needs are listed as low, medium, and high, and are used to delineate five regional climates. The WUCOLS ratings provide a useful guide for designers who want to create plant groupings with similar water needs.

While determining landscape plant water requirements depends on both art and science, accurately applying water in landscape beds may be an even greater challenge. Poorly designed landscapes that create awkward, difficult-to-irrigate areas (see Chapter 2) are among the problems landscape maintenance contractors must confront to meet this challenge. Poor system maintenance and poor decision making by irrigators add to the problems. Considering these factors, efficient irrigation is more than just knowing about plant water requirements.

In some cases, the most efficient way to irrigate landscape bed areas is drip irrigation. Improved water filtration and pressure-compensating in-line emitters have increased the practical value of drip irrigation in commercial landscapes. Water can be applied directly to the root zones of individual plants and is not wasted on bare areas, sidewalks, and roadways.

Reducing Irrigation in Landscape Beds

As simple as it sounds, the best way to reduce the amount of water used for irrigation is to apply less water. Tremendous strides have been made in determining plant water requirements through estimates of ET, and the irrigation industry has improved controllers and created a number of devices to prevent overwatering. Unfortunately, the industry's fascination with ET has inadvertently led to the assumption that irrigated woody landscape plants need regular systematic applications during the entire growing season simply because they use water. This assumption ignores the physiological ability of plants to tolerate drought, and that inevitably has led to overirrigation. This is even apparent in arid regions, where it is common to see mature landscapes planted with native drought-adapted plants being irrigated regularly. In many climates, landscapes will perform just fine with far less irrigation than they currently receive.

Improving Irrigation System Performance

Improving system performance starts with analyzing the irrigation system and studying the plants and the site conditions. Because pop-up spray irrigation systems are designed in the studio and installed when landscape plants are small (and not likely to interfere with water spray patterns), the first thing to investigate is how plant growth has affected water distribution. When mature plants obscure sprinkler throw (Figure 8-12), raise the sprinkler heads or move the heads to allow proper throw. Also straighten the heads and check and clean the nozzles and filters. On older systems, it may be best to systematically replace the nozzles.

Once the system has been adjusted, head pressures can be measured with pitot gauges, and in some situations, uniformity can be tested and precipitation rates can be measured. Where uniformity tests cannot be conducted, manufacturers' tables can be used to estimate precipitation based on nozzle and measured head pressures. If the landscape professional does not know how much water the system is applying, there is no way to apply the right amount of water.

Figure 8-12 Shrub bed irrigation is complicated by growth of plants in the bed. In this case, shrub foliage has distorted the spray pattern, rendering this head ineffective.

While adjusting landscape irrigation systems, it is useful to run adjacent lawn sprinkler systems to see how they are impacting the beds. Lawn sprinklers may have to be adjusted to prevent excessive overthrow into shrub beds. In shrub beds where precipitation rates are above 1.5 inches/h (4 cm/h), it may be worthwhile to change heads to stream rotors with similar throw but much lower precipitation rates. This is an all-or-none option because spray heads and rotor heads cannot be mixed due to different precipitation rates. Finally, study past irrigation programming and calculate how much water has been applied seasonally based on past run times and known precipitation rates. Consider cutting back on days irrigated or run times per irrigation.

For drip systems, check the entire system for line breaks or plugged emitters. With a little digging, it is possible to place containers under emitters to determine if actual drip rates match manufacturer's specifications. On new plantings, make sure emitters are close enough to the base of the plant to actually water the roots. This becomes irrelevant on most mature plants because they get water from shared emitters from adjacent plants or from adjacent lawn areas. Review run times from previous seasons and explore options for reducing days or run times for the upcoming season.

Adjust zone run times according to the type of plants, the bed microclimate, and the maturity of the plants. At some point, determine whether irrigation is even needed for the beds in question. Trees in beds often get all the water they need from surrounding lawn irrigation systems, and no direct irrigation is needed.

As the next irrigation season approaches, wait as long as possible before initiating irrigation. After the peak irrigation season is over, turn off shrub zones as early as possible. In cool temperate marine climates where irrigation is needed from June to early September, it is common to see irrigation systems running as early as March and as late as December. This wastes water and gives the industry a bad reputation.

PRUNING

Most pruning references focus on plant-centered pruning techniques. Plant-centered pruning is based on maintaining a plant's natural form and timing pruning to maximize flowering. Many books include pruning encyclopedias with specific tips on most of the important species (Brickell and Joyce 1996; Brown and Kirkham 2004).

Pruning Shrubs and Ground Covers in Commercial Landscapes

Pruning in commercial settings is always a challenge and reflects a host of limitations such as poorly articulated goals, lack of horticultural knowledge, inadequately trained workers, and constant pressure to reduce time spent on-site.

Commercial pruning of shrubs and ground covers is anything but plant centered. Normally, it focuses on size control and on creating a neat and tidy look at all times. Shrubs are often sheared into cubes, spheres, cylinders, spires, mounds, pom-poms, and any other three-dimensional objects the pruner can dream up (Figure 8-13). The appeal of shearing should be obvious: it is fast; involves little training;

Figure 8-13 In many cases, mindless shearing makes it impossible to determine what the designer was trying to achieve with the plant composition.

and requires virtually no knowledge of plant materials, growth habits, or flower habits. Unfortunately, many plants lose their charm when sheared, and many beautiful plant compositions fail to achieve the desired effect because differences in texture, size, and form do not develop. This situation is another disconnect among designers, owners, and maintenance companies that results in uninteresting and sometimes bizarre-looking landscapes. A more sustainable approach would have designers, owners, and maintenance personnel work together to articulate the design intent and determine an aesthetic and economical way to achieve it.

Pruning Trees in Commercial Landscapes

Tree maintenance in commercial landscapes runs the gamut from untouched, to sheared, to selectively pruned. Large boulevard trees or those in parklike settings are generally pruned selectively by arborists once the trees move beyond the establishment period. These trees are likely to be pruned in natural form except in countries where convention dictates pollarding or other nonnatural styles. Small trees below 15 feet (5 m) are likely to be pruned by landscape maintenance firms in styles ranging from sheared to natural form (Figure 8-14).

Pruning Strategies for Young Trees

Young trees may need regular pruning for 5 to 10 years after planting to develop desirable structure and form in the context of their surroundings. For example, boulevard trees need straight trunks and crowns high enough to provide clearance on adjacent roads and sidewalks. Trees in open areas may need high crowns on a straight trunk or may be allowed to retain lower branches and develop a dense canopy right down to ground level.

The general goal is to produce trees with strong branch attachments without included bark, good branch spacing, and crowns raised slowly to a height appropriate for the location in the landscape.

Figure 8-14 (a) Shearing small trees creates an almost surreal, cartoonish look. (b) Selective pruning produces a more natural look.

Excurrent Trees

Excurrent trees naturally develop a central leader, and many, such as tulip poplar (*Liriodendron tulipifera*) and sweet gum (*Liquidambar styraciflua*), have indeterminate growth. Training involves removing lower branches annually as needed to raise the crown gradually to its desired height (Figure 8-15). Additional annual pruning may be needed to remove competing leaders that may develop or to retrain leaders lost to injury or dieback. This is easy to do because the natural tendency of these trees is to grow with a single leader.

Decurrent Trees

Decurrent trees such as some oaks (*Quercus* spp.) and many maples (*Acer* spp.) naturally lose the terminal leader and develop into multileader trees. If a straight trunk is needed for any period of time, attention has to be paid during the training process. Vigorous trees may maintain a dominant leader for several years, but often competing leaders develop very quickly, making it impossible to develop the desired form. The goal is to maintain a single trunk up to the point where permanent scaffold branches will develop. At that point, emphasis shifts to selecting main branches that are strongly attached to the crown and allowing the natural growth habit to take over. The process is illustrated in Figure 8-16. In field situations, trees can be allowed to develop low crowns with major branches at or near ground level if that suits the desired appearance in the landscape.

Pruning Strategies for Shrubs and Ground Covers

There are several techniques commonly used in pruning shrubs.

Selective Pruning

Selective pruning involves removing a modest number of shoots annually to maintain an overall natural look, maintain a balance between old and new shoots, and manage size (Figure 8-17). Branches are pruned using point-of-origin, drop-crotch, and heading cuts (Figure 8-18).

Figure 8-15 Excurrent trees naturally tend to maintain central leaders. (a) Training involves raising the crown by removing low branches and (b) removing competing leaders when they develop in maturing trees.

Shearing

Shearing, as described earlier, involves trimming plants into geometric shapes using only heading cuts. Once started, shearing has to be done regularly in order to maintain rigid form. Shearing is appropriate for hedges but generally diminishes the beauty of most freestanding shrubs. It also results in a thin dense shell of foliage at the outer edge and a dead zone in the interior of the plant (Color Plate 8-5). Given the prominence of shearing in commercial landscapes, designers may want to rethink their planting schemes by choosing plants that are suited to shearing and have naturally slow growth rates.

Periodic Rejuvenation

Periodic rejuvenation involves cutting plants back near ground level in spring with heading cuts generally just as new growth begins or just after spring flowering shrubs have bloomed. Rejuvenation pruning can be used to create special effects, such as red stems in red twig dogwood (*Cornus sericea*), or to restructure a shrub whose form has been destroyed by shearing (Figure 8-19).

Figure 8-16 Decurrent trees tend to rapidly lose the central leader so regular pruning is needed. (a) Before pruning, numerous branches need to be removed. (b) After pruning, form is re-established. (c) The final goal is to make sure branches are strongly attached and spaced to avoid future structural problems.

Figure 8-17 Flowering shrubs like the bigleaf hydrangea (*Hydrangea macrophylla*) perform best when selectively pruned. (a) Good balance of young and older shoots after pruning leads to (b) attractive form and strong flowering.

Figure 8-18 (a) Thinning cuts remove branches at their point of origin, resulting in normal growth and form. (b) Heading cuts remove branches arbitrarily without regard to their point of attachment and always leave a stub. Regrowth is vigorous from buds located below the cut. Shearing is just frequent heading of all shoots. (c) Drop-crotch cuts remove the main shoot just above a lateral shoot of similar size oriented in the same direction as the parent shoot. Regrowth is intermediate between thinning and heading.

Annual Rejuvenation

Annual rejuvenation involves cutting shrubs back with heading cuts each spring and then allowing them to grow without additional pruning during the course of the growing season. In this case, plants can be pruned to the ground or to a permanent framework of branches chosen by the pruner. This is a useful technique for plants that flower in summer from newly developed shoots such as Bumald spirea (*Spiraea* × *bumalda*) (Color Plates 8-6a and b).

Periodic Mowing of Ground Covers

Periodic mowing of ground covers to keep the height down is a practice that should be used more often. Even low-growing ground covers will eventually begin to mound up on themselves and develop a vertical wall of sheared foliage around the edges topped by interior areas that look wild and unmanageable. The appearance is a little like a haircut, in which the sides are shaved off and the top is long.

Problems Associated with Questionable Pruning Decisions

Maintaining a balance between lower, middle, and upper branches is the key to a natural-looking shrub. Removing too many of the lower branches destroys the natural form and turns shrubs into small, ungainly trees that look top-heavy. Often the only solution is either to rejuvenate the plant or to replace it (Figure 8-20). When plants start to get too big, it is better to reduce the size by starting at the top and working down, leaving as many lower branches as possible. Once the lower branches have been removed, it is hard to get them back except by rejuvenation.

Figure 8-19 Red twig dogwood (*Cornus sericea*) responds to periodic rejuvenation. (a) This plant illustrates appearance after several years' growth without pruning. (b) The plant is cut down to the ground in spring. (c) After a season of regrowth, the new shoots show good winter color.

Waiting too long to prune conifers leads to the awkward quasi-bonsai shrubs seen so often in landscapes. Many conifers are essentially one-way plants because they are not able to produce new shoots when cut back to bare wood. Sheared conifers turn into blobs and lose the qualities that make them distinctive (Figure 8-21a). The key with most conifers is to prune regularly using point-of-origin and drop-crotch cuts throughout the entire canopy (Figure 8-21b). Once conifers get too big, they need to be removed and replaced.

The Impact of Construction and Design Decisions on Pruning

A common landscape construction problem involves laying out plants without consideration of the ultimate size of the plants placed near the perimeter (edge) of a planting area. While plantings may look good initially, it doesn't take long for those near edges to grow into walkways or over roadside curbs. When this happens, offending plants often get sheared off on the outfacing side (Figure 8-22). If the design

Figure 8-20 (a) This viburnum (*Viburnum* spp.) was disfigured by regular shearing. (b) A nearby plant that was cut to the ground in early spring grew back from crown buds to its natural form.

Figure 8-21 (a) Shearing conifers results in round blobs and destroys the character of the plants. (b) With practice, junipers and other conifers can be quickly pruned selectively and retain their natural attributes.

intent was to create a naturally growing cluster of one type of plant, the effect is lost. Parking strips that are narrow should have plants placed in the middle so once they grow they will naturally fit the space. If plants are staggered or planted on a grid, inevitably the edge plants will create pruning problems.

Why this is such a common problem is not clear. It could be an error on the part of the designer, who didn't think about the consequences of the layout scheme. Perhaps too many plants were specified for the area, and installers simply made sure all the plants were used. Possibly construction laborers

Figure 8-22 Plants located too close to the edge of the bed quickly encroach on sidewalks and are sheared to keep them out of people's way. The solution is to plant them farther from the edge of the bed.

were instructed to spread the plants evenly and fill the bed, which indicates poor training and lack of supervision. Figure 8-23 illustrates the impact of this problem.

Failure to articulate the design intent forces pruners to guess what the designer had in mind (Figure 8-24). After studying hundreds of commercial landscapes, we find it is often impossible to determine what (if anything) the designers were trying to accomplish. Difficulty in identifying the design intent is exacerbated when plants die en masse, further obscuring the composition. This leads to ever-expanding mulch beds and complete loss of the overall design (Color Plate 8-7).

Long-term pruning and general maintenance will improve when designers work together with maintenance and construction contractors during and after the planning and construction phases. Designers need to incorporate input from maintenance specialists regarding plant selection, placement, and long-term maintenance. Timely inspections during construction and follow-up annual reviews of maintenance will guide project development and will also improve the final product.

General Pruning Strategies

Mass plantings are created with the assumption that plants will grow into each other (Figure 8-25). One of the advantages of massing plants is less exposed ground and fewer niches for weeds to invade. The

(a)

(b)

Figure 8-23 (a) Junipers (*Juniperus* spp.) planted too close to the edge of the bed will quickly be sheared in order to keep them off the sidewalk. (b) The solution is to remove the entire row of plants next to the edge of the sidewalk and then selectively prune elongating shoots.

Pruning 155

(a)

(b)

Figure 8-24 (a) The natural look as the designer envisioned. (b) As interpreted by the pruning crew. Where was the breakdown in communication?

Figure 8-25 Densely planted beds help reduce inputs of mulch and herbicides and help reduce erosion and compaction.

goals are to keep the dense mass of plants while maintaining proportion to each other and controlling size as needed. Pruning is largely selective and involves thinning cuts (branches removed at points of origin) as needed to keep the planting in bounds. It may also involve periodic rejuvenation of overgrown plants or removal and replacement as needed. Avoid shearing at the perimeter of the planting unless it is part of the design intent. Periodic mowing of ground covers to keep height down may be warranted.

Some plantings may be intended to mimic desert vegetation and contain a mix of small trees and shrubs (Figure 8-26). The goal of this design concept is to allow specimen shrubs to grow naturally with minimal pruning. Pruning is largely selective or uses light shearing prior to major growth to control size but maintain a natural appearance. Specimen plants generally look best when they remain foliated from top to bottom. Avoid shearing individual plants into formal-looking geometric shapes because it ruins the natural desert look.

Defining the edge where ground covers meet sidewalks, curbs, or beds requires regular mechanical edging. If conventional vertical-blade edgers are used, the edge becomes hedged and looks unnatural (Figure 8-23a). Soft edges are created by using string trimmers, but it is easy to obliterate plants at the edges, resulting in a 6 to 8 inch (15 to 20 cm) wide area of exposed soil that looks odd and facilitates weed encroachment (Figure 8-27). Meanwhile, the ground covers themselves begin to build up higher and higher until they look more like shrubs. Ultimately, these become a pruning nightmare as it

Figure 8-26 (a) Desert plants have been randomly sheared with no thought to the overall appearance. (b) Plants have been allowed to grow more naturally, resulting in an attractive planting requiring less effort to maintain.

Figure 8-27 (a) Soft edging with string trimmers where beds meet lawns or curbs potentially looks more natural than hard edges, but often produces a ring of bare ground that looks ugly. (b) A combination of soft and hard edging with periodic mowing produces a more attractive edge.

is difficult to wade into the area to cut back stray shoots. This is a common problem with low-growing junipers (*Juniperus* spp.) and many cultivars of cotoneaster (*Cotoneaster* spp.).

One design strategy to reduce maintenance is to select ground covers that can be mowed periodically to control height buildup (Figure 8-27a). The key is to mow at least annually. This quasi-rejuvenation approach works best during the growing season rather than at the end of the season when regrowth is unlikely. Periodic selective pruning at edges will further reduce the buildup problem. Ground covers other than lawns look best when they appear to just reach the edge of the bed.

MANAGING THE WASTE STREAM

Debris generated from pruning, deciduous tree leaves, lawn clippings, and other organic waste materials, by convention, have been removed from maintenance sites. Decades ago, this material was routinely sent to landfills, where it contributed to excess volume, methane gas production, and leaching into soil. A current and somewhat more sustainable approach involves hauling green waste to local composting facilities for a fee and then repurchasing the finished compost for use in the landscape. Although this approach is a type of recycling, it consumes a great deal of time and energy loading and hauling debris and, ultimately, eats into profits. The advantage is that it allows contractors to leave each site looking neat and tidy at all times. As sustainable options for landscape maintenance are explored, it will be necessary to find better ways to handle the waste stream created from landscape management practices.

A better sustainable goal is to find ways to reduce the amount of waste removed from the site but not necessarily to eliminate it all at once. A 50 percent reduction in waste removal would be significant for most contractors. For example, as pointed out in Chapter 9, clippings can easily be returned to many lawn areas, eliminating a large component of green waste. Clipping removal can still be practiced in high-profile areas, which require higher aesthetic standards. Likewise, pruning debris can be chipped on-site and stored for aging at a discreet on-site location or can be immediately applied to beds that are in less prominent locations than the main entrance. Contractors complain that currently available chippers do not create a product attractive enough to spread on high-visibility beds. This poses an opportunity for chipper manufacturers to find ways to get a more acceptable chip with one pass through the chipper.

Managing Leaf Drop

Currently, deciduous tree leaves are collected and removed from all beds and lawns. While this results

Figure 8-28 When the main leaf drop occurs, use on-site disposal when possible. This area was infested with blackberries (*Rubus* spp.). After removal of vines, the deep mulch of leaves will help slow reinvasion.

in well-groomed landscapes, it is time consuming and costly. It also interferes with the natural organic matter decomposition cycles in bed areas and lawns. In many landscapes, there are beds where leaves can be concentrated without detracting from the site appearance (Color Plate 8-8). Likewise, mulch mowing leaves on lawns where feasible will help recycle leaf organic matter into the soil (Color Plate 8-9). At peak leaf drop, leaves can be collected and used for deep mulching beds or waste areas around parking lots where invasive plants such as blackberries (*Rubus* spp.) are often a problem (Figure 8-28). Designers can facilitate on-site recycling of leaves by including staging areas in discreet locations on corporate campus facilities that accommodate storage and handling of debris. With this practical approach, organic waste can be viewed as an asset rather than as a liability.

SUMMARY

Sustainable maintenance of commercial landscapes involves all parts of the landscape. Proper plant selection and thoughtful plant placement lead to better growth and reduced pruning needs as plants mature. Best planting techniques ensure long-term survival of plants and eliminate problems caused by distorted root systems, stake ties, or maintenance equipment. Intelligent use of fertilizer can speed the growth and vigor of young plants and increase plant survival. Irrigation may be necessary in most landscapes but is often used inefficiently. Sustainable irrigation requires careful system design, constant maintenance and upgrading, and a commitment to avoid overirrigation. Pruning is challenging in commercial landscapes due to lack of time, inadequate staff training, poorly articulated goals, and poor designs. Improved interaction among designers, owners, and maintenance contractors is needed to move away from indiscriminate shearing and toward site-appropriate pruning techniques. Improved waste management solutions should aim to leave waste on-site and incorporate it into the landscape rather than hauling it away to composting facilities or landfills. While challenges are many, so are opportunities for improvement in all aspects of commercial landscape care.

STUDY QUESTIONS

1. Explain the advantages and disadvantages of each of the following in terms of transplanting:
   a. Bare-root stock
   b. Balled-and-burlapped stock
   c. Container stock
2. Why might container plants suffer more from drought stress after planting than bare-root plants? How can this problem be avoided?
3. What is the logic for digging planting holes wide and bowl shaped?
4. Does it make sense to add organic matter to planting backfill soil in all cases? Are there exceptions? Is there anything wrong with adding organic matter?
5. In situations where soil is compacted or otherwise not suitable for planting, what are your options for improving the site?
6. What role do mycorrhizae play in the survival and growth of plants? Does it make sense to add mycorrhizae to planting soils? Explain.
7. If you plant a tree in a lawn and let the grass grow right up to the base of the tree trunk, what impact will the grass have on the growth and vigor of the tree? What is the obvious solution to this problem?
8. Staking is good because it ensures trees will stay straight until they are established. What can go wrong when trees are staked? What is the best way to approach staking?
9. Which is better for plant nutrition, mulch with a high carbon-to-nitrogen ratio or mulch with a low carbon-to nitrogen-ratio? Why?
10. Make a case for fertilizing young transplanted plants. Make a case for not fertilizing young transplants.
11. What is the best time of the year to fertilize? For how many years should plants be fertilized on a regular basis? Which element is most important for growth and color?
12. What is the difference between determinate and indeterminate growth in trees? How does growth style affect response to applied fertilizers?
13. What impact does irrigation of young transplants have on establishment and long-term plant vigor? Do all trees and shrubs require regular irrigation once they have matured? Will the answer to that question change in different regions?
14. What is WUCOLS? How can this system guide irrigation? What are its limitations?
15. What is the major obstacle to accurately irrigating bed areas? What can you do to remedy this problem?

16. What is plant-centered pruning? How does it differ from typical commercial site landscape pruning?
17. Why is indiscriminate shearing so prevalent in commercial landscape work? How can this be changed? Or can it?
18. What is the difference between excurrent and decurrent tree growth habits? How does growth habit affect the initial training and pruning of young trees? Is it important that all trees have a single central trunk? Explain.
19. Explain the basic approach to each of the following shrub pruning styles:
    a. Selective pruning
    b. Shearing
    c. Periodic rejuvenation
    d. Annual rejuvenation
20. How does shearing affect the impact of mass plantings and characteristics of individual plants?
21. A common pruning problem with many evergreens and conifers is the tendency to cut out all the lower shoots, which turns every plant into a small treelike structure. Why is this bad practice? How does it affect bed maintenance?
22. When conifers become overgrown or ugly from years of bad pruning, what is the best option? How can you go about rejuvenating most conifers? Explain.
23. How should ground cover plants be arranged in a planting bed to avoid future pruning problems?
24. How should ground cover beds be handled to avoid the tendency to hedge up the sides while leaving the top to grow wild and tangled? In planning a ground cover planting, what should you look for in selecting the plant material?
25. How can tree leaves be managed in fall to avoid removing them from the site?

Sustainable Lawn Care
Installation & Maintenance Practices for Northwest Professionals

Summary of recommended practices from "Ecologically Sound Lawn Care for the Pacific Northwest" – see that manual for more details and background science, available with "Natural Lawn Care" guide for residents at bottom of web-page: www.seattle.gov/util/ProIPM

Sustainable lawn care practices work with nature to create cost-efficient, healthy lawns. Northwest landscape professionals and scientists have developed and proven these methods on a variety of sites.

Benefits: healthier lawns, happier clients
- Reduced mowing time, water, and fertilizer needs
- Improved turf color, quality, and density
- Enhanced resistance to diseases and weeds
- Improved year-round nutrient availability
- Healthier for people, soil, waterways and wildlife
- Good for business: satisfied customers!

Note: this guide is for soil-based turf. While similar principals apply to sand-based sports turf, practices will differ. Grass species and dates here are for the Pacific Northwest region, west of the Cascades. For other regions, check your local Cooperative Extension publications (see Resources on back).

Key recommendations in this guide
- Realistic expectations: Northwest lawns are a meadow-green color, can have a few weeds, and are thick, wear-resistant and healthy.
- Assess sites to plan practices and soil improvement.
- Choose site-adapted grasses, and maintenance practices.
- Mow regularly: 2-3" on rye/fescue, 1-1½" on bentgrass).
- Mulch mow – leave clippings to improve soil, grass health, drought resistance, and reduce fertilizer needs.
- Test soil every 2-3 years, and correct any deficiencies.
- Fertilize only when needed, with natural organic or slow-release fertilizers – fall is the key time to fertilize.
- Irrigate deeply but less frequently to build deeper roots. Adjust timers for season and weather. Or let low-traffic turf go brown, watering only once each dry month.
- Renovate poor lawn areas with aeration, over-seeding, and compost topdressing. Or fix soil and replant.
- Use Integrated Pest, Weed & Disease Management.

Sustainable Lawn Care for Professionals – summary of Ecologically Sound Lawn Care © 1999 Seattle Public Utilities   revised 10/1/2013

Healthy lawns grow on healthy soil: Northwest lawn assessment

Lawn Care: An Ecosystem Approach

Like forests or prairie grasslands, lawns are dynamic ecosystems: communities of plants, soil, and microbes; insects and earthworms and the birds that feed on them; and humans who mow, water, fertilize, and play on lawns. The interactions of these community members shape the dynamic equilibrium we see as a lawn. Understanding and working within the natural processes that shape the lawn and its soil community can yield a durable, beautiful lawn that is easy to care for. As it turns out, these ecologically sound methods will also help reduce water use, waste, and pollution.

> **Use nature as your model**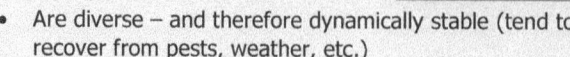
> Natural systems:
> - Recycle everything – water, waste, and nutrients – back into new life
> - Are diverse – and therefore dynamically stable (tend to recover from pests, weather, etc.)
> - Are defined by the resources (sun, soil, water) available on-site
> - Have inherent beauty: elegance, complexity, and balance

Set Expectations and Tolerance Levels

Lawn Color and Weeds: Aim for Healthy Good Looks
Sustainable practices start with educating customers about the value of a healthy, durable, good-looking lawn with:

- A meadow-green color. Dark green is a sign of over-fertilization and/or grass species that won't thrive here.
- Some broadleaf plants (aka "weeds"). Customer surveys show that dense healthy turf with 10-15% mow-able broadleaf plants is very acceptable. Clover is a beneficial nitrogen fixer; other plants such as lawn daisies, yarrow, etc. are included in "eco-lawn" mixes. Target the problem weeds; leave the rest.
- Reasonable mowing height. Mowing too short causes shallow rooting and weed invasion.

Assess Your Site to Plan Practices

Site Analysis: Sun, Soil, Drainage, Traffic & Use Zones
Start by drawing the site conditions, noting sun/shade, soil and drainage, and apparent traffic, wear or use patterns. Note zones that need higher appearance or maintenance, such as near entries, formal beds, or high traffic areas.

- **Sun** Most lawn grasses grow best in full sun to moderate shade. Light shade from deciduous trees may reduce summer water needs. Heavy shade from coniferous trees or buildings will never grow dense grass – alternate ground covers work better in heavy shade.

- **Slope** Moderate slopes work best for lawns, providing some surface drainage and a safe slope for mowing. 1%-6% slope is ideal (1-6 ft. drop in 100 ft. run), but up to 12% is mowable. Steep lawns are also difficult to water.

- **Drainage** Successful lawns have both surface drainage (some slope) and subsurface drainage so the soil doesn't stay waterlogged. Soils that stay saturated will never grow healthy grass – install subsurface drains or switch to a more wet-tolerant ground cover.

- **Visual Evaluation** Stand across the street to judge the lawn's overall condition, then move closer noting color or density variations, and problem weed areas.

- **Grass Species** Older lawns may be mostly bentgrass, which requires lower mowing (1-1½ inches) and less fertilizer. Low maintenance lawns may have a lot of annual bluegrass. Newer lawns are usually a blend of turf-type perennial ryegrasses and fine fescues, which should be mowed higher (2-3") and fertilized more.

- **Zones: Client Use and Appearance Needs** Areas near building entrances and high use areas will often need higher appearance and maintenance levels. Try to match maintenance zones to existing irrigation zones.

Test the Soil
Test soils on new sites and every 2-3 years to identify pH, salt or nutrient problems, and plan fertilizer, lime, water and compost applications. Sample each distinct zone or problem area. Collect several sub-samples in each zone and mix them in a labeled plastic bag (don't use metal containers). Follow sample size and labeling directions from your soil testing lab. Map and label your zones to track changes from year to year. **To find soil test labs, call the Garden Hotline at 206-633-0224.**

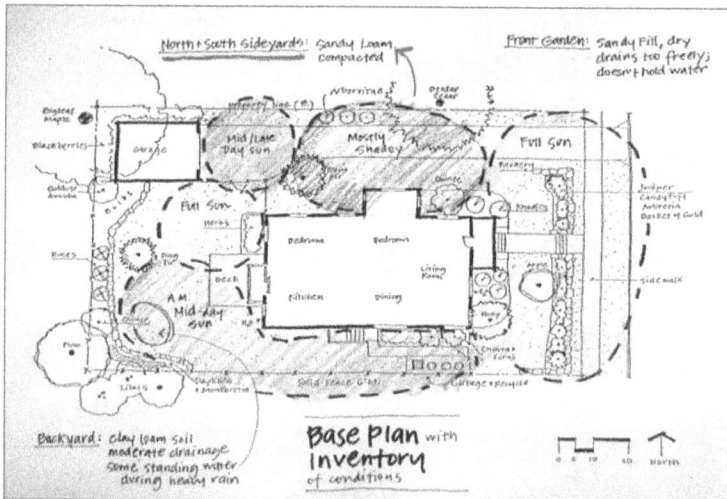

Example site plan, courtesy of Stenn Design

Sustainable Lawn Care: *Installation & Maintenance Practices for Northwest Professionals*

Evaluate Soil and Conditions

Pull several core samples from each lawn zone. Healthy soil is brown, crumbly and sweet smelling, showing deep root development and plenty of earthworms. Look for:

- Soil type (texture): sand, silt, or clay. Sandy soils drain well, but hold less water and nutrients so will need smaller, more frequent fertilization and irrigation. Clay and silt soils drain poorly but hold water and nutrients well. Organic matter improves both sand and clay soils.
- Soil color and odor: tan to brown with sweet smell is healthy; light color indicates low organic; blue or grey with sour smell indicates water-logging or poor aeration.
- Organic-rich (brown horizon) extending at least 6" deep.
- Soil structure: crumbly, with plenty of air space.
- Root development extending at least 6 inches deep, with dense branching and healthy (white to tan) color.

Visual evaluation of lawn condition in different areas, combined with probing soil conditions with a T-handled soil core sampler or shovel, will help you determine lawn restoration and maintenance plans, priorities, and costs.

Common Lawn Problems and Solutions

Lawn Signs	Possible Problems	Potential Solutions
Overall yellowish, thin lawn with many weeds	Unhealthy, infertile soil (sometimes also overwatering and mowing too short).	Soil improvement practices include compost topdressing & aeration, mulch-mowing, and organic fertilization.
Yellow or brown patches	Dog urine damage, fertilizer burn, mower scalping, disease or insect damage.	Water, proper fertilization and mowing height will cure the first three. Use IPM approach to verify disease or insect damage.
Shallow roots (less than 6"), weak root development	Over-frequent watering or drainage problems, shallow soils over hardpan or subsoil, compacted soil, excess thatch.	Correct drainage problems and irrigation frequency. Use all the methods in this guide to improve soil health, structure, and reduce thatch.
Standing water, blue or grey soil, heavy clay, abundance of wet-loving weeds such as buttercup	Poor drainage, causing anaerobic (low oxygen) soil conditions that result in poor lawn rooting and growth and invasion by wet-tolerant species.	Correct subsurface drainage by installing drain tile system, or plant a ground cover that tolerates constantly wet conditions. Correct soil drainage with deep-tine aeration through compost topdressing to "open up" heavy soils (improve structure).
Light-colored soil	Low organic matter.	Organic matter provides homes and food for the billions of beneficial soil organisms. Compost amend or topdress soil.
Hard, compacted soil	Heavy traffic, poor soil structure (possibly from overuse of chemicals resulting in loss of earthworms and soil life), "hardpan" soil.	Spread out traffic. Reduce soluble fertilizer and pesticide use. Aerate and topdress with compost spring and fall until turf improves, or tear out lawn to deeply amend soil, then replant.
No earthworms or other beneficial soil organisms	Overuse of pesticides and soluble fertilizers, or very poorly drained (anaerobic) soils.	Soil life will return over 1-2 years with proper management. Earthworms working the soil aerate, improve drainage, recycle thatch and grass clippings, and build soil microbial life that promotes drought/disease resistance and lush lawns.
Excess thatch (fibrous material) build-up at soil surface (more than ½ inch)	Thatch is grass roots, stems, and stolons that haven't broken down, caused by over-watering, over-fertilization, compacted soils. Bentgrass creates thatch when overfertilized, and false crowns when mowed too high.	Change irrigation and fertilization practices as described in this guide. Switch to grasscycling (mulch-mowing) which helps break down thatch. Mow bentgrass at 1¼" or below and reduce fertilization. If thatch layer is more than 1" thick, mechanically remove it with a de-thatcher or heavy aeration.
Noticeable brown patches in early spring, with heavy feeding on lawn by birds in winter	European crane fly larvae are ¾" long gray-brown grubs called "leatherjackets". This recent invader is only a problem when numbers exceed 25/sq. ft. in late winter.	European crane fly larvae are the only significant insect problem in Northwest lawns. Birds will get most of them during the winter. Stopping lawn irrigation in August-September kills many of the eggs laid at this time. Fertilize and overseed damaged areas in early spring – the lawn will recover.
Moss in lawn	Site is too shady for grass to compete, and/or soil is acidic, compacted, infertile, and poorly drained or overwatered.	Reduce shading and overseed with more shade-tolerant fescue species (or replace with a more shade-tolerant ground cover). Spread lime to correct pH and provide calcium, and iron products to retard moss and promote grass. Use balanced organic fertilizers to help grass compete.
Various grey, white, or red patches (See IPM, page 5)	Turf diseases are common in sand-based short-mowed turf, but on soil-based turf only appear in lawns that are over-fertilized, over-watered, poor soil, or wrong grass species for this region (except for red-thread, which indicates low soil nitrogen availability).	Grasscycling (mulch-mowing), deeper less frequent watering, moderate fall fertilization with organic or slow-release products, and soil-building with compost: these practices all make it harder for disease organisms to compete with the many beneficial bacteria and fungi in the soil and endophytic mycorrhizal fungi in the grasses.

Sustainable Lawn Care: Installation & Maintenance Practices for Northwest Professionals

Maintenance Practices for Healthy Lawns

Maintenance Zones

Identify maintenance zones to match use and client needs. Areas near building entrances often need a higher appearance standard (for instance blowing off clippings after mulch-mowing). High wear areas may also need more attention. Try to match maintenance zones to existing irrigation system zones, adjusting schedules to meet the zone's appearance objectives. Work with clients to identify reasonable expectations for appearance and maintenance standards in different zones (see page 2).

Mowing

Mow higher, mow regularly, and leave the clippings. Mowing higher lets grass grow denser, develop deeper roots, and shade out weeds.

- Rye/fescue lawns: mow at 2-3" (lower will thin the lawn).
- Bentgrass lawns: mow at 1-1½" (above 1¼" bentgrass forms false crowns and grows sideways).
- Slow-grow, meadow, and Eco-lawn mixes are usually mowed above 3" and mowed less frequently, depending on the blend of species.

Mow weekly in spring through early summer, then every 10 days to two weeks through fall. Mow shorter on the last fall mowing (or same time as fall fertilization). Spring growth flush (and thus need to mow more frequently) can be reduced by only fertilizing in the fall, or delaying spring fertilization until May 15.

Mulch mowing builds healthier lawns, saves time and money. Science and northwest professionals' experience agree: mulch mowing ("grasscycling" – leaving the clippings) increases turf density, rooting depth, spring green-up, and summer drought and disease resistance. It saves time bagging and hauling clippings, and saves money by cutting fertilizer needs by 25-50%.

Tips for successful grasscycling:

- Mow when grass is drier, and more frequently in spring.
- Raise mowing heights during the spring growth flush, then lower gradually to normal height in June.
- If clumps appear, mow back over to scatter them – this still saves time over bagging.
- Blow any clippings off lawn surface near building entrances or other high visibility areas, for appearance and to reduce tracking into building. Blow off pavement.
- Reduce fertilization (grasscycling returns at least half the lawn's needs) especially in early spring: wait until May15.
- **Keep mower blades sharp** for clean turf appearance, lawn health, and mulch-mowing success.

Shopping for professional mulching mowers

Good mulching mowers use a combination of deck design and blades with wavy shape and longer sharp edge to recirculate clippings and chop them finely. They blow the resulting mulch down into the turf so it's not visible and is broken down within days by earthworms and soil organisms, returning nutrients to the grass roots within weeks.

Look for:

- Mowers with 20% more power for the deck size: mulching is extra work. Hydrostatic drives adapt well to changing torque requirements of taller grass areas.
- Mowers meeting Cal EPA pollution standards. 4-stroke engines are cleaner, quieter, with a wider torque range. Professional battery electric mowers also exist.
- Easy adjustment of deck height – raising the deck slightly on the fly if clumps appear is a key strategy for spring.
- Easy conversion to bagging – you may never need it, but if lawns are overgrown, bagging once or twice can help. Bagging is also useful for fall leaf collection (reuse those chopped leaves as mulch on beds to control weeds).
- Best mulching performance, especially in wet conditions. Ask other professionals, read reviews, and then test mowers in wet conditions: the best will leave an almost clean surface even in the rain, whereas some mowers sold as "mulch-ready" actually perform poorly. The best mowers really mulch cleanly, year-round.

Fertilizing for Lawn Health

"Feed the soil, not the plant" – key principles:

- Mulch mowing returns most nutrients needed. It feeds the soil life that creates soil structure and stores and recycles nutrients into plant-available forms when needed, increasing lawn rooting depth and density.

- Fall is the key time to fertilize, to build root reserves during slow fall and winter growth. If also fertilizing in spring, use very low nitrogen with iron for early green-up. Delay N application until growth slows in mid-May. This will reduce spring top growth and mowing time.

- The grass species that grow well west of the Cascade Mountains are naturally a meadow-green color. Don't try to fertilize to a dark green color.

- For healthier lawns, apply just enough nitrogen (for the grass species) to promote dense turf and prevent yellowing. Over-fertilization promotes disease, thatch buildup, and excessive top growth (so more mowing).

- Slow-release fertilizers, either from natural organic or non-soluble synthetic formulations, provide longer, better grass nutrition, and are less toxic to beneficial soil life than soluble "quick-release" synthetics. If soluble products are used, they should be "spoon fed" at low application rates. Slow-release products last longer and don't wash away in the rain, saving $ and protecting our waterways.

- Soil testing (every 2-3 years) is the basis for defining a sustainable fertilization program. Depending on soil availability, lawns need an N-P-K (nitrogen-phosphorus-potassium) balance of 3-1-2 or 6-1-4.

- Phosphorus is a serious water pollutant, and many western Washington soils are high in phosphorus. So a 2011 Washington law, HB 1489 prohibits application of phosphorus-containing fertilizers to lawns without a soil test within the last 3 years showing phosphorus deficiency. Compost is exempted from this ban, as are fertilizers used for newly planted or overseeded lawns.

- Lawn grasses need calcium (often leached out in rainy regions) and a moderate pH, so liming every three years is recommended – soil tests will indicate amounts.

How Much? With grasscycling on healthy soil, rye/fescue lawns will need 1-2 lb. N/1000 sq. ft. per year in a balanced organic or slow-release synthetic fertilizer. High-wear ryegrass turf needs a little more. Most should be applied in the fall, with optional mid-spring application. Bentgrass lawns need 1 lb. or less per year. Adjust fertilization based on soil tests and observing lawn condition. See Calendar on back for dates. Apply with a drop-spreader for accuracy, and sweep fertilizer off pavement to reduce water pollution.

Watering

Irrigating for lawn health: deep, slow, less frequent

Grasses are adapted to intermittent dry-season rains, and develop deeper roots with fewer disease problems when the whole root depth is moistened, and then allowed to almost dry out before watering again.

Check sprinkler uniformity by putting out tuna cans and irrigating until 1 inch of water accumulates – that's how much Puget Sound lawns need each week in the hottest weather. Another option on low-traffic lawns is to let them go brown and dormant, watering deeply only once each rainless month to keep crowns alive.

Check running systems monthly, and repair or redirect heads as needed.

Add rain shutoff devices to sprinkler systems. Adjust schedules to reduce irrigation in the cooler early summer and fall months. Learn about irrigation scheduling and get local evapotranspiration information at www.IWMS.org

Integrated Pest Management: Preventive Health Care for Lawns

Healthy lawns crowd out excessive weed growth, out-grow occasional insect damage, and resist diseases. See page 3 for a few common problems and solutions.

If needed, weed control methods include manual control, spot-spraying with least-toxic herbicides, and application of natural products such as corn gluten which inhibits weed seed germination.

Integrated Pest Management (IPM) includes these steps:

1) Correctly identify pests and understand their life cycles.
2) Establish tolerance thresholds: accept some pests/weeds.
3) Monitor to detect and prevent pest problems.
4) Modify maintenance to promote health and reduce pests.
5) If pests (weeds etc.) exceed tolerance threshholds, use cultural, physical, mechanical, or biological controls first. If those prove insufficient, use the least-toxic chemical control and application method that has the least non-target impact, at the most effective time.
6) Evaluate and record the effectiveness of the control, and modify maintenance practices to support lawn recovery and prevent recurrence.

Learn more about specific weed and disease identification and control strategies in the Pro IPM factsheets and in the manual this short guide is based on, *Ecologically Sound Lawn Care for the Pacific Northwest*, both available at www.seattle.gov/util/ProIPM or see Resources on back.

Sustainable Lawn Care: Installation & Maintenance Practices for Northwest Professionals

Renovate: Restore an Old Lawn to Top Condition

Lawn areas that are thin, weedy, or wear-damaged can be renovated to bring them back to health. Renovation practices can fit into the regular maintenance cycle. Renovate in spring (April to mid-May) and/or fall (September to mid-October):

1) **Aerate** Reduce soil compaction, let in air and water, and make spaces to fill with compost by core aerating. Several kinds of larger, tractor-mounted aerators can be used to break up deeper compaction. Leave the cores for organic matter – drag or mow low to break them up.

2) **Overseed** Rake to expose the soil surface. Seed-to-soil contact is essential for good germination. Spread a site-appropriate grass type (see page 7) at 50% of the new lawn coverage rate.

3) **Topdress with compost** Spread ¼ to ½ inch of compost to fill aeration holes and cover the seed. On sand-based turf spread a sand/ compost mix. Hand scatter compost, or use a drop spreader or turf topdressing machine. Rake in compost to fill aeration holes, and to stand up the grass blades through compost layer. Many professionals find that aerating, spreading compost, and then re-aerating through the compost will help incorporate more organic matter into the soil.

Thatch removal (optional) Proper mowing, fertilization and irrigation generally prevents thatch buildup. But on lawns with more than a 1-inch thatch layer, mechanical thatch removal with a de-thatcher or aerator can be useful.

Weed control (optional) These renovation practices will thicken lawns, help grasses compete, and reduce weeds over time. But sometimes the client or location dictates a faster improvement. A one-time spot treatment of problem weeds will help the grass fill in. Use a broadleaf selective herbicide applied directly to the weeds 1-2 weeks before the renovation practices above. Never use "weed & feed" combination products – they are less effective, put chemicals where they aren't needed, damage beneficial soil life, and can wash off easily, harming birds, fish, lakes and streams.

Reasons to Tear Out & Re-install Lawns

Sometimes it's most efficient to re-install a lawn to fix soil problems or other conditions. Reasons to tear out a lawn, amend the soil, and replant include:

- Lawn is over 50% weeds with poor soil conditions.
- Grass species are inferior, not thriving, or disease prone.
- Soil is deeply compacted (more than 2"), low in organic matter, or with hardpan or subsoil within 6" of surface.
- Soil surface is very uneven, or poorly graded for drainage.
- Sub-surface drainage needs to be installed.
- Owner wants and is willing to pay for a rapid improvement.

Sustainable Lawn Care: Installation & Maintenance Practices for Northwest Professionals

Installing New Lawns

Size and Location: How Much is Enough?
Lawns only grow well on well-drained, sunny, moderately sloped sites, and they require frequent maintenance. Talk with clients about where they want lawn for play or appearance, and consider other landscape treatments for sites where lawns won't grow well or are not needed.

Site Requirements: Drainage, Slope, & Sun
If the site is poorly drained, re-grade, install subsurface drainage, or choose a more wet-tolerant ground cover. Place lawns in full sun to moderate shade, on moderately sloped areas (ideally 1%-6% slope, 12% maximum).

Soil Preparation
Unless high quality organic-rich soil already exists, plan to amend and prepare soils:

- Minimum amendment is 2 inches of compost mixed into the upper 6-8 inches of soil. A better installation includes 3-4 inches of compost mixed into the upper 12 inches. Buy compost from a US Composting Council "STA" certified (Seal of Testing Assurance) producer, or verify it is weed-free, mature and stable with a C:N ratio of 20:1-25:1 if not an STA supplier. Use somewhat less compost in heavy clay soils, and somewhat more to amend sand.

- Rake out rocks over 1" diameter.

- Roll lightly to settle, and grade surface well so there are no high or low spots that cause mower scalping.

- Purchasing topsoil is usually not needed – the site soil amended with compost will provide a more sustainable long-term growing environment with deeper root development. Where site soil is too rocky for a lawn surface, rake in 1" of imported topsoil to create the final seedbed, mixing it with underlying amended soil.

Seed Selection
Use a blend of fine fescues and turf-type perennial ryegrasses for Northwest lawns, west of the Cascade Mountains. Fescues are more shade tolerant; ryegrasses tolerate wear but need more fertilizer. Buy from a local, reputable seed supplier, and ask about special blends for higher, less frequent mowing, shade, meadows, etc. Some grasses are pre-inoculated with natural mycorrhizal fungi that increase drought and disease resistance.

Seed or Sod: Pros and Cons
Prepare the soil exactly the same way for seeding or sodding. Sod is quick, but seeded lawns on well-prepared soil usually develop deeper root systems.

Seeding and Care of Young Turf
Ideally, seed in spring or early fall to reduce heat stress. Spread seed twice, at half-rate each time, for uniform coverage. Rake in seed, or cover lightly with compost or topsoil. Compost-amended soil will provide all nutrient needs for the first year, so additional fertilizer is usually not needed. Water newly planted lawns daily in dry weather from germination until 1" high, then every 2-3 days until mowing height is reached. Water weekly through the first summer, to establish a deep root system.

Lawn Alternatives
"Eco-lawn" grass-and-broadleaf seed mixes are becoming increasingly popular in the Northwest. First developed at Oregon State University, they include clovers, daisies, yarrow and other mowable plants, and require higher less frequent mowing and lower fertilization. Just including clover (white, strawberry, or other turf-compatible clovers) in a grass seed mix will reduce nitrogen fertilizer needs. Other alternatives include moss lawns for deep shade, and a wide variety of ground covers for sites where grass won't grow because of shade or poor drainage, or where a lower maintenance ground cover is preferred.

Sustainable Lawn Care: Installation & Maintenance Practices for Northwest Professionals

Calendar of Recommended Lawn Maintenance Practices for the Puget Sound Region

This calendar presents a range of practices, from the minimal maintenance for a healthy lawn to the extra practices that will maintain a high lawn appearance year-round. Additional practices useful on high wear turf such as soil-based playfields are summarized in the third column. These dates are for Puget Sound – please adapt for use east of the Cascades. Each site is unique. The keys to developing an ecologically sound plan for maintenance are careful observation of grass growth, soils, and site characteristics, and a willingness to experiment, learn, and work *with* the natural processes that sustain the lawn ecosystem.

	Low maintenance lawns	*extra practices for* Higher appearance lawns	*additional practices for* High wear turf
Jan. & Feb.	**Sharpen mower blades**, tune up equipment. Plan spring improvements.	Observe thin or damaged areas of lawn – make plans to repair in spring. Test soils.	**Test soils**, and use results to plan annual fertilization & amendments.
Mar.	Correct drainage problems, or consider replacing poorly-drained lawn areas with more wet-tolerant plantings. **Begin mulch-mowing**.	Monitor for crane fly, and red thread disease. **Get soil test every 2-3 years to plan fertilization**. Apply lime if needed, now or in the fall.	**Aerate** regularly through use season. Limit traffic on soggy soil. Look for and correct surface or sub-surface drainage problems.
April	**Leave clippings on lawn all year**. Mow at 2 to 2½ inches on rye/fescue lawns, or 1-1½ inches on bentgrass. Rake thin lawn areas to expose soil and then overseed.	On thin areas, aerate, overseed, and top-dress with compost in spring, fall, or both. If thatch is 1 inch or more thick, dethatch. Test and repair irrigation systems.	**Overseed thin or weedy areas with each aeration**. Locally-adapted perennial ryegrasses stand heavy wear best, but need more fertilizer.
May	Pull (or spot spray) dandelions and other problem weeds to prevent spread.	**Fertilize** (½-1 lb.N) mid to late May when growth slows. Remove weeds April-June. **Use mulching mower** year-round.	Mulch-mow as much as possible throughout the whole growing season.
June	Mow regularly (weekly) until lawn goes brown and dormant. **Limit wear on dormant lawns**.	Mow high (2-2½ inches) and often; leave clippings on lawn. Skip an irrigation cycle when it rains.	**Check irrigation systems** at season's start, to verify uniform coverage with no runoff. Observe and repair heads monthly.
July	If letting lawn go brown & dormant, water slowly & deeply once each rainless month.	Water deep and slow, 1 inch each rainless week. (Sandy soils need more frequent.)	**High wear turf must be irrigated all summer**. Aerate if use is heavy.
Aug.	Mow every 2 weeks on dormant lawn to limit dandelion spread.	Set irrigation to run before dawn to limit disease. Let soil dry between waterings.	Adjust irrigation weekly to heat (evapo-transpiration) and observed grass need.
Sept.	When rains come, rake & **overseed** thin areas. Aerate if compacted. Pull weeds.	**Fertilize** with natural fertilizer (1-2 lb. N /1000 ft²) Sept. to Oct.15th. Pull weeds.	**Renovate** early to mid-fall depending on use (aerate, overseed, topdress).
Oct.	For poor soils/poor lawns, topdress with compost now and/or in April to improve.	**Renovate**/replace lawns from Sept. 1st to Oct. 15th. Aerate, overseed, topdress.	If renovation is not planned, overseed to crowd out weeds, & de-thatch if needed.
Nov.	**Fertilize** September through Oct. 15th with natural fertilizers (1 lb. N/1000 ft²).	**Fertilize** by Oct. 15 with natural fertilizers; or until Nov. 30 with synthetic slow-release	Continue aerating through playing season.
Dec.	**Rake leaves off lawn, or mulch-mow in**. Mow down to 1½ inch on last mowing.	Birds feeding heavily on lawn in fall signal need to monitor for crane fly in spring.	Limit traffic on frozen grass or saturated soils.

For more information contact the Garden Hotline: 206-633-0224 *help@gardenhotline.org*

Resources: WSU Cooperative Extension: http://www.puyallup.wsu.edu/turf/ and http://gardening.wsu.edu/lawns/

Sustainable Landscape Management (2011) by Thomas W. Cook & Ann Marie VanDerZanden

Ecologically Sound Lawn Care for the Pacific Northwest (1999) Manual this summary guide is based on – includes more detail on recommended practices and sources – see link at bottom of page: www.seattle.gov/util/ProIPM

IPM workshops, and factsheets on specific problems and solutions www.seattle.gov/util/ProIPM

Safer products www.GrowSmartGrowSafe.org EnviroStars business certification www.EnviroStars.org

WA Sustainable Landscape Professional certification – search that title at www.wsnla.org

Alternative formats available on request
Voice 206-633-0224, TTY 206-233-7241

Created by:  Seattle Public Utilities

as part of the  Local Hazardous Waste Management Program in King County, Washington

Sustainable Lawn Care: Installation & Maintenance Practices for Northwest Professionals

ProIPM
Integrated Pest Management Solutions for the Landscaping Professional

Welcome to ProIPM, the Green Gardening Program's series of quick reference IPM fact sheets for landscaping professionals. We designed this series both to assist you in the field and to explain to your clients the IPM approach you use on their landscapes. Each sheet in the series gives you the essential facts you need to know about an important Northwest pest or disease problem: identification, life cycle, monitoring, damage threshold, and treatments. Use these fact sheets for easy reference, and feel free to hand them out to your clients as well. We have also included sample monitoring records for your use. Please feel free to photocopy these monitoring sheets if you need additional copies. **These fact sheets are available at www.seattle.gov/util/ProIPM**

IPM Steps
1) Correctly identify the pest (weed, insect, disease, etc.) and understand its life cycle.
2) Establish tolerance/action thresholds: accept some pests, weeds etc.
3) Monitor regularly to detect pest problems.
4) Modify maintenance program to promote plant health and discourage pests.
5) If pests exceed tolerance/action threshold, use cultural, physical, mechanical or biological controls first. If those prove insufficient, use the least-toxic chemical control and application method with least non-target impact, at the most effective time.
6) Evaluate & record effectiveness of control, and modify maintenance or plant choices to support recovery and prevent recurrence.

What is IPM? Integrated Pest Management (IPM) is an approach to pest control that utilizes regular monitoring to determine if and when treatments are needed. IPM employs physical, mechanical, cultural, biological and educational tactics to keep pest numbers low enough to prevent intolerable damage or annoyance. Chemical controls are used as a last resort, and the least-toxic chemicals are preferred. IPM originated in the late 1950s out of research to find predators for introduced agricultural pests. In the intervening years, IPM has evolved and gained acceptance in non-agricultural pest control as well. Now it is widely recognized and utilized in landscaping and structural pest control, as well as agriculture.

Why Use IPM? IPM protects the natural enemies that help to keep pests in check and avoids unnecessary chemical use that may endanger human health and the environment. IPM has been gaining acceptance worldwide and is now mandated by many governmental agencies. For example, IPM has dramatically reduced pesticide use in our National Parks, while maintaining effective pest control. IPM represents the future for the landscaping industry because it is the best long term solution to pest management and plant health. Demand for IPM services is increasing as concern over pesticides grows. Companies that provide IPM services are in an excellent position to prosper in the future. When a client hires an IPM practitioner, they receive expertise, careful monitoring, and labor-intensive cultural practices instead of just chemicals.

What's wrong with a calendar-based spray service? If insecticides and fungicides are applied to the landscape at regular intervals, won't this reduce pest problems? People tend to think of these sprays as "booster shots", as a practice that helps keep plants invulnerable to problems. These calendar sprays, however logical they may seem, are generally ineffective at reducing plant problems. Why?

Most plant difficulties, over 2/3 of them, aren't caused by any living pathogen. They result from soil conditions, watering practices, nutrient imbalance, heat, freezing, or other cultural problems. Sprays, designed to kill living organisms like fungal spores and insects, are wasted on these problems.

If a pathogen or pest is present, it must be treated at the correct time during its life cycle. Many fungal diseases, dogwood anthracnose for instance, require fungicide treatment very early in the season as leaf and flower buds begin to open and at 10 day intervals until full leaf. If a calendar fungicide spray were used on March 15 and June 15, the March 15 spray might be too early and the June 15 spray would undoubtedly be too late. Scale insects, common on many fruit trees and landscape plants, are vulnerable to treatment with insecticides when the eggs hatch into "crawlers" but not at other stages in the life cycle. Remember, disease organisms and insects grow with light, temperature, and moisture, not by watching the calendar.

Spraying every plant in the garden endangers beneficial insects and birds. Broad-spectrum sprays, such as many insecticides, kill many different types of insects, including the larval and adult lady bug, a great muncher of aphids. Healthy, balanced landscapes provide food and shelter for many different creatures. Timed sprays applied to plants "just in case" actually make problems worse when they kill beneficials. *Even if some pests are present, treatment may not be needed.* Most plants can tolerate some damage and just "grow out of it." Using sprays unnecessarily wastes time, money, and materials, but its primary problem is the disruption of a natural garden ecosystem.

Learning when and how to manage garden problems requires more effort and attention than simply spraying by a schedule. See factsheets on monitoring and specific problems and solutions at **www.seattle.gov/util/ProIPM**

(continued on back page)

Fertilizers and IPM

Plants need nutrients in order to grow, and healthy plants are better able to withstand pest and disease attacks. Although some plant species can remain healthy using only the food naturally present in the soil, most plants in home landscapes require at least some additional nutrients. These extra nutrients are provided by soil amendments such as compost and fertilizer. Although not pest controls themselves, fertilizers do affect a plant's susceptibility to pests and diseases, and they can have effects on the environment as well. So the choice of when and how to fertilize is an important component of IPM. The three most important practices for lawn and garden fertilizers are: don't over-fertilize, use slow-release fertilizers, and avoid fertilizer/herbicide mixtures.

Don't over-fertilize. Applying too much fertilizer is harmful in two ways. First, it over-stimulates plant growth. In the case of turf, rapid growth means more mowing and more thatch buildup. Overfertilization can increase aphid problems in susceptible plants, too. The second problem with excess fertilizer is that it can leach or run off into surface water or ground water. For turfgrass, WSU Cooperative Extension recommends no more than 4 pounds of nitrogen per 1000 square feet of lawn per year. This amount of nitrogen can be spread out over four separate applications. Up to one-third to one-half of this nitrogen can be supplied by grasscycling (leaving the clippings), reducing the need for commercial fertilizer.

Use slow-release fertilizers. Slow release fertilizers are designed to provide a slow, steady supply of nutrients. They can be either naturally derived (organic) or synthetically derived. Slow release fertilizers are generally not very soluble in water, so they are less likely to pollute water by runoff or leaching. Top dressing with compost provides soil fertility and helps increase water retention. For turfgrass, WSU recommends a 3-1-2 (N-P-K) ratio. Controlled release fertilizers are preferred to water soluble fertilizers.

Avoid fertilizer/herbicide mixtures (such as "weed and feed" products). Fertilizers with built in weed control are popular because they are convenient, but they are not recommended by WSU Cooperative Extension or the Green Gardening Program. These products are designed to be used whether or not a weed problem exists, and they are broadcast over the entire lawn area. That approach short-circuits the IPM process by ignoring the monitoring step, assuming a zero tolerance for weeds, and not targeting the pest problem. The herbicide ingredients in weed and feed mixtures are highly mobile and inclined to move with water. We suggest keeping fertilization separate from weeding, so that each component can be performed in the optimal manner. Weeds should be removed mechanically if possible, or spot treated with the most appropriate chemical if mechanical methods are impractical. Some tolerance for weeds helps to minimize chemical use.

Disposal of Pesticide Products

Unwanted pesticide products are considered hazardous wastes. They must either be used up as directed (provided the products are still currently registered) or disposed of at a hazardous waste collection facility. Disposal down the drain or in the trash is illegal in Washington State, despite instructions to the contrary on many product labels.

Residents can dispose of unwanted household pesticides free of charge in King County. Collection sites available include the South Transfer Station, the North Seattle and Factoria Haz Sites, or the roving Wastemobile. For information regarding times of operation, location and products accepted, see the website below or call the **Household Hazards Line at 206-296-4692**.

Pesticides generated by small businesses may eligible for disposal at some household hazardous waste sites. For information on hazardous waste disposal for businesses, call the **Business Waste Line at 206-263-8899**. Disposal information for both households and small and large businesses is available at www.LHWMP.org

What is the Green Gardening Program?

The Green Gardening Program is sponsored by Seattle Public Utilities and the Local Hazardous Waste Management Program in King County. The program promotes environmentally-sensitive landscaping practices, with particular emphasis on reducing pesticide use, conserving water, and reusing/recycling landscaping waste. Green Gardening activities have included slide show presentations and brochures for homeowners, professional trainings and resources for landscapers, designers, and nursery staff, and garden tours. For more information, call the Green Gardening Program at 206-343-9759, extension 101.

See the ProIPM factsheets at www.seattle.gov/uitl/ProIPM
Questions about a landscape pests, problems and solutions?
Call the Garden Hotline 206-633-0224, or email *help@gardenhotline.org*

Introduction to the ProIPM factsheet series www.seattle.gov/util/ProIPM *rev. 1/2013*

Plant Health Care (PHC) & Integrated Pest Managment (IPM) flowchart

BASICS OF NATURAL PEST CONTROL

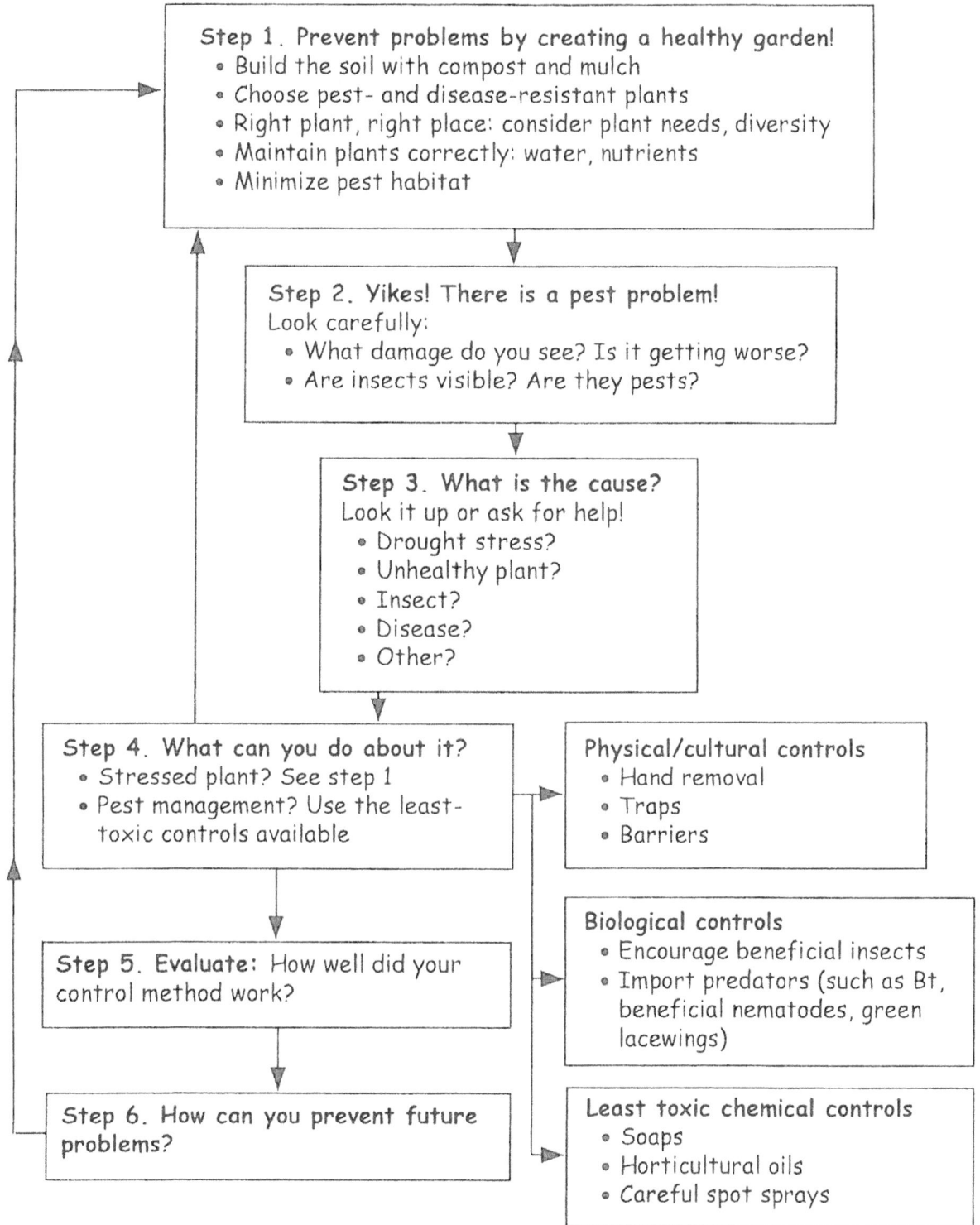

Created by Sage Environmental for the **Green Gardening Program**.
Seattle Public Utilities sponsors the Green Gardening Program in an effort to promote alternatives to pesticides.
Funded by the Local Hazardous Waste Management Program in King County.

www.GrowSmartGrowSafe.org/NaturalYardCare/GardenWithoutPesticides

Garden Without Pesticides

Make your yard and garden healthy and beautiful - without working too hard! Try **Natural Yard Care**

Build healthy soil with compost and mulch. Soil is alive, and soil life matters. Beneficial soil creatures improve soil structure and recycle nutrients. They store water for plants and protect them from pests and diseases. Go to the soil amendments and fertilizer section to learn more about building healthy soil.

Plant right for your site. Get to know your yard. Areas of shade, wet or dry soil, or slope all affect which plants will grow well. Choose plants that will thrive in those areas and that resist insects and diseases. Group plants by their needs for water, sun and soil.

- Thurston County Common Sense Gardening: Plant List – for the earth friendly gardener.
- King County Native Plant Guide: Native plant identification, landscaping plans and how-to articles.
- Elisabeth Carey Miller Botanical Garden: Great plant picks

Practice smart watering. Many plant problems are caused by overwatering. Water plants deeply to promote deep roots. Let the surface of the soil dry out before watering again.

- Saving Water Partnership – water conservation tips for home and business.
- Seattle Public Utilities - Irrigation and sprinkler tips

Learn to live with a few insects. Most bugs in your garden are actually helpful. Killing them all eliminates the beneficial insects too, making the problem worse. Good bugs are a gardener's friend.

Practice natural lawn care. People often use more water and chemicals on their lawns than they need. Try these easy natural lawn care steps instead.

Use pesticides as a last resort. Keep using non-toxic methods and over time you can reduce pest numbers and the damage they cause.

Target your action if pests appear

"Pest" means a lot of different things that cause problems in the yard and garden, including:

- Problem insects
- Weeds
- Slugs and snails
- Critters like deer and moles
- Plant diseases such as black spot

www.GrowSmartGrowSafe.org/NaturalYardCare/GardenWithoutPesticides

Pest problems don't necessarily require pesticides. Identify the problem and your options to deal with it. Start with the expert recommendations on this website and other gardening resources before looking for a product or pesticide.

Traps, barriers or other tools can work as well or better than pesticides. Simple steps like more sunlight or less water may be all the plant needs.

If you use garden chemicals:

- Buy in small amounts. Skip the large "economy" size. Favor ready-to-use products over concentrates.
- Avoid combination products, such as weed and feed, so you don't waste your time and money over-applying one or the other.
- Spot-spray– and only on targeted pests; do not broadcast-apply pesticides over large areas.

Pesticide chemicals can be hazardous to children, pets, birds, fish and other wildlife. Think twice before spraying!

Learn about safer solutions at www.GrowSmartGrowSafe.org

Good Bugs

Good bugs are great for gardens

There are many beneficial insects and pollinators that live in our yards and gardens that perform important tasks. They have the ability to kill or repel harmful insects, pollinate our yards and gardens, and break down dead vegetation so nutrients go back into the soil. There are many ways you can protect beneficial bugs: avoid spraying pesticides on flowering plants, perform pest control work early in the morning or later at night when pollinators are less active, and correctly identify insects prior to any insecticide use to ensure you are targeting harmful insects.

Stop before you spray!

The bug you kill could be a friend. Good bugs:

- Eat pests that harm your plants
- Pollinate fruit trees and berries
- Decompose plant waste and break it down into fertilizer
- Serve as food for birds and animals that also eat pests
- Aerate and improve your soil

For more information on beneficial insects and protecting pollinators, follow these links:

- Beneficial Insects
- http://www.xerces.org/
- https://www.epa.gov/pollinator-protection

SECTION II: WATER MANAGMENT

IN THIS SECTION	PAGE
Managing Stormwater Onsite Source: Seattle Public Utilities	200
Best Irrigation Practices Source: Cascade Water Alliance	204
Efficient Landscape Irrigation Design Checklist	206
Efficient Landscape Irrigation Installation Checklist	208
Efficient Landscape Irrigation System Management Inspection Checklist	209
Landscape Irrigation Schedule Evaluation Checklist	210
Irrigation Evaluation Form	211
Definitions of Efficient Irrigation Terms	212
Resources for Efficient Irrigation Design & Management	215
Elements of an Efficient Irrigation Plan	216
Winterizing & Starting Up the Irrigation System Source: Tacoma Water	217
WAC 246-274-011 Greywater Irrigation Systems Source: https://apps.leg.wa.gov/wac/default.aspx?cite=246-274-011	218

Managing Stormwater Onsite
Low Impact Development practices for landscape & building professionals

What's the problem?
Rain falling on our roofs, roadways, and compacted soil runs off fast down ditches and pipes. This "storm water" can back up and flood homes, cause sewer overflows, and erode hillsides and stream banks. Stormwater also carries dirt, oil and metals from cars, landscape pesticides and fertilizers into Washington's salmon spawning streams, lakes, estuaries, and swimming beaches.

Why manage storm water onsite?
Managing rain where it falls is much more cost-effective than giant pipes and tanks downstream. Simple onsite methods reduce the need for that concrete "gray" infrastructure, by slowing and cleaning rain runoff and soaking it into the soil.

reduce flooding

protect property

restore our waters for people...

...and wildlife

What's the solution?
Rain: Slow it, spread it, filter it, soak it in – restore the sponge. In the forest, rain gets slowed down by tree needles and leaves, then spread out over spongy soils and plants that filter out pollution, slowly letting the rain seep down into the groundwater that keeps our streams running cool all summer. We can help our towns and cities work more like the forest by taking some simple steps during our building and landscape construction, often called "Low Impact Development."

How can we make this...

...work more like this?

What's the role of builders and landscape professionals?
Low Impact Development or "Green Stormwater Infrastructure" practices are required or recommended by Washington State's stormwater manuals, and increasingly by local codes. These regulations apply to new or re-development, but landscape designers, builders, and maintenance professionals can use these same methods cost-effectively on every site. We are all part of the solution.

This guide and other resources are available at www.BuidingSoil.org

rain: slow it, spread it, filter it, soak it in . . .

Low Impact Development toolbox

Protect existing soil and vegetation wherever possible

Planning the site to reduce construction impacts, and fencing off tree root zones and undisturbed soil areas, helps preserve the natural sponge.

Restore disturbed soils with compost and mulch

Breaking up construction-caused compaction to at least 12" deep, and amending with 15-20% compost, restores the soil life that creates structure (the sponge) and grows healthy landscapes that need less water and chemicals. Annual mulching with woodchips stops erosion, weeds, summer water loss, and slowly feeds the soil. Mulch-mowing lawns (leaving the clippings) also builds soil life and structure.

Plant trees

Trees, especially conifers, absorb and evaporate rainfall, slowing runoff. Choose trees that will fit your site when fully grown. Protect tree root zones during construction with fencing, or cover root zone with 4-6 of coarse woodchip, rock, plywood or metal plates.

Reduce paved area, and use porous paving

Consider removing unnecessary paving and restoring the soil. Plan narrower driveway pavement with grass strips at edges or middle. Porous pavers, flagstone, gravel, or reinforced grass-with-paver options all let rain soak through patios, walkways, or driveways into the soil. Permeable concrete and asphalt laid over coarse rock layers soak up rainfall too.

Safely direct pavement and roof runoff into soil and landscape, cisterns, or bioretention "rain gardens"

- ☑ **Make sure that big rain storms can still flow to the storm drain.** When installing a rain garden or cistern, make sure the overflow can drain safely downhill to the street or storm drain, without flooding sidewalks or neighboring properties.
- ☑ **Avoid infiltrating above steep slopes, slide areas, or near building foundations.** In those areas it's better not to use concentrated infiltration methods like rain gardens, rock-filled trenches, or cisterns.
- ☑ **Follow sizing tables** and designs in the WA State Stormwater Manual or local codes to ensure adequate capacity.

Disperse runoff into soil and landscape

Direct roof and pavement runoff away from building foundations. Use a level gravel trench or other method to spread runoff into a large soil and landscape areas downslope, to slowly soak into the soil.

Install a stormwater cistern (detention tank)

Properly sized cisterns will fill during intense rainstorms. They have drain valves that are left open during winter to slowly drain and disperse runoff into the landscape or bioretention areas between storms, so that the cistern is empty when the next big rain comes. Drain valves can be shut in May to fill the cistern for summer irrigation use. Re-open drain valves in September.

Build bioretention swales or cells ("rain gardens")

Bioretention swales and cells are shallow depressions that can pond runoff from roofs and roadways until it soaks in (usually within 48 hours). They have deep compost-amended soils and are landscaped with plants that fit the site's landscape and are adapted to the sun, soil, and moisture conditions: wet-lovers at bottom, drought-tolerant plants at top. Bioretention swales soak up and filter runoff flowing through them. Bioretention cells (aka rain gardens) are designed to infiltrate all the runoff that reaches them, but still have an overflow for big storms.

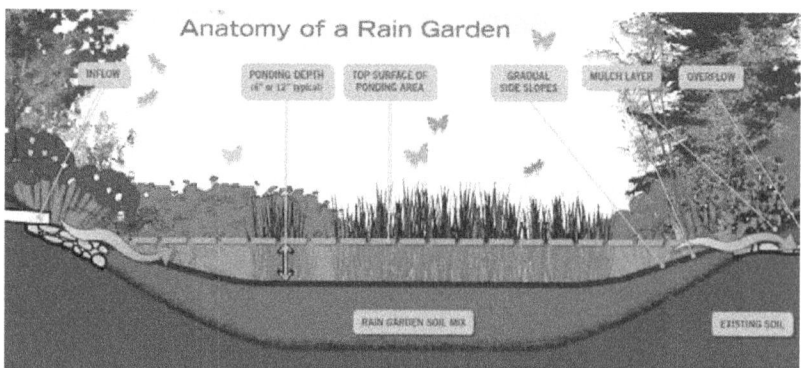

Use a rock-filled trench

In areas too small for a rain garden, a rock-filled trench can help infiltrate roof and driveway runoff into the soil.

Keep it clean – prevent pollution

Besides slowing the flow of storm runoff, it's also important to keep it clean, to protect our streams, lakes, and marine waters. Here's how you can help:

- ☑ **Avoid using pesticides** like "weed & feed" or other weed and bug killers.
- ☑ **Fertilize moderately** – more is not better, and fertilizers can pollute our waterways. Base fertilizer use on soil tests and observed plant need. Look for the words "natural organic" or "slow-release" to find less-polluting fertilizers, for healthier landscapes and waterways.
- ☑ **Prevent concrete wash-off and sediment** from running off-site during construction. Use compost blankets and socks for temporary erosion control, and then till the compost into the soil at end – a 2 for 1 value!
- ☑ **Keep soap, cleaners, paints, etc. out of storm drains**. Direct soapy water into lawns or landscape beds to break down in the soil. Wash vehicles at a car wash. Use the least-toxic cleaning products available.
- ☑ **Fix oil and fluid leaks in vehicles and equipment** – even a little oil can do a lot of harm if it gets into our streams.

Even if your jobsite or property isn't right next to a river, lake, or Puget Sound, that's where runoff from all our towns and yards goes. So let's keep it clean!

Maintain onsite stormwater systems

Whether it's a simple mulch layer, a cistern, or rain garden, your annual maintenance practices will help reduce storm runoff and keep it clean. Renew mulch layers, weed rain gardens, sweep off porous paving, open cistern drain valves in September, and make sure inlets and gutters aren't clogged with dirt or fall leaves. Go out in the first big rain storm of fall, to make sure that everything is flowing where it should. Educate property owners and other professionals. Help keep our storm water drainage system flowing, and our landscapes soaking up the rain!

Resources – learn more about stormwater best practices

- Soil protection and restoration best practices for design, development, and construction, including erosion control www.BuildingSoil.org
- Introductory 2-page factsheets on each of these LID methods, and training resources www.seattle.gov/util/Rainwise   These pages also include Seattle's Green Stormwater Infrastructure resources for professionals.
- *Rain Garden Handbook* for homeowners and landscapers
  https://fortress.wa.gov/ecy/publications/publications/1310027.pdf
- *Low Impact Development Technical Guidance Manual for Puget Sound* – the State-approved guidance for code-required LID (implementing the State stormwater manuals), with details on design, sizing, and technical specs
  www.psp.wa.gov/downloads/LID/20121221_LIDmanual_FINAL_secure.pdf
  Eastern WA LID Manual www.wastormwatercenter.org/ew-lid-guidance-manual
- WA Department of Ecology's *Stormwater Management Manual for Western Washington* (and link to Eastern WA manual too) – State requirements that local governments must follow in building LID into local codes
  www.ecy.wa.gov/programs/wq/stormwater/manual.html
- Low Impact Development (LID) Resources on the WA Dept. of Ecology's website, with many useful local, state, and design resources
  www.ecy.wa.gov/programs/wq/stormwater/municipal/LID/Resources.html

Plants in compost-rich bioretention swales (rain gardens) grow fast! Plan to water, weed and mulch until they fill in – typically 2-3 years. Below is same site after 2 years growth.

based on *RainWise: Managing Storm Water at Home*   ©2013 Seattle Public Utilities   Rev. 2/2014

**CASCADE WATER ALLIANCE
BEST IRRIGATION PRACTICES**

Elements of Efficient Irrigation

- ✓ Efficient irrigation includes the design, installation, maintenance and management of systems that deliver the optimal amount of water needed for healthy plants with minimum waste.
- ✓ Efficient irrigation systems are designed to match the labor, financial and other resources available for the landscape installation and maintenance.
- ✓ Efficient irrigation design integrates other sustainability measures, such as use of stored rainwater and gray-water, use of non-toxic materials, and use of temporary irrigation systems where appropriate to conserve costs and materials.

Benefits of Efficient Irrigation

- ✓ **Promotes healthy plants.** Providing adequate water yields balanced growth. Over- or under-watering can kill plants or make them vulnerable to damage by frost, drought, and other stresses.
- ✓ **Prevents plant disease, pest and weed problems.** Proper irrigation grows healthy plants that resist pests and diseases; and can help prevent weeds, lawn thatch, spread of diseases, and pest problems. Continually saturated soils can promote soil-borne diseases. Drip irrigation can help prevent foliage diseases and weed germination.
- ✓ **Minimizes need for fertilizers and pesticides.** Prevention of plant problems helps reduce the need for inputs. Accurate irrigation limits runoff and leaching of fertilizers.
- ✓ **Saves water and money.** State-of-the-art irrigation equipment and good management can meet plant needs with up to 50% less water than inefficient models.
- ✓ **Reduces labor needs and costs.** Less labor is needed for weeding, fertilization and pest-management, mowing/pruning and disposing of excessive growth.
- ✓ **Conserves materials needed to install systems.** Efficient design can minimize materials needed and save money. Native and drought-tolerant landscapes can often be established using inexpensive temporary irrigation systems that can be removed after 2-3 years—preventing continued unnecessary watering.
- ✓ **Prevents soil erosion, and pollution of ground- and surface water.** Site-appropriate irrigation equipment and scheduling prevents runoff and erosion, and minimizes the need for fertilizers and pesticides that can contaminate surface waters.

Source: Cascade Water Alliance

Sustainable Design

Efficient irrigation requires properly a designed irrigation system including distinct zones for plantings with different needs, efficient sprinklers and drip irrigation, and controls that use weather inputs to modify schedules. A poorly designed system contributes to water waste, plant problems and increased maintenance needs for years to come.

The major components of a well-designed irrigation system are illustrated in *ELEMENTS OF AN EFFICIENT IRRIGATION SYSTEM*.

The *EFFICIENT LANDSCAPE IRRIGATION DESIGN CHECKLIST* describes essential conservation measures to include in systems you design or install, or to require in specifications for contracted systems.

Installation Practices

Ensuring that an irrigation system is laid out and installed as designed, <u>before components are installed or buried</u>, prevents problems that can cause inefficient operation for decades. The *EFFICIENT LANDSCAPE IRRIGATION INSTALLATION CHECKLIST* outlines criteria to specify and confirm, to make sure a system provides the equipment needed to meet plants' needs and for good management.

Management and Maintenance Practices

Regular system check-ups can help identify the most common irrigation problems that waste water and damage plants. It also collects data needed for efficient scheduling and equipment upgrades. The *EFFICIENT IRRIGATION SYSTEM MANAGEMENT INSPECTION CHECKLIST* outlines assessment procedures that can identify problems and record essential information for other management tasks.

Irrigation schedules are the bottom line for efficient water use, whether the rest of the system is state-of-the-art or out-of-date. The *LANDSCAPE IRRIGATION SCHEDULE EVALUATION CHECKLIST* is a guide for assessing if schedules are appropriate and basic conservation features on controllers are being utilized.

Documentation of irrigation zone details and recommended base schedules is essential to good management. The *IRRIGATION EVALUATION FORM* is useful for recording system information that should be posted at the controller; it can also be used for recording system assessment observations and making a punch list of needed repairs.

Definitions of Terms

Important terms needed to understand and discuss efficient irrigation are described in *DEFINITIONS OF EFFICIENT IRRIGATION TERMS*.

Resources

A list of publications and internet *RESOURCES FOR EFFICIENT IRRIGATION DESIGN AND MANAGEMENT* is included at the end of this chapter.

Source: Cascade Water Alliance

EFFICIENT LANDSCAPE IRRIGATION DESIGN CHECKLIST

Include these conservation measures in systems you install or in specifications for contracted systems.

SYSTEM FEATURES	WHAT TO SPECIFY / LOOK FOR
Install irrigation-Only Meter, or Sub-Meter Allows precise tracking of irrigation use.	✓ Separate meter and billing account for irrigation.
Create Irrigation Zones That Match Planting Types and Exposures May be set to run specific day each week, on odd or even dates, or at intervals, such as every third day.	✓ Separate zones for turf, annuals, perennials, woody, and natives/drought tolerant plants. ✓ Separate zones for different micro-climates: Exposed areas on south and west sides of buildings; shady areas on east and north sides, turf in full sun, turf in shade.
Use Drip Irrigation Drip irrigation applies water directly to the soil, so there is no waste by surface evaporation, foliage blocking, overspray on pavement or other areas.	✓ Drip irrigation in planting beds wherever practical. ✓ Entire zone should be drip, not mixed with sprinklers. ✓ Use durable parts like in-line emitters. Minimize fragile emitters, spaghetti-tubing, micro-sprays. ✓ Always install filters and pressure reducers.
Head-toHead Sprinkler Coverage Space sprinklers so spray from each reaches the base of adjacent sprinklers, to prevent uneven watering that floods some areas just to meet basic needs of others.	✓ Use manufacturers nozzle charts to determine proper spacing of sprinklers for the system pressure. ✓ Confirm available flow rates and pressure are adequate to supply all heads in each zone.
Proper Pipe Sizing & Pressure Regulation Ensures adequate water and pressure throughout each zone for uniform application, and allows efficient equipment sizing.	✓ Add flows of all sprinklers or emitters in each zone to make sure supply is adequate. ✓ Calculate pressure losses for the pipe and fittings in each zone, to make sure it is sufficient.
Sprinkler with Check Valves and Other Sealing Components in Heads on Low Parts of Slopes Prevent drain out of laterals through low sprinklers after each irrigation cycle.	✓ Use sprinklers with check valves and strong seals/springs on slopes and at bottom of slopes. ✓ Use sprinklers with integrated pressure regulation or install pressure regulators in pipes on steep slopes.
Use High-Efficiency (HE) Spray Nozzles Apply water more evenly than standard nozzles, and cover an area using 10-20% less water. Allow for larger zones, saving money on pipe and controls.	✓ Use high-efficiency nozzles on all spray heads. ✓ Consider sprays with HE nozzles instead of rotors for residential lawns to save money on components.
Smart Controllers Smart controllers use data from on-site sensors or local weather stations to automatically adjust irrigation schedules to match changing plant needs. Weather based irrigation controls can save 20% or more on annual water use.	✓ For residential or small commercial properties use systems with on-site sensors. ✓ For large sites or multiple properties, consider networked control systems with remote monitoring. ✓ Programming based on plants, soil, exposure and equipment in each zone is critical to success.
Seasonal Adjust Seasonal Adjust on standard controllers resets run times for all zones by a percentage. Monthly adjustment can cut annual usage 20% or more.	✓ Specify controllers with "Monthly Adjust" settings that preset adjustments for each month of the year. ✓ Specify monthly seasonal: July-August 100%, June-September 70-80%, May 50-60%, October-April 0%.
Sensors Rain and soil moisture sensors stop unneeded irrigation when saturated, and can reduce annual water use by 5-20%. Flow sensors detect leaks and stop irrigation in affected zones.	✓ Include rain sensors on all irrigation systems. ✓ Soil moisture sensors should be used only where experience managers are available. ✓ Include flow sensors only where shut downs can be regularly monitored on site or by telecommunications.

Source: Cascade Water Alliance

Master Valves Stops leaks when zones not set to run; or detects main line leaks or zone valves stuck.	✓ Include Master Valves on new systems for added protection.
Temporary Irrigation Systems Native and drought-tolerant plants often need no irrigation after 1-3 years. Temporary irrigation costs less than permanent systems, and components can be removed and reused.	✓ Rotary sprinklers on stands or staked risers, fed by polyethylene tubing, cover large beds or turf areas. ✓ Drip tape is inexpensive, and lasts 1-5 years. ✓ Provide plans to decommission system after 2-3 years, to prevent unnecessary continued use.

Source: Cascade Water Alliance

ecoPRO Required Readings
Best Irrigation Practices - Cascade Water Alliance

EFFICIENT LANDSCAPE IRRIGATION <u>INSTALLATION</u> CHECKLIST

Ensuring that an irrigation system is laid out and installed as designed, <u>before components are installed or buried</u>, prevents problems that can lock in inefficient operation for the life of the system.

Documenting the location of pipes, valves and other system components is <u>essential</u> to enabling regular system maintenance and adjustments needed for efficient operations.

Testing the system identifies problems that could be far more expensive and difficult to fix once the system is buried, and provides information about precipitation rates that is valuable for scheduling.

INSPECTION ITEM	WHAT TO SPECIFY / LOOK FOR
CONFIRM BEFORE TRENCHING	
Confirm Layout Prior to Trenching Stake out (or paint) system layout to compare with plans and allow designer to inspect.	Confirm these items match plans ✓ Water supply size and pressure. ✓ Pipe layout. ✓ Valve locations. ✓ Established tree roots and buried utilities.
CHECK WITH TRENCHES OPEN	
Check and Pressure-Test Pipes Before Burial Before pipes are buried, make sure pipe is sized as specified on plan, and properly installed.	Verify that installed component match plans ✓ Pipe sizes and types match plans and specifications. ✓ Sprinklers and drip risers are properly located per plan. ✓ Number and type of wires are as specified. ✓ Test main line and capped lateral lines for leaks <u>at specified pressures and durations.</u> ✓ Pipe bedding and cover materials meet specification.
TEST AND DOCUMENT WHEN INSTALLATION IS COMPLETE	
Test Sprinkler Coverage Average precipitation rate tests guide accurate irrigation. Distribution Uniformity (DU) tests help identify problems and refine schedules. Both are Irrigation Association (IA) specified methods.	✓ Test precipitation rate (inches per hour) of representative zones to guide scheduling. ✓ Test Distribution Uniformity of representative zones. If less than 60% for sprays or 70% for rotors, identify and fix problems.
Test Drip Irrigation coverage	✓ Check there are emitters by every plant. ✓ Check pressure is adequate at end of laterals.
Sensors Sensors must be set up correctly for efficient watering.	✓ Make sure rain and ET sensors are mounted in full sun. ✓ Make sure soil moisture sensors are located properly, and only linked to zones in similar soils and exposures. ✓ Run flow sensor learning cycle with all zones operating properly (no leaks, stuck valves...)
Document "As-built" System Layout A detailed plan of the system as installed should be provided to the customer and retained by installer.	Show On Drawings ✓ Pipe and wire locations, and sizes. ✓ Valve locations (zone, master, backflow and shutoff) ✓ Nozzle types and sizes
Create and Document Appropriate Schedule Providing an appropriate schedule and suggested seasonal adjustment rates is essential to efficient irrigation. Without a good guide, owners and maintenance contractors may have no idea how to set an effective schedule.	Post at Controller ✓ Description (location, plant and sprinkler types) and schedule for each zone. Drawing of zone locations. ✓ Schedules for 1-3 year establishment period, and for sustainable long-term use. ✓ Recommended Seasonal Adjust. 60% May. 70-80% June & Sept. 100% July—August. 0% October – April. ✓ Copies of Owners Manual and Quick Reference
Temporary Irrigation Systems Provide shut-down and removal schedule and instructions, to prevent unneeded use after plant establishment period.	Identify ✓ Zones that can be shut off, and when. ✓ Show shut off points on plan. ✓ Temporary equipment that can be removed.

Source: Cascade Water Alliance

EFFICIENT IRRIGATION SYSTEM MANAGEMENT INSPECTION CHECKLIST

A basic system check-up including the items below can help identify the most common irrigation problems that waste water and damage plants. It also collects data needed for efficient scheduling and equipment upgrades. *Use the Irrigation Evaluation Form to record observations and recommendations.*

Activity	Steps
Check Meter for Leaks	1. Locate meter. Confirm it is irrigation only. 2. Check leak detector. If leak detected, try to identify sources.

Check Controller Features
✓ Make sure conservation features are being utilized.
✓ Note zones that are not wired, so field observations are recorded accurately.
	1. Locate controllers, and note
	  ✓ Controller type, number of programs capable of running.
	  ✓ Are zone descriptions and schedules posted?
	  ✓ Sensors Active? Rain, flow, soil moisture and/or ET?
	  ✓ Using "Season % Adjust"? Note % setting.
	2. Check wiring
	  ✓ All zones wired? Note zones with no wire on terminal.
	  ✓ Sensors wired?
	  ✓ Master Valve wired?

Review irrigation Schedule ✓ Record zone descriptions / programs. ✓ Identify scheduling problems.	See **IRRIGATION SCHEDULE EVALUATION** for details. ✓ Always compare program on controller to printed schedule —do not assume program is recorded correctly.

Observe Landscape Plantings and Soil
✓ Check soil types and root depths in numerous places—especially trouble spots, to gauge root depths and moisture storage capacity for scheduling.
✓ Select zones to run / observe (if site too large to run all zones)
	1. Turf
	  ✓ Soil type and root depth*
	  ✓ Thatch: Over ½" thick can stop water from reaching roots
	  ✓ Brown areas. May indicate poor soil or broken irrigation.
	  ✓ Soggy areas: May indicate leak or broken sprinklers.
	2. Beds
	  ✓ Soil type and root depth*
	  ✓ Mulch on beds?
	  ✓ Stressed or dead plants: Check for blocked sprinklers.
	  ✓ Established plants, or unplanted areas that no longer need irrigation: May be able to shut off sprinklers or zones.
	
	*Soil and roots
	Sand holds little water-needs frequent watering.
	Clay lets water in slowly—needs multiple short run times.
	Loam good balance of infiltration and storage.
	Shallow soil and roots require frequent watering.

Observe System In Use
✓ Identify leaks, breaks, and problems preventing efficient irrigation
✓ Create maintenance/repair lists
✓ Evaluate if irrigation type and schedule appear appropriate for each area
	1. Note plant type and exposure in each zone
	  ✓ Zones for each planting type—not mixed turf and beds.
	  ✓ Zones for each exposure: N. and E. shadier—shrubs need little irrigation; S. and W. hot and dry
	  ✓ Schedule seems appropriate for plants / irrigation type?
	2. Note obvious problems in each zone
	  ✓ Broken heads or pipes. Misdirected or stuck rotors.
	  ✓ Leaky nozzles or seals
	  ✓ Sprinklers blocked by foliage, too low in turf
	  ✓ High pressure / misting, or low pressure / poor coverage
	  ✓ Wrong pattern nozzle, mixed sprinkler types.
	  ✓ Low-heads drain-out after zone runs
	  ✓ Uneven watering— sprinklers not head-to-head.
	  ✓ Runoff due to high precipitation rate or long run times.

Source: Cascade Water Alliance

ecoPRO Required Readings
Best Irrigation Practices - Cascade Water Alliance

LANDSCAPE IRRIGATION SCHEDULE EVALUATION CHECKLIST

Irrigation schedules are the bottom line for efficient water use, whether the rest of the system is state-of-the-art or out-of-date. Review controller programs carefully—do not assume they are set as intended or recorded correctly. If every zone in a varied landscape is running on the same schedule, it is likely that unnecessary irrigation is occurring that can be remedied with simple adjustments—even without testing sprinkler precipitation rates or efficiency.

CONSERVATION FEATURES	WHAT TO LOOK FOR
Multiple Programs Combinations of watering days and start times should be customized to needs of different plant and soil types, and exposures. Most controllers can run 2-4 different programs.	✓ Different programs used for turf/annual, shrub/tree, and container zones. Zones with daily need should be on separate program from zones with occasional need. ✓ Each zone assigned to <u>just one</u> program. Most controllers <u>can</u> run a zone on two program.
Watering Days Each program may be set to run specific days of the week, on odd or even dates, or at intervals, such as every third day.	"Typical" needs (varies with exposure, soil type & depth) ✓ Turf/annuals: Run 3-5 days a week. ✓ Shrubs/Trees: Run 0-3 days a week (except in extreme conditions like small planters surrounded by paving…) ✓ Dry days between irrigation runs reduce evaporation losses, thatch, disease and weeds.
Run Times Should vary depending on plant type and exposure, soil type and depth, precipitation rate of sprinklers.	Should vary for each zone depending on plants, exposure and equipment. Signs of good scheduling to look for ✓ Shorter run times for sprays than for rotors or rotators. ✓ Reasonable times for drip (20-30 minutes, not hours) ✓ Variation between zones. If all zones set to the same (e.g. 10 or 20 minutes), they likely don't match varied conditions.
Multiple Start Times Splitting each run time into 2 or 3 short cycles helps water infiltrate on slopes or clay soils, and reduces runoff.	✓ Unintended multiple start times on a program? ✓ If program has 2 starts, make sure run times are set to 1/2 of desired total time (1/3 if 3 starts…) ✓ Morning watering reduces evaporative losses from daytime watering, or disease spread from evening runs.
Seasonal Adjust / ET Adjust Seasonal Adjust resets run times for all zones on a program by a percentage, to match weather. ✓ "Monthly adjust" allows preset percentage adjustments for each month of the year. ✓ "ET adjust" automatically varies run times to match weather data from sensors.	✓ Settings appropriate for current month/conditions? ✓ 100% run time should meet typical July-Aug need. Adjust over 100% for unusual hot spells. ✓ Monthly Adjust presets in use, if available? Typical settings: May 60%, June and September 70-80%, July-August 100%, October-April 0%. Necessary? ✓ ET-based scheduling in use, if available?
Sensors ✓ Rain and soil moisture sensors stop irrigation when saturated. ✓ Weather sensors (temperature, solar radiation) provide data used by "Smart" controllers to adjust schedule. ✓ Flow sensors detect irregular flows due to leaks or stuck valves, and shut off affected zones or entire system.	✓ Sensor switch and indicator lights are "On" or "Active". ✓ Battery indicators are green on wireless sensors. ✓ Rain / ET sensors mounted <u>in full sun</u>—not in shade, under trees or overhangs—even if landscape is mostly shaded. ✓ Rain sensors set to activate at ¼" – ½" (check setting on sensor). Higher settings reduce savings, lower settings may stop system after inadequate rain. ✓ Flow sensor/controller must be calibrated. If controller not networked to send alarms, alarm light must be checked almost daily on site so automatic shut-off doesn't kill plants. ✓ Soil moisture sensors placed in typical irrigation and exposure for controlled zone(s)?
Test Functions Many controllers have self-diagnostic modes.	✓ Test wiring for faults.

Source: Cascade Water Alliance

Best Irrigation Practices - Cascade Water Alliance

Irrigation Evaluation Form

Facility/Contractor:						Date:
Controller Location:			PROGRAM	RUN DAYS	Start TIMES	Season Adjust?
Controller Model:			A			
			B			
Zone: Location / Plant Types / Exposure	Irrigation Type	Current Program	C			Appropriate Schedule?
		Run Time	Run Days	Problems / Repairs	Location	
1 ET_____	Prec/hr__	Minutes	1/__ days	Unmatched nozzle/head Broken head/nozzle Adjust pattern / radius Foliage block		
2 ET_____	Prec/hr__	Minutes	1/__ days	Unmatched nozzle/head Broken head/nozzle Adjust pattern / radius Foliage block		
3 ET_____	Prec/hr__	Minutes	1/__ days	Unmatched nozzle/head Broken head/nozzle Adjust pattern / radius Foliage block		
4 ET_____	Prec/hr__	Minutes	1/__ days	Unmatched nozzle/head Broken head/nozzle Adjust pattern / radius Foliage block		
5 ET_____	Prec/hr__	Minutes	1/__ days	Unmatched nozzle/head Broken head/nozzle Adjust pattern / radius Foliage block		
6 ET_____	Prec/hr__	Minutes	1/__ days	Unmatched nozzle/head Broken head/nozzle Adjust pattern / radius Foliage block		
7 ET_____	Prec/hr__	Minutes	1/__ days	Unmatched nozzle/head Broken head/nozzle Adjust pattern / radius Foliage block		
8 ET_____	Prec/hr__	Minutes	1/__ days	Unmatched nozzle/head Broken head/nozzle Adjust pattern / radius Foliage block		
9 ET_____	Prec/hr__	Minutes	1/__ days	Unmatched nozzle/head Broken head/nozzle Adjust pattern / radius Foliage block		
10 ET_____	Prec/hr__	Minutes	1/__ days	Unmatched nozzle/head Broken head/nozzle Adjust pattern / radius Foliage block		
11 ET_____	Prec/hr__	Minutes	1/__ days	Unmatched nozzle/head Broken head/nozzle Adjust pattern / radius Foliage block		
12 ET_____ c_	Prec/hr__	Minutes	1/__ days	Unmatched nozzle/head Broken head/nozzle Adjust pattern / radius Foliage block		

Source: Cascade Water Alliance

DEFINITIONS OF EFFICIENT IRRIGATION TERMS

Central Irrigation Controllers
Control systems that enable monitoring and adjustment of irrigation from a remote computer (or similar device) that is connected to field controllers through a wired or wireless network. Central irrigation controllers often include automated, "Smart", schedule adjustments based on weather data, but some central control systems are simply adjusted manually by operators.

Cycle and Soak
The practice of dividing daily irrigation needs into multiple shorter applications separated by an hour or more, to let water soak into fine-textured soils and thus prevent surface runoff or puddling. Cycle and soak is also used to minimize runoff from slopes. Some irrigation controllers have a Cycle and Soak feature that automatically splits needed run times into two or more briefer runs.

Distribution Uniformity (DU), and Lower-Quarter Distribution Uniformity (LQDU)
Distribution Uniformity (DU) is a measure of how evenly an irrigation device (sprinkler or drip system) applies water. An irrigation zone with 100% DU would apply exactly the same depth of water to every spot in the zone. An irrigation zone with 50% DU would apply twice as much water on average parts as it applies to the parts with poorest coverage, requiring overwatering of most of the zone by 100% in order to adequately water the driest parts. Lower-Quarter Distribution Uniformity is a method used in Irrigation Association (IA) auditing practices to evaluate irrigation zone performance and adjust watering times to adequately water dry portions of the zone.

Irrigation Association Sprinkler Distribution Uniformity Ratings

Sprinkler Type	Excellent (Achievable)	Good (Expected)	Poor (Needs Upgrade)
Multiple Stream Rotors / Rotators	85%	75%	60%
Single Stream Rotors	80%	70%	55%
Sprays	75%	65%	50%

Drip Irrigation
Irrigation devices that discharge water directly to (or under) the soil surface at a controlled rate through "emitters" that are installed on or molded into flexible tubing (usually polyethylene), or attached to hard pipe (PVC). Drip irrigation can meet the needs of plants using 50% less water than sprinkler irrigation because it can apply water very uniformly, avoid overspray to non-target surfaces (pavement, unplanted areas) and minimizes evaporation from foliage, soil surfaces, and misting. Drip irrigation can also be used for precise applications of fertilizers.

Evapotranspiration (ET), and Reference ET (ET_0)
Evapotranspiration (ET) is the sum of water loss from land to the atmosphere by evaporation from surfaces (soil, plant foliage, paving) and by plant transpiration (through leaf stomata). Reference ET (ET_0) is defined as the ET rate from a dense, uniform stand of vegetation (for example, a dense stand of alfalfa mowed at 6" height). Reference ET is estimated daily for a specific location based on measured temperature, humidity, solar radiation and wind speed. Irrigation needs for a specific landscape area can be calculated by multiplying ET_0 times the known needs of specific plants in the area, which are expressed as Plant Factors (see definition below).

Flow Sensor
A gauge that measures the flow rate (gallons per minute) of water in a pipe or channel. When connected to compatible irrigation controllers, flow sensors can be used to track irrigation usage, detect unwanted flows when zones are not programmed to run (from mainline leaks or valves not shutting completely) or irregular flows during programmed irrigation (caused by broken pipes or sprinklers). Many controllers can respond to irregular flows by shutting off irrigation in affected zones and sending an alarm to a central controller.

Graywater
Waste water that has been used in the home for washing, bathing, cooking and other uses—excluding water from toilets, or sinks that may be highly contaminated with food wastes or high soap concentrations. In many locales, codes allow graywater to be used for landscape irrigation, though use is often restricted to sub-surface applications (not sprinklers) on ornamental plants or tree crops—not on herbaceous food crops.

Source: Cascade Water Alliance

High Uniformity Spray Nozzles

High Uniformity Nozzles are engineered to spread water more evenly than standard nozzles, eliminating dry areas and overwatering other areas. They can thoroughly cover an areas using 15% - 20% less water than standard nozzles, compensate for poor zone layout or low pressure, and reduce misting and runoff. Major sprinkler manufacturers (Toro, Rainbird, Hunter) have each developed unique versions of rotating or fixed High Uniformity Nozzles.

Hydrozone

A landscape area comprised of plants with similar water needs. Landscape designs that cluster plants with similar water needs and create irrigation zones including only groups of similar plants in similar exposures, make efficient irrigation possible. Mixed hydrozones that include (for example) annuals and drought tolerant shrubs, cannot be irrigated without either overwatering the shrubs or underwatering the annuals.

Irrigation Association (IA)

A membership organization of irrigation industry professionals, manufacturers, researchers and water utility representatives; that promotes efficient irrigation policies, practices and products. IA offers professional trainings and certification programs, educational materials, and tests and certifies conservation products through the Smart Water Application Technologies (SWAT) program. www.irrigation.org

Plant Available Water Storage

The portion of water stored in soil that is readily available for plants to use. Plant available water storage varies with soil texture, depth and organic matter content. See Table under Soil Water Holding Capacity.

Plant Water Need / Plant Coefficient

The evapotranspiration (ET) rate required for the healthy growth of a particular plant species. Specific Plant Factors have been determined for many crops and ornamental species. However for most landscape applications, the generalized Plant Factors listed in the chart below are used to calculate Water Budgets and irrigation needs.

Plant Factors For Different Plants

Vegetation	Thirsty	Average	Drought Tolerant
Trees / Groundcovers	0.9	0.5	0.2
Shrubs	0.7	0.5	0.2
Turf	0.9	0.75	0.6

Precipitation Rate

The rate of water applied by a sprinkler or sprinkler zone in a defined period of time, commonly expressed as inches of water per hour. Precipitation rate tests or estimates based on manufacturers ratings are useful for estimating irrigation schedules needed to meet plant needs. Precipitation rates for sprinklers are an average of multiple catch points spread uniformly through a zone. Rates for drip irrigation are calculated based on emitter flows and spacing in a zone.

Rain Shut-off Sensors

Sensors that prevent an automatic irrigation controller from starting valves when a set amount of rainfall occurs. Rain sensors can be used with any irrigation controller that runs solenoid valves.

Smart Irrigation Controllers

Irrigation timers that automatically adjust watering schedules based on calculations using current weather data from on-site sensors or sent from regional weather stations, and/or historic data. Smart controllers have been demonstrated to maintain healthy landscapes with 20% less water than standard controllers. However, they **must be** accurately set using information about plants, soil, exposure and irrigation rates in each zone. If they aren't, it is just as likely that the site's water use will be higher, rather than lower.

Soil Moisture Shut-off Sensors

Sensors that prevent an automatic irrigation controller from starting valves when soil is moist. Many soil sensors require the addition of a proprietary control module between the sensor and a controller.

Soil Water Holding Capacity

The specific ability of a particular type of soil to store water, after it is allowed to fully drain. As the chart below illustrates, clay soil stores more than three times as much water per foot of depth than sandy soil, and silts and loams

Source: Cascade Water Alliance

store an intermediate amount. However much of the water stored in clay is held too tightly for plants to access, so they must be watered just as frequently—in small amounts. Loamy soils are able to store the most Plant Available Water.

Moisture Storage, Plant Available Water and Infiltration in Different Soil Types

Soil Texture	Total Water Storage Inches/foot depth	Plant Available Water Storage Inches/foot	Infiltration Rate Inches/hour
Sand	1.2	0.9	2.0+
Sandy loam	1.9	1.6	0.7
Fine sandy loam	2.5	1.7	
Loam	3.2	2.0	0.5
Silt loam	3.5	2.1	
Sandy clay loam	3.7	2.1	
Clay loam	3.8	2.0	0.3
Silty clay loam	3.8	1.7	
Clay	3.9	1.5	0.1

Water Budget

A calculation of the irrigation use expected for a site based on the square footage of landscaping, plant types, and measured efficiency of the irrigation system (or an efficiency goal). Water Budgets <u>based on efficient irrigation assumptions</u> can be compared to the existing water use on a site to gauge the efficiency of irrigation equipment and management. They are also used by municipalities to establish limits on planting of high water use plants at new developments, and by some water purveyors to establish maximum allowable water use for a property.

Source: Cascade Water Alliance

RESOURCES FOR EFFICIENT IRRIGATION DESIGN AND MANAGEMENT

Cascade Water Alliance   http://cascadewater.org/
Water conservation information and commercial equipment rebates for member utilities: Bellevue, Issaquah, Kirkland, Redmond, Sammamish Plateau Water and Sewer district, Skyway Water and Sewer District, Tukwila.

Saving Water Partnership   www.savingwater.org
Water conservation information, links and commercial equipment rebates for member utilities: Cedar River Water and Sewer District, City of Bothell, City of Duvall, City of Mercer Island, City of Renton, Coal Creek Utility District, Highline Water District, Northshore Utility District, Olympic View Water & Sewer District, Seattle Public Utilities, Shoreline Water District, Soos Creek Water and Sewer District, Woodinville Water District; and Water Districts 20, 45, 49, 90, 119, 125.

Irrigation Water Management Services for the Seattle Region http://www.iwms.org/12-swp/28-seattle-area
Conservation tips and calculators, current and historic ET data, and links to upcoming educational event.

Irrigation Association   http://www.irrigation.org

Print versions of training manuals for sale, including:
- ✓ *Landscape Irrigation Auditor Manual 3rd Edition.* $70
- ✓ *Sprinkler Irrigation Efficiency and Management.* $15
- ✓ *Principles of Irrigation* (3rd Edition) $80.

Information about certification trainings on irrigation design, management and assessment.

Smart Water Application Technologies   http://www.irrigation.org/SWAT/

Hunter   http://www.hunterindustries.com/ resourceguide

Design Manuals
- ✓ *Residential Irrigation System* (pdf)
- ✓ *Drip Design Manual* (pdf)
- ✓ *Irrigation Technical Manual* (pdf)

Online Calculators:
- ✓ *Scheduling Calculator*
- ✓ Savings calculator for Pressure Regulation and Check Valve retrofits:

"Product Specialist Training" Online tutorials. www.training.hunterindustries.com

Rainbird   http://www.rainbird.com/landscape/resources
Online Calculators
- ✓ *ET Manager Scheduler Software* (download)
- ✓ *Drip Zone Calculator.* Calculates parts need and zone flow for inline systems

Design Manuals
- ✓ *Landscape Irrigation Design* (pdf)

Qualified Water Efficient Landscaper (QWEL) training program   http://www.qwel.net/
Training Powerpoint presentations available for viewing on line.

Source: Cascade Water Alliance

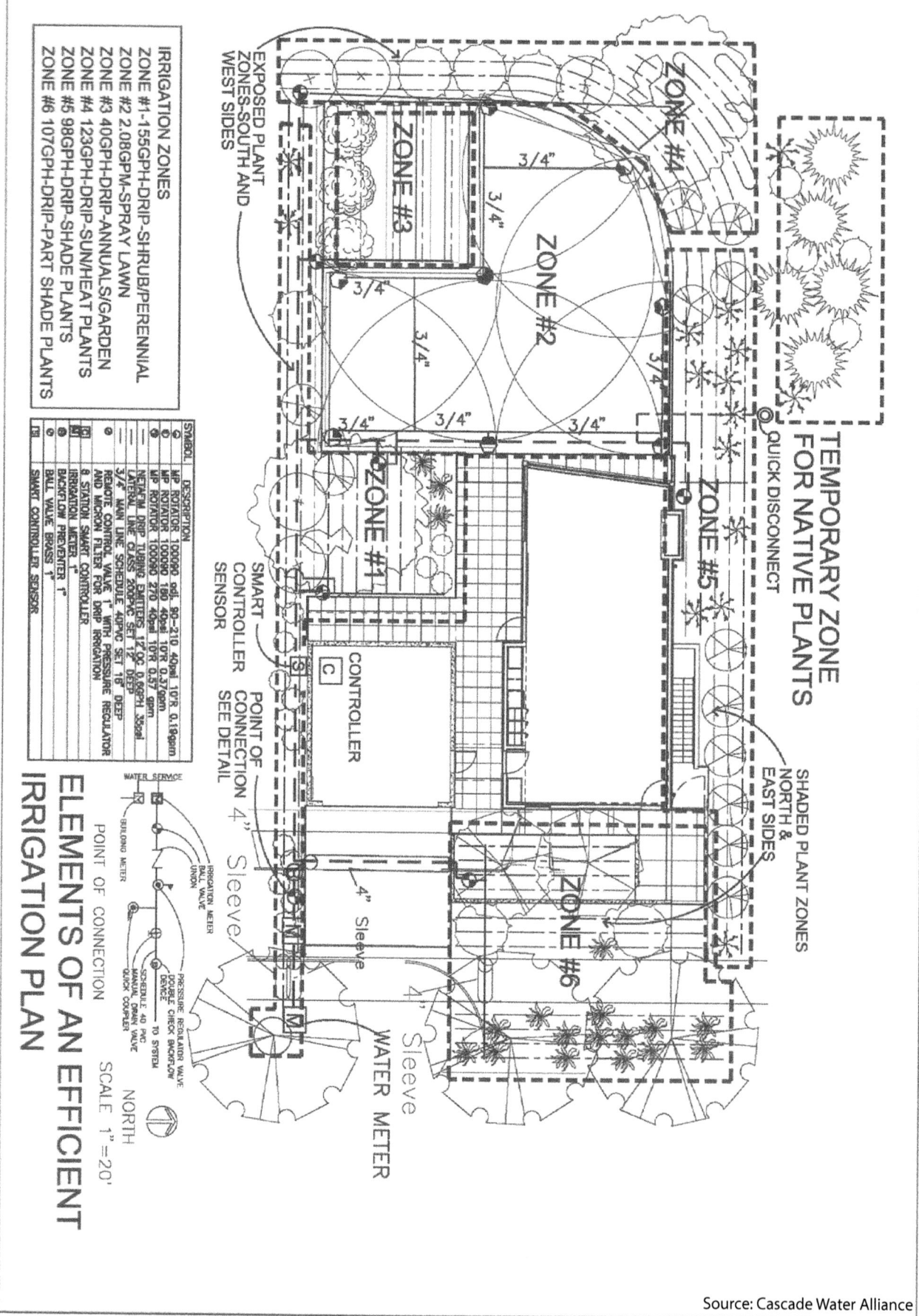

ELEMENTS OF AN EFFICIENT IRRIGATION PLAN

Source: Cascade Water Alliance

Winterizing and Starting up the Irrigation System

Winterizing the Irrigation System

Insulate exposed pipe

Turn water valve off to the site

If you blow out the system:

- Be careful – wear appropriate eye protection and stand away from sprinkler heads
- PVC – not above 80 psi; Polyethylene – not above 50 psi
- Remove flow sensor first
- Do not blow the system from the backflow or pump
- Do not leave manual valves open after blowout
- Turn on each zone beginning with the furthest zone
- Slowly allow air into the main and lateral lines if possible

Open and close backflow isolation valves to ensure water is out of the system - leave valves semi open

Open test cocks on backflow device

Turn off irrigation controller

If the rain sensor has cup or bowl, remove the cup or bowl and cover the sensor

Turning the System on in the Spring

Remove insulation from exposed pipes (optional)

Close isolation valves and test cocks on backflow device

Close all isolation valves on the mainline

Reinstall the flow sensors

Slowly open mainline valve allowing water to reenter the system

Check mainline, backflow, and valves for leaks – make repairs

Turn on irrigation controller and activate rain sensor; ensure settings are appropriate for spring irrigation

Turn on each zone to evaluate leaks and breaks in each station – make repairs as needed

SOURCE: https://apps.leg.wa.gov/wac/default.aspx?cite=246-274-011

WAC 246-274-011
Greywater irrigation systems—General requirements.

(1) The following conditions and restrictions apply to all tiers of greywater irrigation systems:

(a) The greywater must be used only for subsurface irrigation.

(b) The greywater may be used for subsurface irrigation of plants that produce food but must not come into contact with edible portions of any plant.

(c) The greywater must consist of domestic type flows having the consistency and strength typical of greywater from domestic households.

(d) The greywater may not contain toxic substances, cleaning chemicals or hazardous household products derived from the waste from a water softener, activities such as cleaning car parts, washing greasy or oily rags or clothing, rinsing paint brushes, or disposing of waste solutions from home photo labs or similar hobbyist or home occupation activities, or from home maintenance activities.

(e) The greywater may not contain water used to wash diapers or similarly soiled or infectious materials.

(f) The greywater may not contain biomedical waste as defined in chapter 70.95K RCW.

(g) The greywater may not surface in any way, including through ponding or runoff. It must remain below the surface of the ground so that people and animals do not come into contact with it.

(h) The greywater must be used and contained within the property boundary of the building it originates from or on nearby property where it is legally allowed to be used.

(i) The system may be used only during the growing season.

(j) The system must be located in suitable soil.

(k) The system must be located where the land is stable.

(l) The system may not be located in an environmentally sensitive area, as determined by the local health officer.

(m) The irrigation rates may not be greater than the evapotranspiration rate of the irrigation field.

(n) The system must include a readily accessible diversion valve so the greywater can be directed into the approved public sewer system or on-site sewage system when necessary; for example, when soils are saturated or frozen, or blockage, plugging, or backup of the system occurs, or the maximum allowed gallons per day is reached, or when the building owner chooses not to use the system.

(o) The diversion valve must be visibly labeled.

(p) Pipes and above-ground tanks must be labeled with the words: "caution: nonpotable water, do not drink."

(q) If mulch is used, it must be permeable enough to allow rapid infiltration of greywater.

(2) The location of the system must meet the minimum horizontal setback requirements established in WAC 246-274-405, Table I.

(3) If the system fails or is suspected of failing, the owner shall immediately divert the greywater to the approved public sewer system or on-site sewage system serving the building as required under WAC 246-274-445.

[Statutory Authority: RCW 90.46.015. WSR 11-02-011, § 246-274-011, filed 12/28/10, effective 7/31/11.]

SECTION V: HUMAN HEALTH & ENVIRONMENTAL ISSUES

IN THIS SECTION	PAGE
Environmental Issues *Source: Chapter 6 of Sustainable Landscape Management: Design, Construction, and Maintenance*	221
Clean Cities' Guide to Alternative Fuel Commercial Lawn Equiment *Source: U.S. Department of Energy*	239
WA State Noxious Weed Classifications & RCW *Source: https://www.nwcb.wa.gov/washingtons-noxious-weed-laws*	254

chapter 6
Environmental Issues

INTRODUCTION

Environmental concerns about landscape management practices have been raised by environmental groups, governmental organizations, health care professionals, writers, parents, and private citizens. A common viewpoint of critics is that fertilizers and pesticides are overused in the urban environment; are largely unnecessary; and pose unreasonable threats to humans (especially children), pets, and wildlife (particularly fish and birds) (Robbins and Sharp 2003). Traditional approaches to landscaping are criticized for producing ecologically sterile plant monocultures devoid of normal micro- and macroorganisms associated with natural environments (Robbins and Sharp 2003). Finally, use of outdoor power equipment is thought to increase noise pollution and degrade air quality, negating the positive impacts landscapes have on oxygen production and carbon sequestration.

Not surprisingly, the majority of those working in the landscape industry have a different perspective. This group comprises landscape contractors; maintenance contractors; sports field managers; golf course superintendents; and manufacturers of fertilizers, pesticides, irrigation equipment, mowers, and other power equipment. Typically, these stakeholders defend the use of fertilizers and other chemicals as necessary, power equipment as indispensible, and landscape plantings as diverse and overwhelmingly positive environmental enhancers. Many fear that concerns about the environmental impacts of maintenance practices may lead to regulations that will make it impossible for them to provide cost-effective and profitable services to customers.

Because one of the reasons for managing landscapes sustainably is to reduce the environmental concerns associated with management practices, it is important to consider some of the more important landscape management issues and options that exist.

This chapter will discuss the following:

Nutrient leaching and runoff

Pesticide leaching and runoff

Health concerns associated with pesticides

Fish and wildlife issues associated with pesticides

Air pollution due to power equipment emissions

Depletion of water resources

Sustainability and environmental rhetoric

Perspectives on environmental issues regarding pesticide use

NUTRIENT LEACHING AND RUNOFF

Nitrogen and phosphorus are important nutrients for healthy landscape plants. Both are potential pollutants of surface water and groundwater. While both nutrients can cause eutrophication of streams, rivers, and lakes (i.e., uncontrolled algae growth due to nutrient enrichment), much recent research has focused on the role phosphorus plays in eutrophication of urban bodies of water (Petrovic and Easton 2005; Soldat and Petrovic 2008). In urban and suburban areas, potential sources of nitrogen and phosphorus include the following:

- Leaching and runoff from lawns, shrub beds, and flower beds
- Runoff from direct misapplication of chemicals to sidewalks, driveways, and streets
- Leaching from septic systems
- Leaching from lawn clippings and tree leaves that accumulate in or are purposely placed in streets (Figure 6-1)
- Leaching from flower petals, fruits, and nuts of trees (Figure 6-2)
- Deposition of airborne particulate matter, including tree pollen and dust
- Runoff of eroded soil and organic mulch (Figure 6-3)
- Animal urine/feces, roadkill, and food waste
- Soaps and other chemicals

Historically, phosphorus was considered relatively immobile in soils and most likely to move off landscapes only in eroding soil or organic residues. Though quantities are small, it is now clear that phosphorus can also move in dissolved form (Hart, Quin, and Nguyen 2004; Soldat and Petrovic 2008). Nitrate nitrogen from fertilizers leaches readily and is also common in runoff. Research consistently shows that, as fertilizer application rates increase, runoff and leaching increase for both nitrogen and phosphorus.

Phosphorus

Phosphorus is important in all energy reactions occurring in plants. As one of the macronutrients, it is needed in modest quantities by all plants. It is

(a)

(b)

Figure 6-1 (a) Tree leaves and (b) lawn clippings can both contribute to nitrogen and phosphorus pollution if placed in the street.

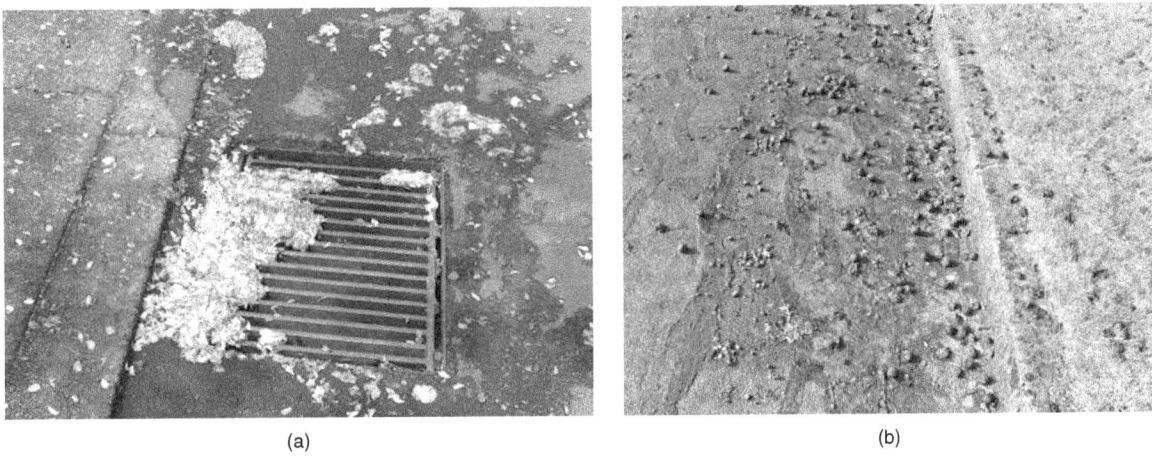

Figure 6-2 (a) Petals from flowering trees often accumulate in storm sewers during spring rains and can contribute to nutrient pollution. (b) Later in the season, fruits from street-side trees can also contribute to nutrient pollution.

included in all complete fertilizers (those containing nitrogen, phosphorus, and potassium). Because plants need much less phosphorus than nitrogen or potassium, it is easy to overapply, resulting in a gradual buildup of phosphorus in soil.

Several states have enacted laws restricting the use of fertilizers containing phosphorus. Extensive soil testing in those states has demonstrated that many lawn soils have accumulated phosphorus far beyond the amount needed for healthy plant growth.

Figure 6-3 Soil from erosion or careless handling during building and landscape construction can be an important source of phosphorus pollution. (a) Properly protected site and (b) improperly protected site.

Figure 6-4 Once nitrogen and phosphorus reach streams or lakes, they stimulate algae growth.

By restricting phosphorus application to lawns, they hope to reduce pollution of lakes and streams (Figure 6-4).

In 2002, Minnesota became the first state to restrict phosphorus and require lawn fertilizers to have 0 percent phosphorus. By law, phosphorus can only be applied to lawns during establishment or if soil tests indicate a deficiency (www.mda.state.mn.us/phoslaw). By 2007, a progress report on the impact of the law restricting phosphorus in Minnesota noted numerous changes, including increased availability of phosphorus-free fertilizers, a 38 percent reduction in the use of fertilizers containing phosphorus, and general acceptance of the regulations by the public. An unintended consequence was a reduction in the number of organic fertilizers available because many organic materials naturally contain relatively high levels of phosphorus (Rosen and Horgan 2005). As of 2007, officials in Minnesota were unable to document the impact of phosphorus-restricted fertilizers on phosphorus levels in water bodies.

Michigan researchers using a statistical modeling program claimed a 25 percent reduction in phosphorus loading (phosphorus accumulating in bodies of water) in lakes and rivers after only one year due to a local ordinance similar to the Minnesota law (Lehman, Bell, and McDonald 2009).

Because other research has shown that increases in phosphorus concentrations in bodies of water are directly related to application rates, it is likely that phosphorus restrictions will reduce the amount of phosphorus loading in lakes and streams due to fertilizer applications. Because there are many other sources of phosphorus in surface waters, including sediments in lake bottoms, it remains unclear just how big an impact laws restricting phosphorus will have on phosphorus pollution (Figures 6-1, 6-2, and 6-3b).

As a result of research, best management practices regarding phosphorus pollution include the following:

- Use soil test data to guide phosphorus applications so as to keep phosphorus levels at the low end of adequate.
- Apply phosphorus at low rates [0.5 lb P_2O_5/1000 sq ft/application (2.5 g P_2O_5/m^2/application)] only as needed and only during the main growing season.
- Time applications to avoid heavy postapplication rainfall events.
- Irrigate enough after application to remove fertilizer from foliage and wash it into the soil.
- Avoid fall applications of phosphorus in climates where frozen soil and snow cover occur in winter.
- Maintain nitrogen fertility high enough to produce dense turf, which reduces dissolved phosphorus runoff and nearly eliminates sediment loss.
- Return clippings when feasible because clippings do not increase phosphorus runoff under turf conditions (Bierman et al. 2009).
- Avoid applying soluble phosphorus sources. Organic sources of phosphorus may result in less runoff loss (Hart, Quin, and Nguyen 2004).

Nitrogen

Nitrogen is the primary nutrient needed to stimulate grass color and growth. Lawns are darker green and denser when nitrogen is applied as fertilizer. Removing clippings from lawns during mowing rapidly removes available nitrogen from the system and increases the need for supplemental nitrogen.

Grasses are very efficient in absorbing nitrogen so the likelihood of large increases of nitrogen in surface water or groundwater due to lawn fertilization is small. In most reports, nitrate losses from watersheds are two to five times higher from agriculture than from suburban/urban landscapes, which, in turn, are higher than nitrate losses from forested areas (Groffman et al. 2004). In the study by Groffman et al. (2004), nitrogen inputs in suburban areas included [10 lb N/acre/y (11.2 kg N/ha/y)] from atmospheric deposition (nitrogen in rainfall and dust) and [13 lb N/acre/y (14.4 kg N/ha/y)] from fertilizer. In a similar study in Arizona (Baker et al. 2001), input from pet waste totaled [15 lb N/acre/y (17 kg N/ha/y)]. This indicates that nitrogen fertilizer inputs over entire urban ecosystems make up about one-third of the total nitrogen entering the ecosystem (Baker et al. 2001). Landscape areas in which lawns were a major component retained 75 percent of added nitrogen in plant and soil material, thus reducing the amount of nitrogen available for leaching or runoff (Groffman et al. 2004).

The ability of lawns to absorb and retain nitrogen changes with age as do lawn nitrogen requirements. As lawns age, more nitrogen is stored in the root zone area, and lawns require less nitrogen for adequate growth. Research indicates that older lawns need less nitrogen and are prone to increased leaching losses if nitrogen application rates remain at establishment levels (Frank et al. 2006). For example, on mature Kentucky bluegrass (*Poa pratensis*), continued high-nitrogen applications of [5 lb N/1000 sq ft/y (24.5 g N/m^2/y)] resulted in a loss of 11 percent of applied nitrogen. Low nitrogen rates of [2 lb N/1000 sq ft/y (9.8g N/m^2/y)] resulted in only 1 percent nitrogen loss.

Pollution potential from nitrogen fertilization of shrub beds has not been extensively researched. One published account compares runoff and leaching between newly established Saint Augustinegrass (*Stenotaphrum secundatum* (Walt.) Kuntze) and a newly planted mixed tree, shrub, and ground cover bed in a tropical environment (Erickson et al. 2001). Runoff was insignificant from both areas, but the landscape bed lost 30 percent of applied nitrogen to leaching while the lawn lost less than 2 percent of applied nitrogen. These results are predictable, because the landscape planting had not achieved 100 percent ground coverage while the sodded lawn covered the entire ground surface immediately. To better understand the dynamics of this situation, additional testing needs to be done over a period of years to see what long-term trends develop.

Best management practices established from research regarding nitrogen pollution include the following:

- Apply nitrogen at times when lawns and other landscape plants are actively growing.
- Avoid late-fall or dormant nitrogen applications.
- Use lowest effective rates of nitrogen, avoiding soluble sources when possible.
- Avoid nitrogen applications prior to expected heavy rainfall events.
- Design lawn and landscape beds so that runoff is retained on-site.
- Reduce applied nitrogen rates when clippings are returned.

For additional details on nutrient management in landscapes, see Chapters 8 and 9.

PESTICIDE LEACHING AND RUNOFF

Pesticides encompass a wide array of chemicals, including herbicides, fungicides, insecticides, miticides, nematicides, moluscicides, rodenticides, and fumigants. Among these chemicals, some are registered for use in landscapes, some for agriculture, and some for structural pests (termites). In general, more chemicals are registered for use on warm-season grasses than on cool-season grasses (see Chapter 10). Because pest species vary from region to region, pesticides commonly used in one area may not be used in another area. Regulations vary by country, so not all pesticides are available in all countries. Understanding the environmental impact of pesticides requires specific knowledge of the site and the chemicals involved.

Most research on pesticide fate in landscapes (whether it accumulates, leaches, runs off, or breaks down) has been directed at lawns and golf course turf. Research aimed at leaching and runoff behavior is generally carried out using a worst-case scenario approach. For example, in many small-plot studies, irrigation is applied at a rate of [2 to 6 inches/h (5 to 15 cm/h)], sometimes within 24 hours after application, to purposely cause runoff or leaching (Baird et al. 2000). In some trials, a preapplication irrigation event is followed by postapplication irrigation (Harrison et al. 1993).

For a short and concise analysis of the fate of pesticides used on turf, see Hull (1995). An in-depth discussion of the fate of pesticides is presented by Balogh and Walker (1992), Racke and Leslie (1993), and Clark and Kenna (2000).

Some general research findings on pesticide fate include the following:

- For commonly used landscape pesticides, runoff is more of a problem than leaching and is more likely to occur if precipitation occurs shortly after application.
- Once chemicals dry on foliage or become bound up in thatch or soil, leaching and runoff potential decrease.
- Leaching potential increases as the solubility and persistence of individual chemicals increases.
- Dense turf or ground cover reduces runoff significantly.
- Most chemicals break down fast in dense vigorous lawns, reducing the potential for leaching and runoff.
- Chemicals purposely or inadvertently applied to concrete or asphalt are extremely prone to runoff and are slow to degrade (Mumley and Katznelson 1999).

Best management practices gleaned from leaching and runoff studies with pesticides include the following:

- Reduce the potential for runoff by designing landscapes that direct runoff to on-site bioswales rather than to storm sewers, streams, or lakes.
- Establish vegetative no-spray buffer zones between treated areas and waterways.
- Avoid application of pesticides when soil moisture levels are high or when heavy precipitation is likely within 24 hours.
- Use pesticide formulations with low runoff or leaching potential. Runoff is generally greater with granular than wettable powder formulations. Water-soluble formulations are more likely to run off than low-water-soluble formulations. Pesticides with high adsorption affinity are less likely to run off or leach than materials that are not adsorbed (Baird et al. 2000).
- Avoid application of pesticides to impervious surfaces such as sidewalks, driveways, and roads.
- Use pesticides only in the context of a well-formulated integrated pest management (IPM) plan (see Chapter 10).

HEALTH CONCERNS ASSOCIATED WITH PESTICIDES

Health concerns associated with pesticide use in commercially maintained landscapes include direct toxic exposure to applicators, human bystanders, and pets; exposure via dislodgeable residues; long-term exposure; and exposure to multiple chemicals. Beyond direct toxic effects, the greatest concern is potential carcinogenicity associated with short- and long-term exposure to pesticides.

The greatest risk to applicators using common pesticides applied in turf and landscape situations comes from insecticides. Fungicides pose less risk and herbicides the least. The actual risk depends on the specific chemical, the dosage, and the extent of exposure (Ottoboni 1997). Licensed applicators who follow all label-recommended safety precautions are unlikely to be exposed to toxic levels of pesticides during mixing and handling (Leonard and Yeary 1990).

Research has generally concluded that bystander exposure to the widely used broadleaf herbicide 2,4-D is unlikely under normal homeowner or professional applicator procedures. According to studies on bystander exposure to herbicides and insecticides, dislodgeable residues drop rapidly in the first 24 hours after application (Sears et al. 1987). In the case of diazinon, a 24-hour re-entry waiting period dramatically reduces potential exposure due to contact with plant foliage. Similar results were obtained in studies using 2,4-D (Thompson, Stephenson, and Sears 1984). Excretion of absorbed 2,4-D by applicators applying product daily as part of their job was well below the established daily dietary intake of 0.3 mg/kg, indicating minimal absorption. In a test of absorption and excretion of 2,4-D in bystanders, Harris et al. (1990) were unable to detect 2,4-D in urine samples from bystanders in the first four days after application.

Although the health impacts from exposure to individual or multiple chemicals are difficult to study, many trials have been conducted on such issues as exposure of children to lead in paint, insecticides applied to foundations for termite control, landscape pesticides, pest strips, and flea collars. Others deal with agricultural pesticide use and potential effects on applicators or the public.

Case-control studies are the most common way to study the health effects (such as cancer) associated with pesticides. Typical studies compare one group of people with cancer to another group of people from the same population who don't have cancer. Participants are asked a series of questions about their use of chemicals and other lifestyle behaviors. The questions may ask participants to recall events that occurred several years to decades ago. Using this data, researchers look for correlations between the history of pesticide use or exposure and the incidence of cancer.

Odds ratios are developed that associate the disease with exposure to one or more chemicals or lifestyle characteristics. Odds ratios above 1.0 indicate that there may be an association of an activity or exposure with the incidence of disease. Case-control studies are not very precise because they don't account for details such as chemical application rates, formulations, actual dates of exposure, and duration of exposure. The odds ratios do not offer any absolute risk factors, only that there may be an association (Ottoboni 1997).

Numerous case-control studies have indicated that 2,4-D appears to be associated with an increased incidence of non-Hodgkin's lymphoma (Blair and Zahm 1995; Buckley et al. 2000; Hoar et al. 1986). Buckley et al. (2000) found a high association of cancer in children of families with a history of high pesticide use but were not able to identify specific chemicals or exposure parameters and suggested more research.

In Canada, Ritter et al. (1997) conducted an in-depth analysis of the relationship between public exposure to pesticides and incidence of cancer. They concluded that phenoxy herbicides (2,4-D and related compounds) may pose a risk to applicators who handle the chemicals regularly but that there was no indication that the general public was at risk from exposure to these herbicides. They also concluded that there was no evidence that lawn and garden pesticides in general are likely to be a major cause of cancer. They called for more sophisticated research studies to better determine the risks associated with pesticide use. It should be noted that, in their opinion, case-control studies have limited value.

There is no consensus among scientists or the public on the relative risks of exposure to pesticides. Groups opposed to pesticides are strong advocates of the precautionary principle in dealing with the potential side effects of pesticide use on human health. The Rio Declaration on Environment and Development (the Rio Declaration) defines the precautionary principle as follows:

> In order to protect the environment, the precautionary approach shall be widely applied by States according to their capabilities. Where there are threats of serious or irreversible damage, lack of full scientific certainty shall not be used as a reason for postponing cost-effective measures to prevent environmental degradation. (Wikipedia 2010)

Simpler interpretations include "better safe than sorry" and "look before you leap." In the context of landscape pesticide exposure, the precautionary principle makes it the responsibility of users to demonstrate that no harm will come from the use of pesticides in landscapes. This has become the crux of an ongoing debate concerning pesticide use because obviously there is no way to demonstrate that no harm will ever come from their use.

The following best management practices reflect concerns raised by the precautionary principle:

- Avoid the use of pesticides as much as possible through a well-conceived IPM plan.
- In all cases, select low-risk pesticides first.
- Take advantage of all available precautions to reduce the exposure to pesticides by applicators and bystanders.
- Use signs to inform bystanders that pesticide applications have been made.
- Alert neighbors of treatments as required by law.
- Avoid re-entry on sprayed properties for 24 to 48 hours or as prescribed by the pesticide label.
- Do not use pesticides in situations where young children or pets are likely to be exposed.

FISH AND WILDLIFE ISSUES ASSOCIATED WITH PESTICIDES

Fish, birds, and other wildlife are potential casualties in areas treated with pesticides (Figure 6-5). In high enough concentrations, insecticides can kill fish or disrupt their reproduction (Mumley and Katznelson 1999). For instance, salmon are susceptible to direct kills at high dosages and suffer from reduced growth when subjected to sublethal doses of organophosphate or carbamate insecticides for exposure periods as short as four days (Baldwin et al. 2009). Bird kills due to direct poisoning have resulted in restrictions on the use of organophosphate insecticides (Stone and Gradoni 1985). Carbaryl (an insecticide) and benomyl (a fungicide) are both toxic to earthworms and can reduce populations in lawns by 60 percent or more for up to 20 weeks after a single application (Potter et al. 1990). In the same study, chlorpyrifos (an insecticide) reduced spider, rove beetle, and

Figure 6-5 Birds are particularly sensitive to insecticide treatments.

predatory mite populations for up to six weeks after a single treatment. Potter (1994) noted that regular pesticide applications to lawns may destabilize the lawn ecosystem and increase the number and severity of pest outbreaks.

To avoid the negative consequences of indiscriminate pesticide use, consider the following best management practices for landscape pesticide use:

- Use pesticides only in the context of a well-conceived IPM plan.
- Determine if the proposed treatment area provides habitat for birds and fish as well as other wildlife and alter plans as needed to avoid their exposure.
- Analyze potential pesticides from a nontarget perspective to avoid inadvertently selecting pesticides posing a high risk to wildlife.
- Create no-spray buffer zones near streams and lakes as defined by local, state, or federal law.
- Avoid regular use of insecticides so arthropod, spider, and mite populations can remain healthy and function properly as beneficial organisms.

See Chapter 10 for additional information on IPM and pest control options.

AIR POLLUTION DUE TO POWER EQUIPMENT EMISSIONS

Landscapes are potential environmental moderators and offer many functional benefits. For instance, Beard and Green (1994) discussed the benefits associated with lawns, including:

- Excellent soil erosion control and dust abatement
- Improved recharge and protection of groundwater quality
- Entrapment and biodegradation of synthetic organic compounds
- Soil improvement and restoration
- Urban heat dissipation–temperature moderation
- Reduced noise, glare, and visual pollution problems
- Decreased noxious pests and allergy-related pollen

In spite of the positive impacts landscapes have on the urban environment, there are drawbacks. Commercial maintenance of landscapes requires the use of noise- and exhaust-producing power equipment. Mowers, edgers, trimmers, chain saws, blowers, chippers, tractors, and trucks are all used regularly or occasionally on commercial landscapes. The internal-combustion engines used to power this equipment create unwanted noise and air pollution.

Until recently, emissions from engines less than 25 hp were not regulated in the United States (U.S. Environmental Protection Agency 1998). The U.S. Environmental Protection Agency (EPA; 1998) estimates indicated that small engines contributed about 5 percent of the total hydrocarbon emissions from internal-combustion engines in the country. In Australia, tests on two- and four-stroke engines indicated that lawn mowers produced 5.2 percent of the carbon monoxide and 11.6 percent of the nonmethane hydrocarbons toward the total emissions in the study region (Priest, Williams, and Bridgman 2000). While both engine types produce significant pollution, studies have demonstrated that two-stroke engines produce from 7 to 20 times more hydrocarbons than four-stroke engines (Priest, Williams, and Bridgman 2000; White et al. 1991).

Small-engine emissions are significant because they are primarily concentrated in residential and commercial areas. In the United States, Phase 1 emission controls were initiated in 1997 by the EPA and involved changes in fuel–air mixing ratios and enhanced exhaust controls. Phase 2 sets stricter exhaust emission levels, beginning in 2011. The new regulations require improvements in fuel systems, engine combustion, and, in some cases, the addition of catalysts (U.S. Environmental Protection

Agency 2008). These changes are predicted to reduce new hydrocarbon and nitrogen oxide emissions by 35 percent and reduce evaporative emissions by 45 percent. Phase 3 standards are in the proposal stage and will bring small-engine emissions in line with those of automobiles.

Other sustainable strategies for engine-powered cars, trucks, and small equipment are being explored by numerous landscape maintenance companies. Some companies have shifted to biodiesel or propane fuel for mowing equipment. Others have replaced fleet vehicles with gas/electric hybrids or more fuel-efficient conventional vehicles. Currently, the most effective way to reduce emissions is to buy new equipment. As technology allows, expect to see more electric mowers and, ultimately, different power sources such as methanol, natural gas, fuel cells, and even hydrogen (Konrad 2009).

Noise issues concern both operators and bystanders. Noise regulations vary by city and country. Noise limits are based on decibel levels at the operator's ear and for specific distances from the source. While there are no universal standards, maximum acceptable decibel levels of 90 at the operator and 60 at 50 ft (15 m) are typical. Larger engines may have higher limits than smaller engines. The nature of small-engine operation makes noise reduction challenging.

DEPLETION OF WATER RESOURCES

Water shortages have long been a concern in arid climates, but humid climates also are increasingly experiencing water shortages as the population increases. In many countries, aging water capture and conveyance systems are inadequate and environmental issues preclude new major water capture projects. With future water supplies uncertain, city utilities will concentrate on protecting existing sources, increasing water reuse, and, in some areas, increasing desalinization (Richardson 2008). Additionally, the use of potable water for irrigation will decrease

Figure 6-6 Where available, treated sewage water can be an important source of irrigation water as on this golf course.

worldwide as higher-priority uses prevail (Duncan, Carrow, and Huck 2009). Nonpotable water from sewage treatment facilities is likely to become more important for landscape uses because it is available in quantity and is close to end users. Golf courses have effectively used treated wastewater for many years (Figure 6-6). Use of nonpotable water for irrigation is discussed in Chapters 2 to 4. Guidelines and details regarding optimal irrigation strategies and options for reducing irrigation are presented in Chapters 8 and 9.

SUSTAINABILITY AND ENVIRONMENTAL RHETORIC

When contemplating life in urban and suburban areas, landscapes seem like the perfect counterbalance to concrete, steel, and asphalt. Imagine life in Manhattan without Central Park. Manicured city parks make life in large metropolitan areas more enjoyable, and attractively landscaped commercial developments make appealing workplaces. If you consider the perspective of the environmental movement, however, it often seems like there is more wrong than right with this landscaped world. Since Rachel

Carson fired the first shots decrying the mindless use of insecticides in forests, the war of words attacking and defending the use of fertilizers and pesticides has been constant. Amid this battle, the truth is hard to find.

Because lawn care is a major focal point for those questioning the use of fertilizers and chemicals in landscapes and because lawns also account for a significant area of commercial landscapes, much of the following discussion will focus on them. Lawns as a symbol of misguided social priorities have been discussed by several authors (Bormann, Balmori, and Geballe 2001; Jenkins 1994; Robbins 2007; Steinberg 2006). Referring to the lawn care reform movement in Canada, Sandberg and Foster (2005) noted that "entrenched battles have inspired civic debate about land stewardship, human health, economic governance, property rights, civic responsibility and aesthetics." They also noted that the "… politics of lawn care reform stand for larger social and cultural dynamics." This theme was carried further by Robbins (2007), who suggested that lawns are something other than "passive products of aggregated consumer choices … to which an industry responds … ." In his view, people are subjugated by lawns because of what lawns demand of them.

Given the level of rhetoric, it is enlightening to examine the claims and counterclaims about lawns and lawn care and their effect on the environment. Following are three examples of rhetoric along with discussion of their veracity, which will demonstrate the types of questions that should be raised when claims are made by either side in the ongoing debate about landscapes and the environment.

Claim:
Lawns are the single largest crop grown in the United States.

Source:
http://www.epa.gov/greenacres/nativeplants/factsht.html#Replacing%20Your%20Lawn.

To determine if this claim is true, the first step is to determine how many acres (square kilometers) of lawns there are in the 48 contiguous states (i.e., the lower 48 states). This is not an easy task because of the complexity of landscape configurations. The most commonly quoted study based on satellite imagery estimates the total area in the lower 48 states covered in some form of lawn at approximately 40,458,600 acres (163,800 km^2) (Milesi et al. 2005). This estimate includes residential, commercial, institutional, and park lawns plus all golf courses and athletic fields and amounts to 1.9 percent of the 48 contiguous states. The study doesn't discriminate between lawn area and shrub beds so it probably more accurately reflects total landscaped area.

The next step is to determine the size of croplands. According to the 2007 U.S. census of agriculture, the total area of farmland is 922,095,840 acres (3,734,488 km^2). Table 6-1 shows how landscapes, which are not part of the U.S. census of agriculture, compare with total cropland, total irrigated cropland, and the five largest crops.

Conclusions:
Landscapes cover a significant land area but are nowhere near the largest crop and are equal to only 4.4 percent of the total farmland in the 48 contiguous states.

Claim:
Lethal lawns: diazinon use threatens salmon survival.

Source:
Oregon Pesticide Education Network (http://www.pesticide.org/diazsalmon.pdf).

An article from the Oregon Pesticide Education Network, titled "Lethal Lawns: Diazinon Use Threatens Salmon Survival," discusses the effects of diazinon on salmon and connects the use of diazinon on lawns directly to salmon health issues. While the general information in this document appears to be accurate and truthful with regard to the effect of diazinon on salmon, the author's attempt to connect diazinon use on lawns with observed levels of diazinon in San Francisco Bay is completely wrong.

TABLE 6-1 Crop Areas in the 48 Contiguous United States

Crop	Total Acres	Total Square Kilometers	Percentage of Total
All crops*	922,095,840	3,734,488	100
All corn*	92,228,203	373,524	10
Soybeans*	63,915,821	258,859	6.9
Forage*	61,455,483	248,895	6.7
Hay*	58,121,003	235,390	6.3
Wheat*	50,932,969	206,279	5.5
Landscapes†	40,458,600	163,800	4.4

*2007 U.S. census of agriculture data.
†From Milesi et al. (2005).

To create the connection, the author refers to a study carried out in Alameda County, California, that determined that diazinon in the bay came from a small number of homes in the surrounding area. According to the lethal lawns report: "The researchers followed up this monitoring study by hiring commercial applicators to apply diazinon to two home lawns in the watershed. This research verified that applications of diazinon at recommended rates and in accordance with directions on the product label caused contamination at the levels that had been measured in the block by block monitoring study." This passage seems to make a direct connection between diazinon use on lawns and diazinon concentration in San Francisco Bay.

The author's statement does not make sense based on research regarding diazinon behavior when applied to lawns. Research has consistently demonstrated that diazinon does not run off lawns because it is bound up in thatch (Niemczyk, Krueger, and Lawrence 1977). Diazinon also has a short residual life (less than a month) in lawns due to rapid breakdown in the lawn canopy (Branham and Wehner 1985).

A review of the original research by Mumley and Katznelson (1999) gives a different version of the final trial. According to Mumley and Katznelson:

"The final stage of monitoring evaluated diazinon runoff from individual homes. Two homes were selected for intensive source area sampling. Diazinon was applied to each home at recommended rates and in accordance with label instructions. Source area samples were collected from roof drains, patios and driveways following rainfall events for fifty days after application." They concluded with the following: "The largest source areas were patios and driveways, followed by roof drains." Lawns were never mentioned in this report. The authors applied diazinon to driveways, patios, and roof drains, which explains why runoff could be measured for 50 days after application.

Conclusions:
In this case, there was no relationship at all between diazinon use on lawns and diazinon runoff into San Francisco Bay. The product was applied by the researchers and not professional applicators, and applications were made directly to the driveways, patios, and roof drains to control ants. Lawns were never treated. A better title for the report would have been "Lethal Driveways and Patios: Diazinon Application to Impervious Surfaces Threatens Salmon Survival."

PERSPECTIVES ON ENVIRONMENTAL ISSUES REGARDING PESTICIDE USE

In the ongoing debate between environmental advocates and the landscape industry, environmental groups have become proactive while the landscape industry has been more reactive. Environmental groups force the action by challenging the industry in the courts of law and public opinion. The industry groups react with counterclaims, lobbying, and lawsuits via manufacturers and industry groups. Meanwhile, the EPA and its counterparts in other countries are charged with trying to satisfy both sides. This awkward arrangement has resulted in ongoing changes in testing requirements, increasing restrictions on pesticide use, and loss of registration for products demonstrated to cause unacceptable health or environmental damage (Table 6-2).

Claim:
All of our pesticide products are legal and registered by the EPA as practically nontoxic.

Source:
Promotional material used by some pesticide applicators, distributors, and manufacturers (U.S. General Accounting Office 1990).

In 1990, the U.S. General Accounting Office (GAO) submitted a report to the U.S. Senate concerning the ongoing use of prohibited safety claims by manufacturers, distributors, and users of landscape pesticides. It pointed out that, despite clearly stated rules on what can and cannot be said about pesticides, prohibited claims were continuing. EPA regulations prohibit statements that are "false or misleading" and claims "as to the safety of the pesticide or its ingredients, including statements such as 'safe,' 'nonpoisonous,' 'noninjurious,' 'harmless' or 'nontoxic to humans and pets' with or without such a qualifying phrase as 'when used as directed.'"

In the 1990 report, the GAO criticized the EPA for not taking enforcement action against manufacturers and distributors for making prohibited claims. The GAO also criticized the Federal Trade Commission (FTC) for failing to protect consumers against false advertising and failing to take enforcement action against applicators, manufacturers, and distributors.

In 2003, the state of New York levied a $2 million fine against Dow AgroSciences for making prohibited safety claims about its pesticide products from 1995 to 2003. In addition to the financial penalty, Dow AgroSciences was required to stop making safety claims about its products and to implement a compliance program (http://www.ag.ny.gov/media_center/2003/dec/dec15a_03.html).

Conclusions:
By law, prohibited safety claims about pesticides cannot be made. Because the EPA is not an enforcement organization, violations of these regulations have seldom been prosecuted.

TABLE 6-2 Partial List of Pesticides Banned or Severely Restricted from Use in Landscapes*

United States[†]	Canada[‡]	European Union[§]
Herbicides	**Herbicides**	**Herbicides**
2,4,5-T	2,4-D all forms	2,4,5-T and its salts and esters
2,4,5-TP	Amitrole	Simazine
2,4-D isooctyl ester	Dicamba	
4,6-Dinitro-o-cresol	Dichlobenil	
Bromoxynil butyrate	MCPP	
Calcium arsenate	Simazine	
Dinitrobutyl phenol		
Dinitro-o-cresol		
Insecticides	**Insecticides**	**Insecticides**
Aldrin	Carbaryl	Acephate
Chlordane	Endosulfan	Alachlor

(Continued)

TABLE 6-2 (Continued)

United States[†]	Canada[‡]	European Union[§]
DDT	Malathion	Aldicarb
Diazinon	Phosalone	Aldrin
Endrin	Pyrethrins	Arsenic compounds
Gamma-lindane	Rotenone	Carbaryl
Heptachlor		Chlordane
Lead arsenate		DDT
Sodium arsenate		Diazinon
Sodium arsenite		Dieldrin
		Endrin
		Heptachlor
		Lindane (gamma-HCH)
		Malathion
		Permethrin
Fungicides	**Fungicides**	**Fungicides**
Cadmium compounds	Captan	Mercury compounds
Mercury compounds	Copper sulfate	Zineb
	Ferbam	
	Folpet	
	Thiophanate-methyl	
	Zineb	

*This list is intended only as an example and is not intended to be exhaustive.
[†]http://scorecard.org/chemical-groups/one-list.tcl?short_list_name=brpest.
[‡]http://www.ene.gov.on.ca/en/land/pesticides/class-pesticides.php.
[§]http://www.pan-uk.org/PDFs/Banned%20In%20The%20EU_April%20Update.pdf.

In Canada, the debate has heated up in recent years as indicated by attempts to ban or restrict cosmetic pesticide use in landscapes. Compare the following comments from Health Canada's Pest Management Regulatory Agency (PMRA) with the campaign by environmental groups.

"After undertaking a detailed review of 2,4-D, the PMRA (2008) determined that 2,4-D meets Canada's strict health and safety standards and can be sold and used in Canada." The PMRA noted that its findings were consistent with regulations in the United States, New Zealand, and countries of the European Union, as well as the World Health Organization.

In closing its report, the PMRA noted that "Health Canada understands that the public may have concerns over use of pesticides and would like to convey that all registered pesticides undergo a thorough science-based risk assessment and must meet strict health and environmental standards before being approved for use in Canada." PMRA's reasoned and scientific assessment did little to assuage the fears of the public.

Environmental and health groups throughout Canada campaigned vigorously against cosmetic pesticides in Quebec and Ontario and, most recently, New Brunswick. Each of these provinces passed legislation to ban pesticides on home lawns and restrict their use on golf and sports turf. In announcing the New Brunswick ban, the Canadian Association of Physicians for the Environment (CAPE) singled out 2,4-D along with other products and noted that over 700,000 citizens were now protected from unnecessary spraying and that the province's ecosystems were safer (Khan 2010). To garner support for the ban of pesticides, a CAPE fund-raising letter noted that people exposed to pesticides are at increased risk for brain, prostate, kidney, and pancreatic cancer, and children are at increased risk for leukemia. The letter also noted that polls showed 8 out of 10 New Brunswick residents were in favor of a ban on nonessential pesticides and that they believed they posed potential health risks to humans. Finally, the CAPE fund-raising letter stated the following: "With overwhelming support from the public, health groups and the environmental community, it makes perfect sense for governments to do away with lawn poisons." The PMRA findings were not even mentioned. CAPE's goal is to ban lawn pesticides throughout Canada.

Campaigns to ban or restrict pesticides generally focus on the public's fear of cancer and the overuse of unnecessary pesticides. It is challenging to prove these claims but easy to invoke the precautionary principle to encourage people to err on the side of caution.

There is also the question of overuse. Just as fast-food restaurants make money by selling fast food, spray companies make money by spraying chemicals. Because they are in the business of spraying pesticides, they are responsive to the desires of owners and site managers who have their own standards for aesthetic quality. It is easy to assume that every lawn at every site is being deluged with chemicals, but a detailed and systematic study of pesticide use in commercial landscapes that would confirm or deny this assumption has yet to be conducted.

The question of pesticide use in landscapes for cosmetic purposes is more complicated than just safety or overuse claims. For example, attitudes about the appropriateness of lawns as the main element in landscapes appear to be changing (Bourdieu 1984; Hirsch and Baxter 2009). No longer does the entire public subscribe to the standard of a pure grass lawn, free of weeds. Those who do strive for perfect lawns often simply want to fit in and avoid conflict with their neighbors. This contributes to the use of pesticides in landscapes (Robbins and Sharp 2003). This idea is supported by Hirsch and Baxter (2009), who found three key implications based on their study:

1. "Environmental health risk policy should consider the notion that social and contextual influences can more powerfully affect the way laypeople think than risk perceptions alone."
2. "Residents may desire change, such as reductions in neighbourhood pesticide use, but are unwilling to engage in antagonistic relations with neighbours."
3. Mandatory bans versus voluntary ones "… deflect much of the responsibility for alternative yard aesthetics away from the individual homeowner."

The constantly increasing pressure to ban or further restrict pesticides has definitely put the landscape industry on alert. In some cases, it has split commercial lawn care providers into two factions: one side is adamant that there is no scientific reason to ban the use of pesticides deemed necessary by applicators (Gathercole 2009); the other side maintains that it is fruitless to oppose the changes taking place nationwide and it is time to move away from business as usual and embrace IPM and alternative strategies for lawn and landscape care (Lanthier 2009). At this time, there does not appear to be a consensus of opinion within the industry.

If the changes in Canada reflect a change in global attitudes about pesticide use, then they also present an opportunity for innovative sustainable landscape management practices. The following excerpt from a paper by an agronomic and arboricultural consultant in British Columbia regarding pesticide safety sums up the attitudes and concerns about pesticide spraying among commercial applicators in Canada at the present time:

> The horticulture industry is under scrutiny over the use of pesticides in urban areas. The public opinion is that pesticides are dangerous and that we (the users) are not careful enough. Part of that criticism is valid. It will remain valid as long as some people spray without protective clothing, in contravention of common sense and in contravention of the label itself.
>
> We need to tell our story. We need to tell the public we require these products to manage serious problems, and we use these products only when justified and following recognized safety practices. But we also need to answer the public concern of unnecessary pesticide use. Our industry associations must encourage on-going training on non-pesticide methods that are effective in commercial programs.
>
> I say "let's move on." Let's respect the pesticide labels, which say to wear protective clothing…. Let's respect provincial legislation,

which says we must use IPM and seek non-pesticide methods of control. Let's respect the public opinion, which says we must use less pesticides and more natural methods. It may not be easy, but it can be done. (Lanthier 2009)

SUMMARY

Environmental issues in landscape management are real and need to be dealt with in a professional manner. Leaching of nitrogen and phosphorus from landscapes can be managed by design and through best management practices. Likewise, leaching and runoff of applied pesticides can be controlled using integrated pest management strategies and best management practices during and after application. Health concerns associated with pesticide use primarily affect applicators but are equally important for bystanders, pets, and wildlife. To minimize potential hazards, pest control activities need to be carefully thought out and executed with safety utmost in mind. The industry needs to develop alternative methods for effective pest control. Air pollution associated with power equipment is decreasing due to new emission control regulations and will continue to decrease as new technology and regulations evolve.

Water resources are in a state of flux, and landscape access to potable sources of water will continue to decline as higher-priority uses emerge. In addition, alternate sources of water need to be developed for use in landscapes.

Agenda-driven rhetoric makes it very difficult to know what is true in the debate over the environmental impact of landscaping practices. Careful analysis is needed to arrive at the truth. The examples presented in this chapter demonstrate how important it is to look behind claims. With perspectives on environmental issues diverse and often extreme, moderate voices are often not heard. The final guidelines presented here offer a blueprint for maximizing environmental health while achieving acceptable landscape quality.

STUDY QUESTIONS

1. How do the views of environmental groups differ from those of many landscapers with regard to environmental issues?
2. What are the basic goals of sustainable landscape management as far as environmental issues are concerned?
3. Nitrogen and phosphorus fertilizers have been targeted as potential sources of water pollution. What can managers do to reduce the possibility that these nutrients will end up in streams, rivers, and lakes?
4. To date, how effective have phosphorus fertilizer bans been in reducing phosphorus levels in water?
5. What are the potential problems associated with the use of pesticides in landscapes? How can you manage applications to minimize these problems?
6. Who faces the greater risk from pesticides used in landscapes, the applicators or the bystanders? What can managers do to limit bystander exposure to pesticides?
7. What is the significance of case-control studies regarding the risk of cancer in humans? What are some of the drawbacks to case-control studies?
8. What is the precautionary principle and how does it relate to the discussion about health risks associated with the use of pesticides?
9. What problems do landscape pesticides (insecticides mainly) pose for wildlife? Is it possible to use pesticides without endangering fish and birds? Explain.
10. As long as we use power equipment for maintenance, there will be air pollution. Based on current technology, what is the most effective way to minimize that pollution?
11. Where do landscapes fall on the priority list for using potable water? How does that impact our approach to design and maintenance of future landscapes?

12. As the saying goes, "Don't believe everything you read." How does that apply to the ongoing environmental rhetoric? Why don't both sides simply strive to find the truth? In your opinion, does the end goal justify the means?
13. Find three examples of environmental rhetoric and analyze each one to determine just how truthful the claims are. See if you can find the truth behind the claims.
14. Based on the discussion about pesticide bans in Canada, what do you think the likelihood is that the same thing will happen in the United States?
15. How will lawn and shrub bed care be impacted if pesticide use is banned in those areas in commercially maintained landscapes in your climate zone?
16. Which of the following regions would have the toughest time producing attractive landscapes at existing sites if pesticides were banned for cosmetic purposes?
    a. Northern Europe
    b. Southern Italy
    c. Northwestern Australia
    d. Virginia and North Carolina
17. Is there a place for pesticides in sustainable landscapes? In your opinion, how should the pesticide issue be addressed in your region?

U.S. DEPARTMENT OF ENERGY | Energy Efficiency & Renewable Energy

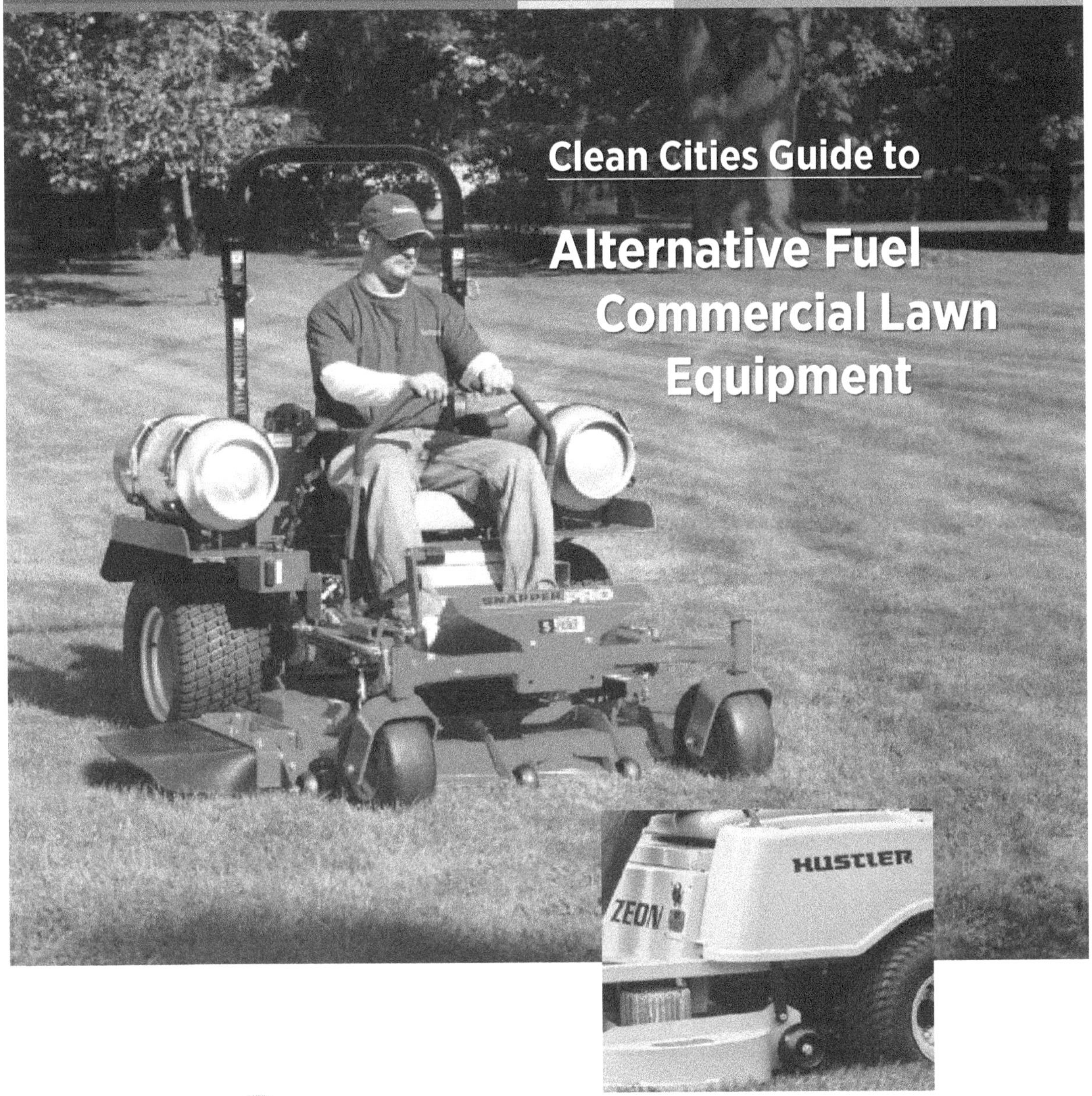

Clean Cities Guide to
Alternative Fuel Commercial Lawn Equipment

Photo from Ferris Industries

Clean Cities Guide to
Alternative Fuel Commercial Lawn Equipment

A single commercial lawnmower can annually use as much gasoline or diesel fuel as a commercial work truck. Powering commercial lawn service equipment with alternative fuels is an effective way to reduce petroleum use. Alternative fuels can also reduce pollutant emissions compared with conventional fuels. Numerous biodiesel, compressed natural gas, electric, and propane mowers are available to help keep the grass green and the nation clean.

Contents

Introduction	4
Compressed Natural Gas	6
Biodiesel	6
Electricity	7
Propane	8
Incentives	14
Special Considerations	14
Resources	15

Clean Cities Guide to Alternative Fuel Commercial Lawn Equipment

Introduction

Photo from iStock/6334062

Turf grass is a fixture of the American landscape and the American economy. It is the nation's largest irrigated crop, covering more than 40 million acres. Legions of lawnmowers care for this expanse during the growing season—up to year-round in the warmest climates. The annual economic impact of the U.S. turf grass industry has been estimated at more than $62 billion.

Lawn mowing also contributes to the nation's petroleum consumption and pollutant emissions. Mowers consume 1.2 billion gallons of gasoline annually, about 1% of U.S. motor gasoline consumption. Commercial mowing accounts for about 35% of this total and is the highest-intensity use. Large property owners and mowing companies cut lawns, sports fields, golf courses, parks, roadsides, and other grassy areas for 7 hours per day and consume 900 to 2,000 gallons of fuel annually depending on climate and length of the growing season. In addition to gasoline, commercial mowing consumes more than 100 million gallons of diesel annually.

Alternative fuel mowers are one way to reduce the energy and environmental impacts of commercial lawn mowing. They can reduce petroleum use and emissions compared with gasoline-

Clean Cities Guide to Alternative Fuel Commercial Lawn Equipment

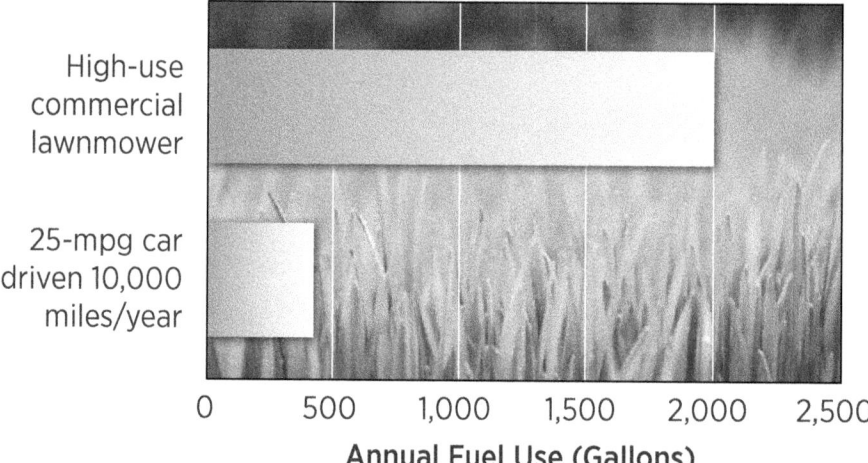

Commercial lawnmowers can consume more fuel than a typical car. Photo from iStock/6751109

and diesel-fueled mowers. They may also save on fuel and maintenance costs, extend mower life, reduce fuel spillage and fuel theft, and promote a "green" image. And on ozone alert days, alternative fuel mowers may not be subject to the operational restrictions that gasoline mowers must abide by.

To help inform the commercial mowing industry about product options and potential benefits, Clean Cities produced this guide to alternative fuel commercial lawn equipment. Although the guide's focus is on original equipment manufacturer (OEM) mowers, some mowers can be converted to run on alternative fuels. For more information about propane conversions, see page 8.

This guide may be particularly helpful for organizations that are already using alternative fuels in their vehicles and have an alternative fuel supply or electric charging in place (e.g., golf cart charging stations at most golf courses). On the flip side, experiencing the benefits of using alternative fuels in mowing equipment may encourage organizations to try them in on-road vehicles as well. Whatever the case, alternative fuel commercial lawnmowers are a powerful and cost-effective way to reduce U.S. petroleum dependence and help protect the environment.

Clean Cities Guide to Alternative Fuel Commercial Lawn Equipment

Compressed Natural Gas

Virtually all natural gas consumed in the United States is produced in North America. And compared with gasoline and diesel engines, natural gas engines can produce lower amounts of harmful emissions, including the greenhouse gas carbon dioxide. The cleaner-burning nature of natural gas may result in reduced maintenance requirements, such as less-frequent oil changes, and extended mower life. In addition, natural gas does not spoil or clog fuel systems in lawn equipment during seasonal storage, whereas liquid fuels can.

Natural gas must be compressed and stored at high pressure to enable adequate mowing time. This sealed and pressurized fuel-storage system has the advantage of eliminating evaporative emissions and spillage, as well as the potential fuel theft sometimes associated with liquid-fueled lawn equipment.

In 2011, there were more than 900 compressed natural gas (CNG) fueling stations in the United States with stations in almost every state. See a national map of CNG stations and find stations near you using the Alternative Fuels and Advanced Vehicles Data Center (AFDC) at *www.afdc.energy.gov/afdc/fuels/natural_gas_locations.html*. Over the past decade, CNG has been the least expensive U.S. motor fuel.

Dixie Chopper

- Website: *www.dixiechopper.com*
- Dealer Locator: *www.dixiechopper.com*

   Xcaliber Eco-Eagle
   - Cutting Deck Size: 66 in.
   - Engine: Generac 990 cc
   - Manufacturer's Suggested Retail Price (MSRP): $20,599
   - Basic Commercial Warranty: 5 years

Photo from manufacturer

Biodiesel

Biodiesel is a renewable alternative fuel produced domestically from a wide range of vegetable oils and animal fats. It is nontoxic and can reduce pollutant emissions compared with petroleum diesel. It also improves engine operation by raising diesel fuel's lubricity and combustion quality. Biodiesel blended with petroleum diesel can be used to fuel diesel vehicles without modifying the vehicles in most cases—20% biodiesel and 80% petroleum diesel (B20) is the most popular blend. B20 or other biodiesel blends are

CNG and Biodiesel

approved for use with some diesel-powered commercial lawnmowers without modification. Contact mower manufacturers to determine if B20 is approved for use in their diesel products.

Electricity

Electric power is quiet, requires little maintenance, and produces no tailpipe emissions. Electric mowers connected to an electricity supply with a cord or powered with rechargeable batteries are popular for residential use, but the rigors of commercial mowing have limited their use for this application to date. However, recent improvements in battery technology have resulted in new products with potential commercial application. Hustler Turf's Zeon—the first all-electric, zero-turn-radius mower—provides up to 80 minutes of continuous mowing time, enough to mow more than an acre. The Ariens AMP Rider provides up to 75 minutes of continuous mowing time.

Ariens

- Website: *www.ampbyariens.com*
- Dealer Locator:
    http://apache.ariens.com/cgibin/pnrg0140a

AMP Rider

- Cutting Deck Size: 34 in.
- Propulsion: Traction Drive,
    4 horsepower (HP), 48 volts (V)
- MSRP: $2,329
- Basic Commercial Warranty: 1 year for battery,
    2 years for other components

Hustler Turf

- Website: *www.hustlerturf.com*
- Dealer Locator:
    www.hustlerturf.com/find-a-dealer.html

Zeon

- Cutting Deck Size: 42 in.
- Propulsion: Hydro-Gear, 48 V,
    82 foot-pound maximum torque
- MSRP: $6,999
- Basic Commercial Warranty: 1 year

Photos from manufacturers

Propane

Also known as liquefied petroleum gas or LPG and autogas, propane is a widely available alternative transportation fuel in the United States. There are more than 2,600 propane vehicle fueling stations with locations in all 50 states. See a national map of propane stations and find stations near you using the AFDC's Alternative Fueling Station Locator (*www.afdc.energy.gov/afdc/fuels/propane_locations.html*). Most propane consumed in the United States is produced domestically, and, compared with gasoline and diesel engines, propane engines can produce lower amounts of some harmful emissions, including carbon dioxide. The cleaner-burning nature of propane may result in reduced maintenance requirements, such as less-frequent oil changes, and extended mower life. Also, like CNG, propane does not spoil or clog fuel systems in lawn equipment during seasonal storage, which can be the case with gasoline and diesel.

Propane is stored as a liquid under relatively low pressure and becomes a gas at normal pressure (meaning it enters the engine as a gas). The liquid storage gives it a high energy density, so a mower can run a long time on a tank of fuel, while the sealed and pressurized storage has the advantage of eliminating evaporative emissions and spillage as well as potential fuel theft.

There are two options in the propane arena: Buying an OEM propane mower, or converting a conventional one to run on propane. One company, Enviro-Gard, patented the propane technology found on OEM mowers from many manufacturers, converts gasoline mowers (and other gasoline-powered equipment) to propane, and supplies full propane engines to be installed in aftermarket mowers. The company's conversion kits range from 6.5 HP to 37 HP.

Like OEM products, the conversions are certified by the U.S. Environmental Protection Agency. Contact the company to locate the nearest conversion center. Propane mower conversions cost $1,000 to $2,500, including parts and labor. For more information about EnviroGard, visit *www.onyxsolutions.com/lawn-care.php*. To find other companies that could perform propane mower conversions, contact your state's Propane Gas Association (see *www.npga.org/i4a/pages/index.cfm?pageid=544* for a list of association websites) or use the Propane Education & Research Council's (PERC) Find a Propane Retailer tool (*www.usepropane.com/fpr.aspx*).

Ariens/Gravely

- Website: www.gravely.com
- Dealer Locator: www.gravelymower.com/locator

Pro-Master 260H XDZ LP

- Cutting Deck Size: 60 in.
- Engine: Generac 28 HP
- MSRP: $13,049
- Basic Commercial Warranty: 2 years

Bob-Cat

- Website: www.bobcatturf.com
- Dealer Locator:
  www.bobcatturf.com/Dealer_Locator

Predator-Pro LP

- Cutting Deck Size: 61 in. and 72 in.
- Engine: Generac 30 HP
- MSRP: $13,372 (61-in. model)
  $14,279 (72-in. model)
- Basic Commercial Warranty:
  2 years/2,000 hours or 5 years/500 hours

Cub Cadet

- Website: www.cubcadet.com
- Dealer Locator: www.cubcadet.com

TANK S LP

- Cutting Deck Size: 60 in. and 72 in.
- Engine: Kawasaki 852 cc (60-in. model)
  Kawasaki 999 cc (72-in. model)
- MSRP: $15,199 (60-in. model)
  $16,199 (72-in. model)
- Basic Commercial Warranty: 3 years

Photos from manufacturers

Propane

Cub Cadet continued

Z Force S LP
- Cutting Deck Size: 48 in. and 60 in.
- Engine: Kawasaki 726 cc
- MSRP: $6,399 (48-in. model)
  $7,199 (60-in. model)
- Basic Commercial Warranty:
  3 years/180 hours

Dixie Chopper
- Website: *www.dixiechopper.com*
- Dealer Locator: *www.dixiechopper.com*

Xcaliber Propane
- Cutting Deck Size: 66 in. and 74 in.
- Engine: Generac 990 cc
- MSRP: $14,199 (66-in. model)
  $14,299 (74-in. model)
- Basic Commercial Warranty: 5 years

Exmark
- Website: *www.exmark.com*
- Dealer Locator: *www.exmarkdealer.com*

Turf Tracer S-Series Propane
- Cutting Deck Size: 48 in. and 52 in.
- Engine: Kawasaki 20 HP
- MSRP: $8,499 (48-in. model)
  $8,699 (52-in. model)
- Basic Commercial Warranty: 2 years

Photos from manufacturers

Propane

Exmark continued

Turf Tracer X-Series Propane
- Cutting Deck Size: 52 in. and 60 in.
- Engine: Kawasaki 24 HP
- MSRP: $9,898 (52-in. model)
  $9,998 (60-in. model)
- Basic Commercial Warranty: 2 years

Lazer Z S-Series Propane
- Cutting Deck Size: 60 in. and 72 in.
- Engine: Kawasaki 29 HP
- MSRP: $12,899 (60-in. model)
  $13,399 (72-in. model)
- Basic Commercial Warranty: 3 years

Lazer Z X-Series Propane
- Cutting Deck Size: 60 in.
- Engine: Kawasaki 29 HP
- MSRP: $13,599
- Basic Commercial Warranty: 3 years

Ferris Industries
- Website: *www.ferrisindustries.com*
- Dealer Locator: *http://ferris.via.infonow.net/locator*

IS3100ZP
- Cutting Deck Size: 61 in. and 72 in.
- Engine: Briggs & Stratton 895 cc
- MSRP: $14,799 (61-in. model)
  $15,499 (72-in. model)
- Basic Commercial Warranty: 2 years

Photos from manufacturers

Propane

Husqvarna

- Website: *www.husqvarna.com*
- Dealer Locator: *www.husqvarna.com/us/landscape-and-groundcare/dealers/dealer-locator*

PZ6029PFX

- Cutting Deck Size: 60 in.
- Engine: Kawasaki 29 HP
- MSRP: $11,499
- Basic Commercial Warranty: 3 years

SCAG Power Equipment

- Website: *www.scag.com*
- Dealer Locator: *www.scag.com/locator*

Turf Tiger LP

- Cutting Deck Size: 52 in. and 61 in.
- Engine: Kohler
- MSRP: $12,900 (52-in. model)
  $13,065 (61-in. model)
- Basic Commercial Warranty: 2 years

Turf Tiger Dual Fuel

- Cutting Deck Size: 61 in.
- Engine: Kubota Dual-Fuel 31 HP (gasoline), 29 HP (propane)
- MSRP: $18,425
- Basic Commercial Warranty: 2 years

Photos from manufacturers

Propane

Snapper Pro

- Website: *www.snapperpro.com*
- Dealer Locator:
  http://snapperpro.via.infonow.net/locator

S200xp

- Cutting Deck Size: 61 in.
- Engine: Briggs & Stratton 895 cc
- MSRP: $10,999
- Basic Commercial Warranty: 2 years

Toro

- Website: *www.toro.com*
- Dealer Locator: *www.toro.com/en-us/locator*

Z Master G3 Propane Powered

- Cutting Deck Size: 60 in. and 72 in.
- Engine: Kawasaki 29 HP
- MSRP: $14,888 (60-in. model)
         $15,443 (72-in. model)
- Basic Commercial Warranty:
   5 years/1,200 hours

Zipper Mowers

- Website: *www.zippermowers.com*

STS-28 LP

- Cutting Deck Size: 64 in. and 74 in.
- Engine: Kawasaki 28 HP
- MSRP: $12,799 (64-in. model)
         $13,499 (74-in. model)
- Basic Commercial Warranty: 5 years

Photos from manufacturers

Propane

Zipper continued

ETS LP

- Cutting Deck Size: 50 in. and 60 in.
- Engine: Kawasaki 31 HP
- MSRP: $10,699 (50-in. model)
          $11,499 (60-in. model)
- Basic Commercial Warranty: 5 years

Photo from manufacturer

Incentives

Various financial incentives may be available for alternative fuels and alternative fuel mowers. For example, the Propane Council of Texas provided incentives for the purchase of dedicated propane mower purchases or conversions. See *www.txpropane.com/propanetexasfueltexasproudpropanelawnmower.html* for more information about this program. A similar program run through the Central Texas Clean Cities Coalition incentivized 55 propane mower conversions and purchases. PERC offered incentives for the purchase of new propane mowers through its Propane FEED (Farm Equipment Efficiency Demonstration) program. See *www.agpropane.com/FEED* for more information.

Alternative fuel mowers also may be eligible for some federal and state incentives that are available for alternative fuel vehicles. See the AFDC's Federal and State Incentives and Laws section at *www.afdc.energy.gov/afdc/laws* for more information about other incentives that may apply to alternative fuel mowers.

Another incentive is the unrestricted use of clean alternative fuel mowers on "ozone action days" in some cities. These are days when high ozone pollution levels trigger restrictions on operation of conventional fuel mowers, but alternative fuel mowers are left to operate freely because of their clean-burning characteristics. This gives alternative fuel mower operators an advantage over competitors who use conventional fuels only.

Special Considerations

Some mower engines are designed to run on alternative fuels with little or no modification. Others are not. Using alternative fuels or fuel blends that are not specifically approved for your equipment can cause serious damage to the engine or significantly reduce performance. To ensure alternative fuel or fuel blend use won't damage your mower, be sure to consult your equipment's owner's manual or contact the manufacturer or dealer.

Photo from iStock/3358788

Visit the following websites for more information about alternative fuels and alternative fuel lawnmowers.

All Propane Mowers: *www.allpropanemowers.com*

Alternative Fuels and Advanced Vehicles Data Center: *www.afdc.energy.gov/afdc*

AmeriGas: *www.amerigas.com*

Blossman Gas: *www.propanemowerfueling.com*

Ferrellgas: *www.ferrellgas.com*

Heritage Propane: *www.heritagepropane.com*

Metro Lawn: *www.gogreenmetrolawn.com*

National Propane Gas Association: *www.npga.org*

Natural Gas Vehicles for America (NGVAmerica): *www.ngvc.org*

Propane Education & Research Council: *www.propanecouncil.org*

Texas Propane Gas Association/Propane Council of Texas: *www.txpropane.com*

U.S. DEPARTMENT OF
ENERGY

Energy Efficiency &
Renewable Energy

EERE Information Center
1-877-EERE-INFO (1-877-337-3463)
www.eere.energy.gov/informationcenter

Prepared by the National Renewable
Energy Laboratory (NREL), a national
laboratory of the U.S. Department of
Energy, Office of Energy Efficiency and
Renewable Energy; operated by the
Alliance for Sustainable Energy, LLC.

DOE/GO-102011-3364
October 2011

Printed with a renewable-source ink on
paper containing at least 50% wastepaper,
including 10% post consumer waste.

U.S. Department of Energy

*Front cover photos (top to bottom)
from Snapper Pro, Hustler Turf,
Ferris Industries*

https://www.nwcb.wa.gov/washingtons-noxious-weed-laws

Washington's Noxious Weed Laws

Weed laws establish all property owners' responsibility for helping to prevent and control the spread of Noxious Weeds. Since plants grow without regard to property lines or political jurisdictions, everyone's cooperation is needed – city gardeners, farmers, government land agencies, foresters, and ranchers all have a role to play.

Washington's weed laws spell out these responsibilities and create the government infrastructure needed to educate citizens and ensure that the laws are respected.

Washington's weed laws also direct the state Noxious Weed Control Board to create and maintain the state's official list of noxious weeds that landowners may be required to control.

RCW 17.10.090: State noxious weed list—Selection of weeds for control by county board.
(1) Each county noxious weed control board shall, within ninety days of the adoption of the state noxious weed list from the state noxious weed control board and following a hearing, select those weeds from the class C list and those weeds from the class B list not designated for control in the noxious weed control region in which the county lies that it finds necessary to be controlled in the county.

(2) The weeds thus selected and all class A weeds and those class B weeds that have been designated for control in the noxious weed control region in which the county lies shall be classified within that county as noxious weeds, and those weeds comprise the county noxious weed list.

(3) Nothing in this chapter limits a county noxious weed control board, or other branch of county or city government, from conducting education, outreach, or other assistance regarding plant species not included on the state noxious weed list if the county or city determines that the plant species causes localized risk or concern.
[2011 c 126 § 2; 1997 c 353 § 11; 1987 c 438 § 9; 1969 ex.s. c 113 § 9.]

Washington State's Noxious Weed List is Organized into 3 Classes of Weeds: Class A, B & C.
Class A Weeds:
- Class A weeds are mostly newcomers to Washington, and are generally rare.
- The goal is to completely eradicate them before they gain a foothold.
- Landowners are required to completely eradicate Class A weeds. (Eradicating weeds means getting rid of the plants altogether, including plant roots.)

Class B Weeds:
- Class B weeds are those that are widespread in some parts of the state, but limited or absent in other parts of the state.
- The goal with Class B weeds is to prevent them from spreading into new areas, and to contain or reduce their population in already infested areas.
- The State Weed Board designates Class B noxious weeds for control in those parts of the state where they are limited or absent and threaten to invade. Click here to view how Class B noxious weeds have been designated for control in Washington. Designations are based on this region map. Additionally, a County Weed Board may select a Class B non-designate for control if it is considered a local priority.
- Landowners may be required to control Class B noxious weeds, depending on how widespread the species is and/or whether the species is a local priority. Check with your County Noxious Weed Control Board for more info on which Class B species you must control.

Class C Weeds
- Class C weeds are often widespread, or are of special interest to the agricultural industry.
- The State Weed Board does not require control of Class C noxious weeds.
- The State and many County Weed Boards provide information on identification and best management practices for these species.
- A County Weed Board may require landowners to control a Class C weed if it poses a threat to agriculture or natural resources. Check with your County Noxious Weed Control Board for more info on which Class C species you must control.

SECTION VI: ecoPRO Resources

IN THIS SECTION	PAGE
ecoPRO Glossary of Terms	256
ecoPRO Required Reading List, Supplemental Materials & Additional Resources for Study	262

ecoPRO GLOSSARY
Revised January 2020

Beneficials

Include insects, nematodes, microorganisms, animals, and plants that support or are vital to the health, growth, and fruitfulness of plants.

Carbon Cycle

In the carbon cycle, plants absorb carbon dioxide from the atmosphere and use it, combined with water they get from the soil, to make the substances they need for growth. The process of photosynthesis incorporates the carbon atoms from carbon dioxide into sugars. Animals eat the plants and use the carbon to build their own tissues. Animals return carbon dioxide into the air when they breathe and when they die, since the carbon is returned to the soil during decomposition. The carbon atoms in soil may then be used in a new plant or small microorganisms. The same atoms can be recycled for millennia. Best landscape practices tend to increase soil carbon content in living and dead organic matter.

Chemical Pesticides

Chemically and industrially manufactured products that kill pests or inhibit the growth of pest populations including plants, insects, fungi, algae, and mammalian species. An umbrella term for insecticides, herbicides, fungicides, mollusk killers, rodent controllers, etc.

Closed System Management

Self-sustaining processes and practices within a defined area.

Compost

Organic materials combined under controlled aerobic conditions that create humus from the raw ingredients. Composts from Washington State-permitted facilities meet additional process and contaminant standards. (See https://ecology.wa.gov/Waste-Toxics/Reducing-recycling-waste/Organic-materials/Managing-organics-compost

Compost Blanket

Medium coarse compost applied at depth of 1-3 inches to prevent erosion primarily on slopes. (See specifications at http://www.buildingsoil.org/tools/Erosion_Control.pdf)

Compost Filter Sock

A type of contained compost filter berm; a mesh tube filled with composted material that is placed perpendicular to sheet-flow runoff to control erosion and retain sediment in disturbed areas.

Compost Teaw

A liquid extract of compost that contains plant growth compounds and beneficial microorganisms.

Design

The underlying plan or conception that affects and controls the function and development of the landscape.

Drip Irrigation

Irrigation devices that discharge water directly to (or under) the soil surface at a controlled rate through "emitters" that are installed on or molded into flexible tubing (usually polyethylene), or attached to hard pipe (PVC). Drip irrigation can meet the needs of plants using 50% less water than sprinkler irrigation because it can apply water very uniformly, avoid overspray to non-target surfaces (pavement, unplanted areas) and minimizes evaporation from foliage, soil surfaces, and misting. Drip irrigation can also be used for precise applications of fertilizers.

Ecoregion

Ecoregions are areas that reflect broad ecological patterns occurring on the landscape. In general, each ecoregion has a distinctive composition and pattern of plant and animal species distribution. Abiotic factors, such as climate, landform, soil, and hydrology are important in the development of ecosystems, and thus help define ecoregions. Within an individual ecoregion, the ecological relationships between species and their physical environment are essentially similar. Washington State is generally considered to encompass nine ecoregions. http://www.landscope.org/washington/natural_geography/ecoregions/

Embodied-energy

Measure of the total energy consumed by the product through its whole life--creation, use, and disposal.

Fertilizer

A substance containing one or more of the 16 recognized plant nutrients that is used to promote plant health and growth.

Forest Stewardship Council (FSC) Certified Wood Products

Wood products are certified by the Forestry Stewardship Council (FSC), a group of 12 global certifiers that evaluate both forest management activities (forest certification) and tracking of forest products (chain-of-custody certification). https://us.fsc.org/en-us/certification

Genetically Modified Organisms (GMOs)

An organism whose genetic material has been altered through the use of genetic engineering techniques. These techniques, generally known as recombinant DNA technology, use DNA molecules from different sources, which are combined into one molecule to create a new set of genes. This DNA is then transferred into an organism, giving it modified or novel genes.

Graywater

Waste water that has been used in the home for washing, bathing, cooking and other uses—excluding water from toilets, or sinks that may be highly contaminated with food wastes or high soap concentrations. In many locales, codes allow graywater to be used for landscape irrigation, though use is often restricted to sub-surface applications (not sprinklers) on ornamental plants or tree crops—not on herbaceous food crops.

Green Stormwater Infrastructure (GSI)

Using green solutions to help reduce overflows by allowing stormwater to infiltrate slowly into the ground and cutting the volume of stormwater entering the system.

Heat Island Effect

As urban areas develop, changes occur in their landscape. Buildings, roads, and other infrastructure replace open land and vegetation. Surfaces that were once permeable and moist become impermeable and dry. These changes cause urban regions to become warmer than their rural surroundings, forming an "island" of higher temperatures in the landscape. Mitigation strategies include: 1) increasing tree and vegetative cover; 2) installing green roofs (also called "rooftop gardens" or "eco-roofs"); 3) installing cool—mainly reflective—roofs; and 4) using cool pavements.

Humus

The dark organic material in soils, formed by the microbial decomposition of vegetable or animal matter, and essential to soil fertility.

Hydrology

The study of the movement, distribution, and quality of water – the water cycle.

Hydrozone

A landscape area comprised of plants with similar water needs. Landscape designs that cluster plants with similar water needs and create irrigation zones including only groups of similar plants in similar exposures, make efficient irrigation possible. Mixed hydrozones that include (for example) annuals and drought tolerant shrubs, cannot be irrigated without either overwatering the shrubs or underwatering the annuals.

Integrated Pest Management (IPM)

Integrated pest management is an effective and environmentally sensitive approach to pest management that relies on a combination of common-sense practices, including pest monitoring, setting thresholds of acceptable damage, and using cultural and pest control methods with the least non-target impact. IPM programs use current, comprehensive information on the life cycles of pests and their interaction with the environment. This information, in combination with available pest control methods, is used to manage pest damage cost-effectively, with the least possible hazard to people, property, and the environment.

International Society of Arboriculture (ISA)

The International Society of Arboriculture certifies arborists and publishes information about tree care. (http://pnwisa.org)

Irrigation Association (IA)

A membership organization of irrigation industry professionals, manufacturers, researchers and water utility representatives; that promotes efficient irrigation policies, practices and products. IA offers professional trainings and certification programs, educational materials, and tests and certifies conservation products through the Smart Water Application Technologies (SWAT) program. (http://www.irrigation.org/)

Landscape Management Plan

A written plan outlining the utilitarian, ecological, and aesthetic objectives for a specific landscape. The plan describes the specific practices and products that will be used to implement the landscape management plan, along with a schedule of annual maintenance practices. (See www.seattle.gov/util/LandscapeProfessionals - "Maintenance Plans")

Low Impact Development

LID is an approach to land development (or re-development) that works with nature to manage stormwater as close to its source as possible. LID employs principles such as preserving and recreating natural landscape features, minimizing effective imperviousness to create functional and appealing site drainage that treat stormwater as a resource rather than a waste product. There are many practices that have been used to adhere to these principles such as bioretention facilities, rain gardens, vegetated rooftops, rain barrels, and permeable pavements. By implementing LID principles and practices, water can be managed in a way that reduces the impact of built areas and promotes the natural movement of water within an ecosystem or watershed. Applied on a broad scale, LID can maintain or restore a watershed's hydrologic and ecological functions. LID has been characterized as a sustainable stormwater practice by the Water Environment Research Foundation and others.

Material Safety Data Sheet (MSDS)

An MSDS contains information on safe working procedures when handling chemical products, provides hazard evaluations on the use, storage, handling, and emergency procedures for specific materials within a product formulation and the potential health and environmental impacts of exposure to chemicals or other dangerous substances in that formulation. An MSDS is prepared by the manufacturers of chemical products, and is required to be made available to workers who handle these substances. MSDS information is available from the manufacturer and also through online resources.

Mulch

A layer of material applied to the surface of an area of soil to conserve moisture, improve the fertility and health of the soil, reduce weed growth, and/or enhance the visual appeal of the area. A mulch is usually, but not exclusively organic in nature. It may be permanent (e.g. bark chips) or temporary (e.g. plastic sheeting). It may be applied to bare soil, or around existing plants. Mulches of manure or compost will be incorporated naturally into the soil by the activity of worms and other organisms. The process is used both in commercial crop production and in gardening, and when applied correctly can dramatically improve soil productivity.

Mulch Mowing

Mowing with equipment that disperses cut grass clippings over the mowed area during the mowing process in order to decompose and return to the soil naturally.

Mycorrhiza

The symbiotic association of the mycelium of a fungus with the roots of a seed plant.

Native Plant

A native plant is one that occurs naturally in a particular region, ecosystem, or habitat without direct or indirect human intervention. We consider the flora present at the time Europeans arrived in Washington State as native. Native plants include all kinds of plants from mosses and ferns to wildflowers, shrubs, and trees. Definition derived from: http://www.usna.usda.gov/

Naturally Derived Fertilizers

Plant nutrients derived from naturally occurring plant, animal, microbial, or mineral sources.

Natural Lawn Care

Soil and turf installation and maintenance practices that create healthy, deep-rooted turf that resists damage from pests, weeds, traffic and drought, with minimal chemical and water inputs and waste outputs. Key practices include appropriate site and species selection, soil preparation with compost, mulch-mowing at proper heights, moderate fertilization with organic sources based on plant needs, watering deeply but less frequently, integrated pest and weed management, and renovation practices including aeration, compost topdressing, and over-seeding to restore dense turf. (See Ecologically Sound Lawn Care for the Pacific Northwest)

Noxious Weed List

Washington State Noxious Weed Control Board updates a statewide list by area annually. (See http://www.nwcb.wa.gov)

Onsite Infiltration

Stormwater retention and treatment encouraged for Low Impact Development (LID). Includes compost-amended soils, trees, rain gardens and bioretention areas, vegetated swales, pocket wetlands and stormwater wetlands, vegetated landscaping, and vegetated buffers.

Organic Matter

Matter composed of organic compounds that has come from the remains of once-living organisms such as plants and animals and their waste products in the environment.

Pest

The term "plant pest" has a very specific definition in terms of the International Plant Protection Convention and phytosanitary measures worldwide. A pest is any species, strain, or biotype of plant, animal, or pathogenic agent injurious to plants or plant products (FAO, 1990; revised FAO, 1995; IPPC, 1997).

PEX Pipe

Cross-linked polyethylene pipe, durable for extreme temperatures. Creep deformation in PEX is caused by long-term exposure to stress and chemical attack from acids or alkalis. PEX degrades when exposed to sunlight and is not recyclable.

Plant Available Water Storage

The portion of water stored in soil that is readily available for plants to use. Plant available water storage varies with soil texture, depth and organic matter content.

Plant Communities

Groups of plants that tend to occur together in particular local environments.

Plant Health Care (PHC)

An emphasis of plant health over pest management. PHC takes an ecosystem approach that emphasizes working with nature instead of fighting nature, and it sees proper culture as the foundation of a healthy landscape. PHC has evolved from IPM: It still incorporates all IPM principles, but goes beyond it.

Pollinators

Animals such as birds, bees, bats, butterflies, moths, beetles, or other animals, that move pollen within flowers or carry pollen from flower to flower. Plants can also be pollinated by abiotic factors such as wind and water.

Rain Shut-off Sensors

Sensors that prevent an automatic irrigation controller from starting valves when a set amount of rainfall occurs. Rain sensors can be used with any irrigation controller that runs solenoid valves.

Smart Irrigation Controllers

Irrigation timers that automatically adjust watering schedules based on calculations using current weather data from on-site sensors or sent from regional weather stations, and/or historic data. Smart controllers have been demonstrated to maintain healthy landscapes with 20% less water than standard controllers. They must be accurately set using information about plants, soil, exposure and irrigation rates in each zone; if they are not, it is likely that the site's water use will be higher, rather than lower.

Soil Interfaces

Layers of the soil profile that are composed of very different soil texture and density that interfere with movement of water, nutrients, and roots.

Soil Management Plan

Site plan (drawing) showing both (1) vegetation and soil protection zones (to be fenced and protected from disturbance during construction and (2) areas that will be disturbed during construction and then restored, typically by de-compacting and amending soil with compost or bringing in compost-amended topsoil. Soil management plans should also include a worksheet showing how much compost, topsoil, and/or mulch will be used in each soil restoration area. They should be communicated to all construction personnel to ensure that protection zones are maintained during construction and that all disturbed areas are restored at the end of construction. (See Building Soil manual at http://www.soilsforsalmon.org/pdf/Soil_BMP_Manual.pdf)

Soil Moisture Shut-off Sensors

Sensors that prevent an automatic irrigation controller from starting valves when soil is moist. Many soil sensors require the addition of a proprietary control module between the sensor and a controller.

Soil Water Holding Capacity

The specific ability of a particular type of soil to store water, after it is allowed to fully drain. Clay soil stores more than three times as much water per foot of depth than sandy soil; silty and loamy soils store an intermediate amount. However much of the water stored in clay is held too tightly for plants to access, so they must be watered just as frequently—in small amounts. Loamy soils are able to store the most Plant Available Water.

Synthetic Fertilizers

Plant nutrients manufactured by chemical and industrial processes. These include products not found in nature or products synthetically compounded or simulated from natural sources.

Volatile Organic Compound (VOC)

Organic chemicals that have a high vapor pressure at ordinary room temperature. VOCs include both human-made and naturally occurring chemical compounds. Most scents or odors are of VOCs. Some VOCs are dangerous to human health or cause harm to the environment. Anthropogenic VOCs are regulated by law, especially indoors, where concentrations are the highest. Harmful VOCs typically are not acutely toxic, but have compounding long-term health effects.

Water Budget

A calculation of the irrigation use expected for a site based on the square footage of landscaping, plant types, and measured efficiency of the irrigation system (or an efficiency goal). Water Budgets based on efficient irrigation assumptions can be compared to the existing water use on a site to gauge the efficiency of irrigation equipment and management. They are also used by municipalities to establish limits on planting of high water use plants at new developments, and by some water purveyors to establish maximum allowable water use for a property.

REQUIRED READING LIST, SUPPLEMENTAL MATERIALS, & ADDITIONAL RESOURCES

This document details the following:
1. **Required Reading List** for the ecoPRO certification training and exam: All required readings are found in the ecoPRO Required Readings, booklet (for purchase through https://ecoprocertified.org); some of the readings can also be found online – see links below. Please read the information PRIOR to attending the training and/or taking the exam. Most of the certification exam is based on information from these readings.
2. **Supplemental Study Materials**: Materials that support the Required Reading List and are <u>highly recommended</u> as supplemental study materials.
3. **Additional Resources**: Materials, hotlines, and other resources to learn more or use as references.

This document is updated periodically and available online at https://ecoprocertified.org .
Updated: July 2020

1. REQUIRED READING LIST

All of the Required Reading can be found in the ecoPRO Required Readings booklet. Many of the readings can also be found online (see links below).

- **ecoPRO Guiding Principles and Sustainable Best Practices.** Revised 2020.

- *Sustainable Landscape Management: Design, Construction, Maintenance.* Thomas W. Cook and Ann Marie Vanderzanden, 2011, chapters 1, 3, 4, 5, 6, 7, and 8. *(Included in the ecoPRO Handbook publication)*

- *The Case for Sustainable Landscapes.* read pages 5-11, available online at
  https://landscapeforlife.org/wp-content/uploads/2017/09/The-Case-for-Sustainable-Landscapes-Brochure.pdf
  or watch the "Introduction to SITES" video at http://www.sustainablesites.org/resources

- *Designing the Sustainable Site: Integrated Design Strategies for Small Scale Sites and Residential Landscapes.* Heather L. Venhaus, 2012. (Included in the ecoPRO Handbook publication)

- **Soils and Soil Testing.** WSU Cooperative Extension. Read "Estimating Soil Texture by Hand."
  http://puyallup.wsu.edu/soils/soils/ and watch the "Determining Soil Texture" video at that site

- www.SoilsforSalmon.org and BuildingSoil.org Washington's soil protection & restoration best practices. Read these 2-page fact sheets on that site:
  - **Soil BMP Summary**
  - **When to Amend?**
  - **Erosion Control with Compost**
  - **Managing Stormwater Onsite**

- **Regional Pruning Guides.** Plant Amnesty. Read Northwest Pacific Maritime and Eastern Washington guides (available online only to www.PlantAmnesty.org members, in the Resources section) or watch pruning videos at https://www.youtube.com/c/plantamnesty/playlists

- **Best Irrigation Practices.** Cascade Water Alliance, 2013.

- **Winterizing and Starting Up the Irrigation System.** Mark Guthrie, Tacoma Water, 2014.

- **Clean Cities' Guide to Alternative Fuel Commercial Lawn Equipment.** U.S. Department of Energy. http://www.afdc.energy.gov/pdfs/48369.pdf

- **Sustainable Lawn Care: Installation and Maintenance Practices for NW Professionals**. Seattle Public Utilities, January 2012. http://www.seattle.gov/util/landscapeprofessionals click on "Lawns, Plants & Trees"

- **Introduction to IPM** and **PHC/IPM steps flowchart.** Developed by Green Gardening Program, Seattle Public Utilities, updated January 2012. http://www.seattle.gov/util/landscapeprofessionals click on "Integrated Pest Management"

- **Grow Smart Grow Safe**. Regional website for practical pest, weed & disease management and safer product selection. www.GrowSmartGrowSafe.org click on "Natural Yard Care" and read "Garden Without Pesticides."

- **Natural Landscaping: Design, Build, Maintain.** Seattle Public Utilities, September 2007. 8-page summary of landscape best practices, source of the ecoPRO BMPs. http://www.seattle.gov/util/landscapeprofessionals

2. SUPPLEMENTAL STUDY MATERIALS

These are optional resources that support the Required Reading and are highly recommended as supplemental study materials.

- **Design.** Video: "Designing the Sustainable Site" (by Heather Venhaus, on her book in the above Required Reading List) http://vimeo.com/53430426

- **Soils & soil testing.** Videos (WSU Cooperative Extension). http://puyallup.wsu.edu/soils/soils/

- **Soils for Salmon.** Resources, factsheets, video, slide show: www.SoilsforSalmon.org

- **Pruning.** Videos: How-to pruning videos (Plant Amnesty). https://www.youtube.com/c/plantamnesty/playlists

- **Sustainable landscaping.** Videos, click on "Training" at http://www.seattle.gov/util/landscapeprofessionals

- **IPM.** Weed Control Calendar; individual ProIPM fact sheets, and many resource links at http://www.seattle.gov/util/landscapeprofessionals click on "Integrated Pest Management"

- **IPM.** Grow Smart Grow Safe website. http://www.GrowSmartGrowSafe.org/

3. ADDITIONAL RESOURCES to learn more or use as references

* Asterisk marks resources that are also included in the ecoPRO Required Reading list.

HOTLINES – Expert consultation for professionals or clients – email photos for pest and problem ID

- **Garden Hotline** 206-633-0224 help@gardenhotline.org many resources at www.gardenhotline.org
- **Plant Answer Line** (UW Botanic Gardens Miller Library) 206-897-5268 hortlib@uw.edu
http://depts.washington.edu/hortlib/resources/resources.php

GENERAL

- **WSU Extension Master Gardener** http://gardening.wsu.edu/ extensive library of information
- Seattle Public Utilities websites: **Natural Yard Care** http://www.seattle.gov/util/yard/
and **Landscape Professionals** on soil, plants, pests, landscape maintenance plans, IPM etc.
http://www.seattle.gov/util/landscapeprofessionals
- Documenting the value/benefits of sustainable landscapes:
The Value of Green infrastructure covers air, water, energy, climate, and community benefits
https://www.americanrivers.org/conservation-resource/value-green-infrastructure/
Green Cities: Good Health – a comprehensive searchable database of research-proven human benefits
http://depts.washington.edu/hhwb/
- **Ecological Landscaping Association LinkedIn Group** – landscape professionals around the nation communicating about sustainable, ecological landscaping experience. Register through LinkedIn.

DESIGN

- * *Natural Landscaping: Design, Build, Maintain* http://www.seattle.gov/util/landscapeprofessionals
- * **The Sustainable Sites Initiative** (or SITES™) www.sustainablesites.org is the site and landscape equivalent of the US Green Building council's LEED™ green building system.
Download the free *SITES Rating System* and see videos at http://www.sustainablesites.org/resources
Landscape for Life http://landscapeforlife.org/ has SITES-based guidance for the general public, including a curriculum with slide-sets with instructors manual, and **The Case for Sustainable Landscapes*
- **ASLA Sustainable Landscapes** – case studies, design resources, & more
http://www.asla.org/sustainablelandscapes/
- **King County Native Plant Guide – landscape plans** for a variety of site conditions
http://green.kingcounty.gov/GoNative/
- *Sustainable Landscapes and Gardens: good science-practical applications* book with local authors
http://www.sustainablelandscapesandgardens.com/

SOIL

- * www.SoilsforSalmon.org has background science and basic information for builders and landscapers on Washington's soil protection and restoration requirements, including the *Building Soil Manual*, compost calculator, erosion control, project sequencing for soil restoration, and a short slideshow useful for orienting staff and customers *Soil Strategies for Landscape Success*

- * **WSU Cooperative Extension Soil Information for Gardeners.** https://puyallup.wsu.edu/soils/gardening/ including how-to on soil sampling and understanding test results, soil texture, Washington soils, and more
- **Soil Biology Primer** – excellent illustrations & text on how soil works; available online or book https://www.nrcs.usda.gov/wps/portal/nrcs/main/soils/health/biology/
- ecoPRO professional instruction videos (45 min each):
  Healthy Soils Part 1, Soil Science *and* **Healthy Soils Part 2, Soil Restoration**
  www.seattle.gov/util/landscapeprofessionals click on "Training" and look on right side of that page

WATER & IRRIGATION

- *Going Green with Irrigation System Maintenance*. Tim Wilson, 2009.
- www.SavingWater.org water conservation and healthy landscape practices
- **Irrigation Association** educational resources, http://www.irrigation.org/ (click on "Resources") including comprehensive Turf & Landscape Irrigation Best Management Practices for design, installation, maintenance, and management of irrigation systems, and irrigation designer and installer Professional Certification
- **Irrigation Water Management Society** http://www.iwms.org/ –click on "Seattle' for local ET data & more

STORMWATER

- * **Managing Stormwater On Site** – 4-page summary for professionals, at www.SoilsforSalmon.org and see videos at www.seattle.gov/util/landscapeprofessionals click on "Training" and look on right of that page. See also Seattle's Green Infrastructure www.seattle.gov/util/greeninfrastructure
- *Low Impact Development Western Washington Technical Guidance Manual for Puget Sound* (also available is the *Eastern WA Manual*) – complete guidance on green stormwater infrastructure methods https://www.wastormwatercenter.org/lid-manuals-guides/
- *Rain Garden Handbook for Western WA*, 2013 ed. and other WSU resources https://extension.wsu.edu/raingarden/homeowner-resources/
- **Low Impact Development Technical Training Workshops** and similar certificate and training programs around the US see WA Stormwater Center http://www.wastormwatercenter.org/training-resources/
- **WA Dept. of Ecology's LID page** with many useful links www.ecy.wa.gov/programs/wq/stormwater/municipal/LID/Resources.html

IPM/IPC – Integrated Pest Management, Integrated Plant Care

- * **ProIPM factsheets** on common NW problems, workshop presentations on IPM, plant selection and more, click on "Integrated Pest Management" at http://www.seattle.gov/util/landscapeprofessionals
- * www.GrowSmartGrowSafe.org practical pest, weed & disease management and safer product selection
- **WSU IPM & Pesticide Safety Education** – many useful resources are linked from https://pep.wsu.edu/
- **UPEST- School IPM** http://schoolipm.wsu.edu/
- **UC IPM** pest & solutions, from University of California http://www.ipm.ucdavis.edu/

- The **Garden Hotline** and **Plant Answer Line** (listed under Hotlines at top) can help with pest, weed, & disease identification (call, or email them a photo) and least toxic control methods
- **Common Sense Pest Control**, Olkowski, Daar and Olkowski. Book.

PLANTS

- *Arboriculture: Integrated Management of Landscape Trees, Shrubs, and Vines (4th Edition).* Richard W. Harris, James R. Clark, Nelda P. Matheny, 2004.
- www.GreatPlantPicks.org – NW adapted plants listed by site condition and other criteria
- **King County Native Plant Guide** – plant list, planting plans, plant site requirements
  http://green.kingcounty.gov/GoNative/
- **WSU Extension Native Plants database** http://pnwplants.wsu.edu/
- **WA Native Plant Society** http://www.wnps.org/
- *Tree Protection on Construction and Development Sites: A Best Management Practices Guidebook for the PNW*, EM 8994 December 2009 http://www.dnr.wa.gov/Publications/rp_urban_treeprtctnguidbk.pdf

LAWNS

- *Ecologically Sound Lawn Care for the Pacific NW* – 90-page manual
  or see the 8-page summary *Sustainable Lawn Care for Northwest Professionals*
  http://www.seattle.gov/util/landscapeprofessionals click on "Lawns, Plants & Trees", look on right side
- *WSU EB0482 Home Lawns* for public https://puyallup.wsu.edu/turf/publications/ , and
  many resources linked from WSU Master Gardener Library / Lawns http://gardening.wsu.edu/lawns/

URBAN AGRICULTURE / EDIBLE LANDSCAPING

- **Growing Food in the City** – basic food gardening information in 14 languages
  http://www.seattle.gov/util/yard/ click on "Food Gardening"
- **Tilth Alliance** – classes, demonstration gardens, and volunteer opportunities www.TilthAlliance.org/
- **Master Gardeners** – Washington State University Extension http://gardening.wsu.edu/
- *Gardening for Good Nutrition* basic guide, and other urban food and agriculture resources at
  https://www.solid-ground.org/get-help/food-resources/
- **Urban Farm Hub** – urban agriculture news and resources for the Northwest http://www.urbanfarmhub.org/
- **Edible Landscaping Basics,** book by pioneer Rosalind Creasy – hard copy only
- Search "Edible Landscaping Northwest" for books by Marianne Binetti & others, blogs, etc.

LANDSCAPE PROFESSIONAL TRAINING & CERTIFICATION PROGRAMS

- **ecoPRO Certified Sustainable Landscape Professional** training program https://ecoprocertified.org
- **EnviroStars** business certification http://www.envirostars.org/
- **WA Association of Landscape Professionals** (WALP) education http://www.walp.org/

- **WA State Nursery & Landscape Association** (WSNLA) http://www.wsnla.org/
- **WA Chapter of the American Society of Landscape Architects** (WASLA) state licensure and continuing education http://www.wasla.org/
- **WA Chapter of the Association of Professional Landscape Designers** (APLD) certification and education http://apldwa.org/
- **International Society of Arboriculture** (ISA) certification https://www.isa-arbor.com/Credentials and Pacific Northwest Chapter continuing education https://pnwisa.org/classes-events/
- **Irrigation Association** (IA) certification for designers and installers http://www.irrigation.org/

Sustainable or organic landscape professional certification programs around the U.S.

- **ecoPRO Certified Sustainable Landscape Professional** https://ecoprocertified.wordpress.com/
- **Bay Friendly Landscaping** https://rescapeca.org/ and **Bay Friendly Guidelines** https://rescapeca.org/wp-content/uploads/2016/01/Bay-Friendly-Landscaping-Guide.pdf
- **NOFA Organic Land Care** http://www.organiclandcare.net/
- **Society for Organic Urban Land Care** https://organiclandcare.ca/

www.ingramcontent.com/pod-product-compliance
Ingram Content Group UK Ltd.
Pitfield, Milton Keynes, MK11 3LW, UK
UKHW051259180426
11947UKWH00020B/1808

9 781119 819882